Safe Within the Walls

Ellis Amdur, M.A., N.C.C., C.M.H.S.

Communication, Control, and De-escalation of Mentally Ill and Aggressive Inmates

A Comprehensive Guidebook for

Correctional Officers in Prison Facilities

An Edgework Book
www.edgeworkbooks.com

Notes and Notices

SAFE WITHIN THE WALLS: Communication, Control, and De-escalation of Mentally Ill and Aggressive Inmates
A Comprehensive Guidebook for Correctional Officers in Prison Facilities

By Ellis Amdur, M.A., N.C.C., C.M.H.S. © 2019

A Message to Our Readers
Edgework is committed to offering the best of what our years of experience and study have taught us. We ask that you express your respect for these intentions and honor our work by adhering strictly to the copyright protection notice you will find below. Please know that by choosing NOT to reproduce these materials, you are supporting our work and making it possible for us to continue to develop materials that will enhance both officer and public safety. We thank you sincerely for your vigilance in respecting our rights!

Notice of Rights
All rights reserved. No part of this book may be reproduced or transmitted in any form by any means, electronic, mechanical, photocopying, recording, or otherwise, without the explicit prior written permission of the author and publisher. For information on getting permission for reprints, contact Edgework: Crisis Intervention Resources PLLC (www.edgework.info)

Limited Liability and Disclaimer
This book is informational only and is not to be considered an official policy manual. By purchasing this book, you agree that you will hold the author and publisher harmless from all claims arising out of or related to your access or use of, or inability to access or use, this book or the information contained herein.

The information in this book is provided for general information only and provided "AS IS" to the fullest extent permitted by law, without express or implied, including, but not limited to, any warranty of fitness for a particular purpose. The author and publisher make no warranties about the accuracy, completeness, or timeliness of the content, services, text, graphs, and links appearing in this book.

Credits
Photographs by: Dreamstime.com
Illustrations by: Shoko Zama
Design: Soundview Design
Cover photograph by: Stomac, Wikimedia Commons

Contents

Published Works by the Author vii
In Gratitude For Previous Collaboration ix
In Gratitude For Expert Critique xi
Introduction xiii
A Note on Terminology xv

Section I	**Inmates Suffering From Mental Illness** 1	
Chapter 1	Mental Illness Within the Prison System 3	
Chapter 2	Threat Assessment: How Do We Know Someone Is Dangerous? 13	
Section II	**Core Requirements For De-Escalation And Control Of Inmates Who Are Agitated, Aggressive, And/Or Suffering From Mental Illness** 17	
Chapter 3	The Development of a Safety Mindset 19	
Chapter 4	Training Your Intuition (Correctional Awareness) to Pick Up Danger 27	
Chapter 5	Honing Your Intuition Through Awareness of Personal Spacing 29	
Section III	**Centering: Standing With Strength In Crisis Situations** 33	
Chapter 6	Introduction to Centering 35	
Chapter 7	A Fair Witness: Peer Support Is a Survival Tactic 37	
Chapter 8	It's Not Personal Unless You Make It So 39	
Chapter 9	Circular Breathing: Be the Eye in the Center of the Hurricane 45	
Chapter 10	The Intoxication and Joy of Righteous Anger 53	
Section IV	**Dealing With Inmates Who Have Unusual Or Intense Communication Styles** 55	
Chapter 11	Overview of Section IV 57	
Chapter 12	Rigid Personality: High Functioning Autism and Other Similar Disorders 59	
Chapter 13	Tell It Like It Is: Communication with Concrete Thinkers 65	
Chapter 14	Information Processing and Retention: Consolidating Gains 67	
Chapter 15	Coping with Stubborn Refusals 69	
Chapter 16	Stuck: Coping with Repetitive Demands, Questions and Obsessions 71	
Chapter 17	The Need for Reassurance 73	
Chapter 18	Dealing with Mood Swings 75

Chapter 19	They Aren't Moving: What to Do?	77
Chapter 20	Should a Correctional Officer Ever Apologize?	79
Chapter 21	Useful Tactics for Dealing with Symptoms of Paranoia and Persecution	81
Chapter 22	Feces Smearing... and Worse	85

Section V — Recognizing The Strategies Of Opportunistic And Manipulative Inmates ... 87

Chapter 23	Divide and Confuse: Borderline Personality Disorder and Splitting	89
Chapter 24	Bad Intentions: Recognizing the Strategies of Opportunistic and Manipulative Inmates	93
Chapter 25	Tactical and Safety Considerations Related to the Supervision of the Sociopathic Inmate	97

Section VI — Communication With Inmates That Have Severe Mental Illness Or Other Conditions That Cause Severe Disability ... 103

Chapter 26	Overview of Section VI	105
Chapter 27	Struggling in a Fog: Dealing with the Symptoms of Disorganization	107
Chapter 28	Latency: The Unresponsive Inmate	111
Chapter 29	Withdrawal from Intoxicating Substances	115
Chapter 30	Psychosis: Delusions and Hallucinations	119
Chapter 31	Communication with Inmates Experiencing Delusions/Hallucinations	123
Chapter 32	Welcome to the Rollercoaster: Tactics for Dealing with Symptoms of Mania	133
Chapter 33	Communication with Inmates with Dementia (The Elderly)	139

Section VII — Suicide ... 141

Chapter 34	Suicide in Prison	143
Chapter 35	The Basics of Intervention with an Inmate Who May Be Suicidal	147
Chapter 36	Essential Questions	151
Chapter 37	Self-Mutilation	157

Section VIII — Recognizing Patterns Of Aggression ... 161

Chapter 38	The Cycle of Aggression	163
Chapter 39	Why Would an Inmate Become Aggressive?	171
Chapter 40	What Does Aggression Look Like?	175

Section IX — De-Escalation Of Angry Inmates ... 183

Chapter 41	Preemptive De-escalation	185
Chapter 42	Physical Organization in the Face of Aggression	187
Chapter 43	Tone and Quality of Your Voice	195
Chapter 44	Across the Spectrum of Anger	197
Chapter 45	Diamonds in the Rough: Essential Strategies for De-escalation of Anger	203

Chapter 46	Tactical Paraphrasing: The Gold Standard with Angry and Agitated Inmates Suffering from Mental Illness	211
Chapter 47	Big Mistakes That Seemed Like Such Good Ideas at the Time	219

Section X — Managing Rage and Violence 223

Chapter 48	Preface to Rage and Violence	225
Chapter 49	Chaotic Rage: A Consideration of Rage Emerging from Various Disorganized States	227
Chapter 50	Terrified Rage	235
Chapter 51	Hot Rage	239
Chapter 52	Predatory or Cool Rage	253
Chapter 53	De-escalation of Inmates with Developmental Disabilities	259
Chapter 54	Mob Rage: Feeding Frenzy	263
Chapter 55	Deceptive Rage: Snake in the Grass	265
Chapter 56	The Aftermath: What Happens to the Aggressive, Mentally Ill Inmate After an Aggressive Incident?	267
Chapter 57	Managing Threats to Your Family	269
Chapter 58	Conclusion	273

Appendices 275

Appendix A	The Question Of Positional And Compression Asphyxia—By Dr. Gary Vilke	277
Appendix B	Suggested Response Protocol Concerning Suspected Excited Delirium/Chaotic Rage Incidents—By Ret. Lieutenant Michael Paulus	281

Endnotes 297
About The Author 299

Published Works By Ellis Amdur

Published by Edgework www.edgework.info

On the De-escalation of Aggression, Crisis Negotiation & Other Psychological Areas

BODY AND SOUL: Toward a Radical Intersubjectivity in Psychotherapy – Ellis Amdur

COOLING THE FLAMES: Communication, Control, and De-escalation of Mentally Ill & Aggressive Patients
A Comprehensive Guidebook for Emergency Medical Services – Ellis Amdur & John K. Murphy

EVERYTHING ON THE LINE: Calming and De-escalation of Aggressive and Mentally Ill Individuals on the Phone
A Comprehensive Guidebook for Emergency Dispatch (9-1-1) Centers – Ellis Amdur

FROM CHAOS TO COMPLIANCE: Communication, Control, and De-escalation of Mentally Ill, Emotionally Disturbed and Aggressive Offenders – *A Comprehensive Guidebook for Parole and Probation Officers* – Ellis Amdur & Alan Pelton

GUARDING THE GATES: Calming, Control and De-escalation of Mentally Ill, Emotionally Disturbed and Aggressive Individuals
A Comprehensive Guidebook for Security Guards – Ellis Amdur & William Cooper

GRACE UNDER FIRE: Skills to Calm and De-escalate Aggressive and Mentally Ill Individuals in Outpatient Settings: 2nd Edition
A Comprehensive Guidebook for Health and Social Services Agencies, and Individual Practitioners – Ellis Amdur

IN THE EYE OF THE HURRICANE: Skills to Calm and De-escalate Aggressive and Mentally Ill Family Members: 2nd Edition – Ellis Amdur

SAFE BEHIND BARS: Communication, Control, and De-escalation of Mentally Ill and Aggressive Inmates
A Comprehensive Guidebook for Correctional Officers in Jail Settings – Ellis Amdur, Michael Blake & Chris De Villeneuve

SAFE HAVEN: Skills to Calm and De-escalate Aggressive and Mentally Ill Individuals: 2nd Edition
A Comprehensive Guidebook for Personnel Working in Hospital and Residential Settings – Ellis Amdur

SAFETY AT WORK: Skills to Calm and De-escalate Aggressive and Mentally Ill Individuals
A Comprehensive Guidebook for Corporate Security Managers, Human Resources Staff, Loss Prevention Specialists, Executive Protection, and others involved in Threat Management Professions – Ellis Amdur & William Cooper

SHAPESHIFTING FOR LAW ENFORCEMENT CNT/HNT: Effective Scenario Training for Crisis/Hostage Negotiation Teams – Ellis Amdur & Ret. Sgt. Lisbeth Eddy

SHAPESHIFTING FOR CORRECTIONAL FACILITY CNT/HNT: Effective Scenario Training for Crisis/Hostage Negotiation Teams – Ellis Amdur & Ret. Sgt. Lisbeth Eddy

THE ACCORD AGENT: Managing Intense, Problematic Social Interactions Within Business Environments – Ellis Amdur & Robert Hubal

THE COORDINATOR – 2nd Revised Edition: Managing High-Risk High-Consequence Social Interactions in an Unfamiliar Environment – Ellis Amdur & Robert Hubal

THE THIN BLUE LIFELINE: Verbal De-escalation of Mentally Ill and Emotionally Disturbed People
A Comprehensive Guidebook for Law Enforcement Officers – Ellis Amdur & John Hutchings

THREAT DE-ESCALATION: HOW TO EFFECTIVELY ASSESS AND DIFFUSE DANGEROUS SITUATIONS (Book & DVD)
A Publication of the United States Concealed Carry Association – Ellis Amdur

Published by Freelance Academy Press, Inc. www.freelanceacademypress.com

DUELING WITH O-SENSEI: Grappling with the Myth of the Warrior Sage – *Revised & Expanded Edition* – Ellis Amdur

HIDDEN IN PLAIN SIGHT: Tracing the Roots of Ueshiba Morihei's Power –*Revised & Expanded Edition* – Ellis Amdur

OLD SCHOOL: Essays on Japanese Martial Traditions – *2nd Expanded Edition* – Ellis Amdur

Fiction

THE CIMARRONIN: A SAMURAI IN NEW SPAIN: *A Graphic Novel* – Neal Stephenson, Charles Mann, Ellis Amdur & Mark Teppo

THE GIRL WITH THE FACE OF THE MOON (A Novel) – Ellis Amdur

In Gratitude for Previous Collaboration

SAFE WITHIN THE WALLS is a follow-up work from my previous book, SAFE BEHIND BARS: Communication, Control, and De-escalation of Mentally Ill and Aggressive Inmates *A Comprehensive Guidebook for Correctional Officers in Jail Settings*. The system of management and resources within a jail environment is so significantly different from a prison that this necessitated this present work. My two collaborators for SAFE BEHIND BARS were subject-matter experts, Sergeant Michael Blake and Chris DeVilleneuve. I have taken that book and reworked it for the prison environment, and then further received the help of a number of critical readers, all experts in the field, to hammer the book into its present form.

In particular, I retained a number of the scenarios and incidents that Sergeant Blake drew from her own career, as well as her basic typology of five patterns of behavior that one can observer among individuals in custody who are suffering from mental illness.

Sergeant Michael Blake earned her Bachelor's Degree in Law and Justice from Central Washington University in 1993. While in College, she volunteered for the local Crisis Line and completed an internship with the Attorney General's Office. That internship included compiling statistics for the FBI's Uniform Crime Reporting and she was introduced to the Homicide information and Tracking System (HITS Program) in which crime statistics are coupled with GPS in order to solve Crime in Washington State. Since 1994, she has been employed off and on in Corrections with the Yakima County Department of Corrections in Washington State. In 2002, she promoted to Corporal and in 2003, began working as one of the Training Coordinators for the Department. During her tenure as Training Coordinator, she wrote the first training model for corrections officers based on the Reno Model for training Law Enforcement officers. She also co-authored promotional training models for Corporals and Sergeants with her partners in training. All three of these training models were accepted and approved by the Washington State Criminal Justice Training Academy as qualified curriculum for certification processes. In 2007, Michael promoted to Shift Sergeant, running a team of thirty plus officers where she remained for two years, helping to guide her shift through several crisis events, including the death of an officer. She continues in this position, adamant that it is the most rewarding job in corrections.

Chris De Villeneuve holds an MBA/HCM in healthcare management, a Master's degree in Educational Counseling and a Bachelor's degree in Psychology. He has worked integrated care and behavioral health for -31years. He is the Division Director for Behavioral Health and Integrated Care at Catholic Charities Serving Central Washington for the past three years. Prior work has been as a Director with

Comprehensive Health working at clinical sites across Central Washington. He was a Designated Crisis Responder (DCR) in the State of Washington and was a volunteer hostage negotiator for the Yakima Police Department for thirteen years. Chris is a happily married father of two children (Johnathan – 12-years of age and Vivian 9-years of age).

In Gratitude for Expert Critique

The following professionals have closely reviewed this book. With their rigorous critique, I have corrected errors of fact, added new information, and fine-tuned the manuscript. One of the qualities of a good correctional officer is the understanding that the task supersedes protecting someone's feelings; therefore, I have appreciated all their direct criticism.

All responsibility for this book, however, must lie in my hands. Any errors, in particular, are my responsibility. Given that lives can be on the line in work such as this, please don't hesitate to contact Edgework Books (www.edgeworkbooks.com) if you believe that any part of this book is inaccurate or requires additional material. The book will be revised, if needed, in future editions.

Joseph Johnson, CCTP, CCFP, is currently a Correctional Officer for the State of Oregon in a medium security facility. He has been in that position for the last 12 years. Joseph has a background as a First Responder, and has worked as a Firefighter, Reserve Police Officer, and in the Parole/Probation field. Joseph is also an adjunct instructor at the local community college in the Criminal Justice department. Joseph has a combined experience of eighteen years in adult corrections between county and state levels. Joseph holds numerous instructor certifications, including Excited Delirium/Agitated Chaotic Events Instructor. Joseph is also currently working on his Master's degree in Clinical Mental Health Counseling. Joseph has held many positions throughout his career, including Field Training Officer (FTO), member of both the Intelligence Team and Extortion Investigation Team, and is currently a member of his facility's Peer Support Team. At the state corrections level, Joseph has worked in Disciplinary Segregation, Intensive Management, and General Population. Upon completion of his Master's degree, Joseph plans to focus his work on First Responders and Veterans.

Peter Kelly was a prison custodial officer from 2006-2010 at Risden Maximum security prison in Hobart, Tasmania. During his time in this role, Peter worked predominantly in the High-Dependency unit, attached directly to the mental health unit of the prison. Peter is currently the international chief instructor for *Aikido Yuishinkai,* and now travels the world teaching and disseminating this martial art.

Chris Mortensen earned his Bachelor's degree in Psychology from Western Oregon University in 2014. He began his career in Corrections for the Oregon Department of Corrections as a Correctional Officer from 2006- 2013. During his tenure as an Officer, he helped oversee the Institution Security Threat Group and served as a Field Training Officer. In 2013, Chris transitioned to the Professional Development Unit as a Training and Development Specialist II tasked with training new Correctional Officers through the Basic Corrections Course Academy and Annual Training for Agency Staff. In 2016, he joined the Oregon State Penitentiary S.W.A.T. team, where he is still currently a member. In addition, he is the Medic First Aid Training Center Director for the Oregon Department of Corrections.

Patrick Samples earned his Bachelor's Degree in Education in 1991 from the University of West Georgia. He began his career as an Educator and held a variety of jobs in the Education Sector including; Educational Software Prototype Developer, Consultant, and GED Training Coordinator for the state of GA. In 2005, Patrick was hired by the Oregon Department of Corrections as a Training Development Specialist II, and has served on the Crisis Negotiation Team since 2007. During his tenure as a Negotiator his duties have included Technical Systems Officer and most recently, Assistant Team Leader. Patrick is also a Certified Crisis Intervention Specialist II (CCIS II), and is instrumental in the design and delivery of Crisis Intervention Training (CIT) for Correctional Staff.

Phil Soward earned his Bachelor's Degree in Corrections and Psychology from Western Oregon State College in 1992. He completed his Internship with the Oregon Department of Correction establishing a Gang Management Task Force as well as an Intake Testing Program consisting of Psychological Evaluations, Drug and Alcohol Screening, Education Basics Testing and Hostility Screenings. The program allowed Counselors to assign appropriate programs, and together with a complete evaluation performed by Intake Health Services, place the individual at the specific institution most appropriate to their needs. From 1989-1996 he continued Proctoring Intake Testing to men and women entering the correctional system. In 1995 he became ODOC Correctional Officer. In 2003 he joined the OSCI Crisis Negotiation Team. He soon became the Assistant Team Leader, and held that position for over ten years. Since 2014 he has been an Adjunct Instructor for the annual ODOC In-Service Training.

Joseph Steinfeld, MSW, LCSWR, worked as a psychiatric social worker and a social work supervisor for the New York State Office of Mental Health within the state prison system from 1992 - 2016. Duties included evaluation of the mental health needs of inmates entering the prison system in the reception center, clinical coordination of a program integrating seriously inmates suffering from mental illness into the general population, supervision of clinical staff, provision of testimony in disciplinary hearings regarding mental health issues, and training of mental health as well as corrections staff in mental health issues. Joe was an expert reviewer for the journal *Hospital and Community Psychiatry* on the topic of management of violence, and taught that topic in a variety of settings. He has also been an adjunct professor with Marist College and with Adelphi University School of Social Work. Joe has achieved rankings in judo and aikido, is a former Kennedy King Games judo champion, and has provided training on the management of violence in a variety of settings. He is currently retired from state civil service and works on call as an assistant with a veterinary ambulance service, and as a handler with an animal talent agency.

Introduction

This book is designed to address the unique challenges facing Institutional Correctional Officers (referred to as "correctional officers" in this text) responsible for supervision of inmates suffering from mental illness incarcerated in prison settings. It is intended to increase officer and inmate safety by introducing specific identification and response strategies to manage distressed, threatening or aggressive inmates quickly and safely. The strategies and techniques presented in this book are to be used as a foundation upon which the individual correctional officer, and indeed entire agencies, can improve outcomes and increase safety.

The behaviors of individual suffering from mental illness or other emotional disturbance can be quite bizarre. Through understanding such behaviors, you will become more skillful in assessing if an inmate is truly dangerous, and in many situations, you will have the ability to calm and deescalate such an individual. Often, you will find your presence alone prevents a situation from escalating, with inmates complying with directives willingly, with some even anxious to meet your approval or gain your respect.

Throughout this book I speak of officer safety. Officer safety is a subject that goes far beyond managing how to survive a shift uninjured. In addition to the threat of violence, correctional officers routinely face serious job-related pressure including a lack of adequate staffing, mandatory overtime, rotating shift work, etc. However, dealing with inmates manifesting bizarre, profoundly distressed and perhaps dangerous behaviors can exponentially add to the rigors of the job. If correctional officers have confidence that they know the best way to communicate with these most confusing and sometimes dangerous inmates, their very stressful job will become less so, and therefore, safer in the bargain.

This author previously co-wrote SAFE BEHIND BARS: Communication, Control, and De-escalation of Mentally Ill and Aggressive Inmates *A Comprehensive Guidebook for Correctional Officers in Jail Settings*, with Michael Blake and Chris De Villeneuve. That book focused on two areas: tactical de-escalation and control of inmates suffering from mental illness and systemic issues. Only the first of those topics, interactions between officer and inmate, is covered in this book. The reason for the added focus on systems issue in the jail book is that inmates held in jails often cycle in a round from hospital to outpatient treatment to contact with police to jail to the courts to probation and back again. Each 'contact point' must integrate their services with the others if the misdemeanant individual (or pre-trial detainee) suffering from mental illness is well-served. In this sense, one cannot write about individuals suffering from mental illness within a jail setting without considering all the other institutions just enumerated.

Prison is different. First of all, it is a closed, insular world. All services are held within its walls. Many thousands of books, scholarly and otherwise, have been written about systemic issues within prisons. Beyond that, policies can be quite different within federal and state prisons, within prisons at different levels of security and private institutions as well. As my critical readers emphasized, policies about disciplinary hearings, write-ups and rules on drug use, much less discharge planning and institutional policy are completely out of the hands of the front-line correctional officer.

One thing is universal, however. The dilemma of the front-line correctional officer whose responsibility is to maintain the safety of inmates, of fellow officers and other staff and, of course, himself or herself. Therefore, this book will focus on face-to-face encounters with aggressive inmates, particularly those who are emotionally disturbed, intoxicated or suffering from mental illness.

It is the hope of the author, whose professional experience encompasses over thirty years of interaction in face-to-face encounters with mentally ill and emotionally disturbed individuals, that this book will be invaluable in readying both newer officers and experienced veterans for such encounters. You may find, however, that reading this book is not sufficient. For those interested in more hands-on training, I provide direct instruction, traveling to your location to provide not only basic de-escalation training, but advanced training in such areas as strategic communication with individuals with character disorders or anti-social traits, and along with subject-matter expert associates, combined training in both physical and verbal tactics to ensure safety. (See www.gullaamdur.com)

A Note on Terminology

The question of terminology can be something of a minefield. At its worst, it can develop into a 'toxic political correctness,' where the use of the 'wrong' term can be used by others to define the speaker as immoral or prejudiced. Such an environment can become quite dangerous, not only to one's career, but literally to one's safety. If officers are concerned that everything they say is being monitored, a mistrust between supervisory and line officers can develop, as well as tension between front-line staff. If correctional officers are at odds with one another, if group solidarity between officers is damaged, the prison will become an even more dangerous environment. Not only is it unsafe for officers, it will be unsafe for inmates as well.

Therefore, a basic principle should be: **Default to good intentions.** There needs to be policy on terminology, particularly that used in regards to inmates. But if an officer, particularly seasoned officer who has lived his or her life using certain language with no ill intention whatsoever, uses a certain term that is no longer the 'correct' one, *remind them rather than attack them*. Only if an officer clearly expresses, by word or deed, that they are using language in order to damage an individual's sense of self-worth or respect, or in order to create strife or pain, then should this be regarded as an act of verbal abuse.

Of course, there are words that are always abusive that must be forbidden: ethnic slurs or obscenities. But particularly when trying to institute a change of program or correctional culture, the changes in terminology should be introduced and enforced by reminding officers, not sanctioning them.

Which leads to several terms used in this book: throughout my entire career, I have referred to 'mentally ill patients,' 'mentally ill inmates,' etc. I have never, in using this term, intended to demean the person I am discussing. Of recent years, however, such terms as 'patient with mental illness,' or 'inmate suffering from mental illness,' are now encouraged. After a caution from one of my critical readers, I have written this book striving to use the latter terminology. I'm sure some of my readers are rolling their eyes at this point—it seems like such a trivial change, and if you are used to the older way of speaking, you know you will 'slip up' at one point or another. As I said above, one should be given the benefit of the doubt in cases like this as the change in language becomes more natural over time. But there is a really significant question at the heart of this: is the inmate an illness or a person? If the inmate is sick with pneumonia, you don't say, 'That pneumonia inmate;' you say, 'the inmate with pneumonia.' Mental illness should not be different. If you will have any chance of influencing the inmate—and by influence, I mean that your interactions cause him or her to be less of a danger to others—it is only through treating him or her with respect (without compromising safety, of course). Talk to the person who has an illness—don't talk to the diagnosis.

A number of new approaches are being tried on both a state and federal level: new models of incarceration, new strategies of incarceration, etc. And with them come new terms used within each model. One example of this, part of the so-called Norway model, is a suggestion to change the term 'inmate' to 'adult in custody' (AIC). It is possible that, in the future, this term will become the norm, just as inmate has largely (but not entirely) replaced the term 'prisoner' in the United States, at least. At the point of this writing (2019), however, AIC is not standard terminology. If I were to use this term, either in full or by the abbreviation, officers from many states will have to constantly remind themselves what I'm talking about because that term is not used in their state. Therefore, I will continue to use the term, 'inmate,' the most common term used throughout the United States. If AIC—or some other term—becomes the norm sometime in the future, I will change it in future editions.

SECTION I

Inmates Suffering From Mental Illness

CHAPTER 1

Mental Illness Within the Prison System

Something not in the Basic Job Description
There is a range of reasons why someone chooses the field of corrections. For some, it is a calling: serving and protecting their community. Unfortunately, no one mentions the mentally ill until they are already hired. Inmates suffering from mental illness are often in the wrong place, housed with the wrong people, and given the severe overcrowding that is endemic in most prisons in the United States, get lost among the numbers. At the same time, they have been incarcerated because they have committed felonies—serious crimes—and present a danger to their community.

> **1.1 From a Veteran Correctional Officer: The Need for Dedicated Staff for the Inmate suffering from Mental Illness**
> In some of the prisons I worked, access to mental health nurses and doctors was very limited, and quite frankly, there were occasions when I observed abusive behavior from correctional officers towards inmates suffering from mental illness. I believe that most of this was due to officers being poorly trained to deal with such inmates, some of the most challenging within our prison system. The officers felt frustrated and helpless. I therefore insist that the correctional officers that work within the units that house the mentally unstable must be hand-picked and well-trained. They must understand the special nature of the people that they are dealing with, and have the personality to deal with this unique situation.

Smaller correctional facilities do not require advanced degrees to work in corrections, and many of the officers have not been educated on even the basics about how and why a mental illness manifests itself. Unless the facility dedicates expensive training time specifically for dealing with inmates suffering from mental illness, officers may never gain the skill or knowledge to successfully work with potentially one of the most difficult and dangerous populations--unless they educate themselves on their own time.

Concrete skills, such as Taser™, defensive tactics, threat identification and cuffing are often easier to learn than tactical communication and body language, even though the last two skills are an almost constant requirement in correctional institutions. Just as with physical skills, you must strive to train your verbal responses into 'pseudo-instinct,' where you don't have to think before you effectively react, something that takes a lot of practice. It is not a matter of simply knowing the "right" thing to say; experts at de-escalation must have the fluidity to move from one style into another if the first doesn't work. In fact, 'prepared' responses are often the worst thing to do, especially with veteran or character disordered inmates with finely tuned 'bullsh*t meters.'

> **1.2 From a Veteran Correctional Officer: You Can't Do it By Script**
> I recall an inmate whom I'd known for years. I worked pretty well with him and got a little complacent. He was on meth, in crisis, and I was trying to de-escalate him using a kind of scripted technique that I'd just learned in a training seminar. He immediately keyed in on the 'new tactics' I was running on him, called me out on it and blew up.

If the only individuals suffering from mental illness that an officer sees are in the prison environment, it's easy to forget that the vast majority of people with mental illness are productive members of their communities. Only a small number of individuals with mental illness ever end up in prison. Despite the care they may have received pre-sentencing, in jail or in other facilities, they may come into prison in a bad way. Some are violent for a myriad of reasons. On the other hand, mental illness does not affect intelligence. (Try to convince someone with a quantum physics degree that there are not demons in his room or better yet, that you aren't a demon!) When we **look at behavior rather than diagnosis**, incarcerated inmates suffering from mental illness roughly divide into five populations.[1] Of course, these categories are a general overview of the most prevalent populations):

Inmates with Chronic Mental Illness. These are inmates who, before their felony conviction, may have committed a string of misdemeanor crimes. Some have moved in and out of mental health facilities, and many have also abused drugs. They generally have a history of trauma, sometimes lifelong, and may have been homeless for considerable periods of time.

Developmental Delayed Inmates. This population of inmates has developmental disabilities (intellectual disability or fetal alcohol syndrome, for example) that affect their cognitive abilities and maturity levels. They may also have mental illnesses beyond their developmental disability. The felonies that get them imprisoned are often severe, crimes of sexual or physical violence, because more minor offense are usually pled down due to their disabilities.

Inmates with Psychotic Disorders and/or Paranoia. These inmates can be highly violent and aggressive. They generally fall into one of two categories: those that are experiencing hallucinations or delusions (psychosis) (CHAPTERS 30 & 31), and those inmates that will not cooperate with the simplest of directives because they resist your control. (CHAPTER 21). It must be remembered, however, that violence is almost always contextual—it doesn't appear in a vacuum. Mental illness, alone, does not make an individual violent.

Crisis Inmates. These are the inmates who have hit a breaking point, due to some crisis. This might be something 'outside,' such as divorce, a death in the family, etc., or it may be something 'inside,' such as pressure from prison gangs or rape.

Victimized Inmates. These individuals may have been actively involved in criminal activities, but, once inside, are controlled by others (either an individual or a gang). They are victimized and exploited by the controlling individual(s). They may have come into prison with psychological disorders, but very often, they develop such disorders as depression, anxiety, post-traumatic stress disorder, to name a few, due to their experiences within prison.

Because mental illness affects and manifests itself differently in each person, there are inmates that will not fit into these five categories, or may fit into more than one. There are also driving factors that may move them from one category to another, much like a sliding scale.

The Inmate with Chronic Mental Illness

This inmate is generally not overtly aggressive, but can be if they feel threatened or pressured. They have often lost support or even contact with their family and friends. They often don't like or believe in the value of medications, or sometimes, because they think they are cured, discontinue taking those that are prescribed.

Some officers may have good rapport with them and may be the 'go-to' people to intervene when they are in crisis. They can get fixated on other officers, and get ramped up when they see them. Over time, officers will know what verbal interventions either calm them down or flame them up.

The Inmate with Chronic Mental Illness will often spend more time in prison than an inmate who is not mentally ill who commits the same crime, as they stack up new charges or disciplinary infractions while inside.

These inmates often have their own ideas about their situation—essentially making it up as they go along, while completely believing everything they say. One of the author's associates, Sgt. Michael Blake, refers to this as 'speaking into being,' meaning, "If I said it, it's real." This is clinically referred to as 'magical thinking.' If such inmates tell you they were wrongly convicted, you are never going to convince them otherwise, even if you have court record or evidence in your hand. If they feel that you have wronged them in even the slightest way, you will only get back in their good graces if another person does something worse (in their mind) to take the spotlight off of you—and that might not work either. You might stay on their 'enemies list' for life. Sometimes you will have no idea what caused them to turn on you. You may have dealt peacefully with them for years, but suddenly, for no apparent reason, it's your turn to be the bad guy.

1.3 The Distinction Between Delusions, Magical Thinking and Manipulative Lying

There are distinctions between delusions, magical thinking and 'sociopathic lying.' A delusion is a fixed, irrational, non-reality-based idea, that doesn't change over time. Magical thinking is also non-reality-based, but is more like the fantasies of a child, based on what they *feel* is true. For example, this author once met a slightly developmentally disabled man, who was obsessed with a famous country music singer, and he would proclaim that she was his lover. He fantasized about her so much that he felt it *should* be so, and then when he was challenged, he would get very angry. He shifted between, "It could be so if I only met her,' to "It should be so," to "It is so," depending on his emotions at the time.

That said, it is very hard to distinguish between an inmate who has a *delusion* that he or she is innocent of a crime, and *magical thinking*, where one *feels* something so strongly that they believe it in the moment. <u>In any event, officers' interventions with such individuals are largely the same, whether it is labeled a delusion or magical thinking.</u>

With manipulative lying, on the other hand, the individual tells a lie and then, when not believed or contradicted, becomes morally outraged when they're not believed. This is due to a kind of entitlement, as if to say: "If I say the sky is red, you have to believe me, because I said it. It doesn't matter if it's true or not. What matters is that I said it."

Delusions are by definition totally fixed and inflexible, even when they defy reason, whereas the lies of the anti-social/sociopathic individual are altered glibly and smoothly to gain advantage. The latter individual's frame of mind is a kind of toxic narcissism. They have a right to lie because they are the only thing of importance in the world—and your questioning their statement is an attack, therefore, on the only thing that matters. (CHAPTERS 24 & 25)

Some such inmates are known for stripping down naked in their cells, or at best, wearing only underwear. They are often isolated from general population due to disruptive behaviors, and they tend to stay naked in their isolation cells until they are released. Some inmates go one step further and smear their own fecal matter all over the cells and sometimes themselves, sometimes for months on end. Even more horribly, some eat their own excrement. (CHAPTER 22) They often have to be moved from their cells with force so the officers can clean it. These inmates are then pushed into showers as they refuse to clean themselves. (How many days can you leave an inmate smeared in their own fecal matter before it becomes negligence, both concerning the inmate's own health, but also concerning other inmates who may have to suffer from the noxious smell? How many such occurrences does it take before officers become burned out, or worse, regard such inmates with contempt or even hatred?). Some officers are more stressed by these inmates than any others: they feel completely helpless in dealing with them, yet they are forced to witness and experience humanity at its most degraded. To make matter even worse, these profoundly ill people are also some of our highest risk inmates for self-harm and aggressive behavior.

The Developmentally Disabled Inmate

These inmates, moderately to severely cognitively impaired, are not frequently found in a prison setting—when they are, it is usually for a serious crime of violence or sexual assault. Statistics are all over the map, but Goldman sites studies that approximately 2% of inmates are developmentally disabled. However, he notes that the number may be far higher.[2] Concerning their behavior associated with their crime, as one law enforcement officer stated," "They are the last to leave the scene, the first to get arrested, and the first to confess."[3]

Developmentally Disabled Inmates often have a history of being taken care of, or at least lived with family members, and they may have had a considerable history of assault against them. Given that they often strike out against the people closest to them when aggravated—family and other caregivers—this becomes particularly problematic for officers, because you are now their 'family.' Developmentally Disabled Inmates, childlike, have a difficult time in prison: they are easily victimized, rarely treatable, and often lack a basic understanding of the world and other people—let alone a prison.

No one really knows what how best to manage Developmentally Disabled Inmates within a prison setting. They are not really 'mentally ill.' Either from birth or due to injury, they are impaired on a neurological level. Although a mental health professional, or a trained correctional officer can help deal with case management issues with such an inmate, there is nothing they can do to cure or change them. We can offer therapy or medication to an individual suffering from mental illness; we cannot restructure a brain. In most states, the system for developmentally disabled individuals is even more underfunded and under-resourced than the mental health or corrections systems. Often, no one available is trained to deal with such inmates, and for that reason, no one *wants* to deal with them.

Inmates with Psychotic Disorders and/or Paranoia

Such inmates make up one of the smallest portions of incarcerated inmates suffering from mental illness. This is fortunate because these inmates burn up time and resources quickly. An inordinate amount officers' time will be taken up with them, to the detriment of all other inmates in the prison.

Such inmates will have episodes where they are medically at risk and at risk to others: dehydrated, violent, and fighting. They may have gone many days without sleeping, eating, or drinking. This drains even more resources as medical intervention may be necessary when the inmate becomes physically compromised. Time and resources will be taken up at the judicial level, too, if a court order is needed to use injectable medications for the inmate's well-being. Officers will more than likely have to wrestle the inmate to the floor in order to give them the medications.

Other such inmates will not comply with the simplest directives. Whether hearing voices or seeing hallucinations (CHAPTERS 30 & 31) or not, they are very paranoid (CHAPTER 21), and very angry towards anyone they perceive as controlling them in any way. These inmates will get offended at the slightest thing, "Why are you looking at me like that?" "Why did you look away when you were talking to me?" "Is that a smirk on your face?" "Get out of my room!" "Don't touch my stuff!" "Don't touch me!" Anything and everything may set them off. For the person dealing with them, there is no right answer; nothing will please this inmate or calm them.

Such inmates are unimpressed by consequences. If you take away their books, they will write on their uniforms. If you take away their pencils, they will rip their uniforms. If you take away their uniforms, they will rip apart their cells. If you restrain them they may try to kill themselves, or urinate and defecate all over themselves and the chair and try to spit on you and bite you. Sometimes they will take bites out of their own flesh. When you try to take them out of restraints and try clean them up, they will fight you. If you leave them naked in a cell, they flood the cell. If you turn off the water, they will fill their toilets with fecal matter. When you come into unplug it, they will throw fecal matter, urine, and/or blood on you. If you don't try to unplug it or tell them to unplug it, they will smear the room and themselves with fecal matter. They may even eat it.

Even while looking straight into a weapon, these inmates will often not back down. Why would they comply with an officer or case manager when they are receiving messages from God or threats from Satan? All too many physical interactions with inmates suffering from psychotic symptoms or acute paranoia will end up in a use of force, or at least a verbal altercation—at least until they are psychologically stabilized.

Inmates with Psychotic Disorders are some of the highest risk inmates in any correctional population. If they can't hurt another person, they may just as readily hurt themselves. These inmates will often have multiple 'use of force' events involving a Taser™ or pepper spray whereas most inmates will, after only one use of force with either of these less-than-lethal weapons, decide that they do not want to re-experience it.

The Crisis Inmate

This population of inmates is the polar opposite of the Inmate suffering from psychosis or paranoia. Crisis Inmates may have been functioning adequately within the prison, either in a state of ordinary health or perhaps with a treatable mental illnesses. They may have quit taking necessary psychiatric medications for any one of a number of reasons, or intolerable levels of stress cause them to reach a 'breaking point.' Crisis Inmates may have families who are deeply worried for them. Often, their first crisis is what brought them to prison—they have murdered or assaulted a family member or business associate, embezzled large sums of money—some kind of 'one-time event' that causes profound damage, resulting in them being placed in an environment that is as alien to them as the Amazon jungle or an Arctic island.

Crisis Inmates are ill equipped to deal with real criminals or the prison environment. They are at risk for victimization in correctional facilities, and above and beyond their current charge, would not normally be leading a life of crime. Crisis Inmates can receive secondary trauma simply from the process of incarceration. In this sense, they are psychologically fragile individuals, and any serious crisis, occurring 'outside' in the world they left behind, or 'inside' the prison, may cause them to break down emotionally or psychologically.

The Victimized Inmate

Victimized Inmates aren't as common as some of the other types of inmates suffering from mental illness in correctional facilities, but they are certainly one of the saddest for professionals to deal with. These inmates may have mental illnesses that are treatable, and could conceivably live relatively stable lives; however, a combination of such things as mental illness, trauma, developmental disabilities and a lack of survival skills leads them become part of a criminal milieu, and eventually, commit one or more serious felonies. For some, their move into criminality may have started with victimization 'outside.' For example, many people with mental illness cannot be gainfully employed, but receive monthly disability or Veterans' checks. The government funds that are meant to help a debilitated member of our society have instead placed a very large target on those needing it, visible to anyone of the many criminals who want to make a dollar or have the perverse urge to control and corrupt the life of another person.

The easiest way to control such a vulnerable person is through 'love' or drugs—or both—and you will definitely see this inside the prison. The criminal manipulates or forces his victim to beg money from their family and their friends. Beyond that, criminals isolate Victimized Inmates from family and friends on the outside, and those in the prison who might be able to help them on the inside. Soon the criminal or gang is the only person they have access to. All information coming in or going out of the relationship is carefully monitored and sifted by the criminal—after all, knowledge is power. They may also control their prescription medication (if they allow the person to take them) and any other drugs: generally, they may sell their prescriptions to other inmates. The criminal eventually will turn the Victimized Inmate to criminal activity within the prison—as well as sexually exploiting them through prostitution and rape.

To Sum Up

Incarceration can be traumatizing to some, and irrelevant to others (Many sociopaths don't really give a damn where they are; for them, prison is 'just another place'). For many, it is somewhere in-between. For some inmates suffering from mental illness, prison may be the safest, most comforting place they know. For others, it is hell.

For most inmates with mental illness even the physical environment is an assault on their senses. It is a land of walls, uncompromising rules and fluorescent lighting. It is too loud, too bright and too noisy. Couple this with insufficient 'nourishing' human interaction (in the form of programs, medication management and therapy); these inmates become more and more ill.

Prisoners with mental illness are generally at the lowest strata of the prison inmate hierarchy. Often disheveled in appearance, destitute of funds to purchase inmate commissary commodities, lacking familial resources including, sadly, even visits from family members, unable to hold the higher paying jobs in prison, due to both emotional instability and impaired cognitive abilities, the inmate suffering from mental illness is often unprepared to navigate the difficult and sometimes treacherous waters of a prison.

More often than not, Crisis Inmates do not possess the mindset or skills to successfully navigate the prison environment or the justice process. They frequently *become* Victim Inmates if a criminal gets their claws into them or if their family or support network cuts off contact with them. Because of prison culture, they often cannot even ask for help. For example, if a Crisis Inmate were threatened by a gang member, and reported the threat to a correctional officer, they would be marked as a snitch and then be at risk from nearly all the inmates.

Crisis Inmates have to be separated from most general population inmates until that crisis is resolved. General population inmates make fun of them, victimize them, steal from them, and/or beat them. On the other hand, they often exhibit behaviors that are annoying or frightening to other inmates, or evoke the bullying impulse.

Inmates suffering from psychosis or acute paranoia cannot function inside a correctional facility. They break the rules wherever they are, and wherever they go. The simplest directive such as, 'flush your toilet' is met with a verbal outburst, if not a physical one. These are the inmates that will hit and kick the walls if they can't hit you, even to the extent of breaking their own bones. They are not, however, usually at risk of victimization, unless placed in a general population unit where more than one inmate can gang up on them. Even then, the consequences may be dire for the attackers. This type of inmate, male or female, will often keep getting up and attacking, no matter what the cost to himself or herself.

1.4 Why Do Inmates Suffering from Mental Illness Stop Taking Their Medication?

There are many reasons inmates resist taking their medications, discontinue them, or take them intermittently. Among them are:

- **Unwelcome Side Effects.** Among possible side-effects are muscle spasms, intolerable itching/crawling sensations in the limbs, tongue thrusting, tremors, impairment of sexual functioning, dry mouth, weight gain, weight loss, skin disorders, even life-threatening disorders that must be monitored through such invasive procedures as regular blood-draws, to name but a few.
- **No Effect (or so it seems).** Many psychiatric medications are not 'felt' beyond their side-effects. They don't make the inmate 'high,' or even 'better.' Apart from the side-effects, the inmate simply 'feels like him/herself.' Feeling good, therefore, one draws the natural conclusion that the drug has done its job, or in other cases, does not work, and therefore can be discontinued.
- **No Effect (in truth).** Many of the medications simply don't work for a specific inmate. They may have had very high hopes that the medications would have helped, even cured them. All that they got, instead, were the sides-effects.
- **The Illness Is Better Than the Cure.** Sometimes, even apart from noxious side-effects, the illness can feel better than the 'cure.' Many psychotic individuals find that the medications muffle or suppress delusions and/or hallucinations, but they don't make them disappear. Furthermore, the medications often do not touch the belief system around the delusions. Life on medications, for such people, is like living under a sodden blanket. What is reality to them may be muffled, tranquilized, and constricted, but not otherwise changed. For such people, the medications may help them live a more stable, uneventful life, but just as we shake off constricting bedding when we are too hot and constricted, psychotic individuals may discontinue medications, simply to have, in their view, air to breathe.
- **Mania, the 'Up-Side' of Manic-Depression.** This can be a state of high-energy and ecstasy. Medicated life, on the other hand, can be flat and boring. **(CHAPTER 32)**
- **Intoxicants Preferred to Medication.** The inmate's use of illicit drugs and/or alcohol leads them to discontinue their prescribed medications.

CHAPTER 2

Threat Assessment: How Do We Know Someone Is Dangerous?

Subsequent to intake, an inmate may be moved up or down the custodial risk scale from their initial classification. This secondary assessment process is where officers' experience and intuition can play a valuable role in assessing the inmates risk level. The officer may override previous assessments, and recommend a more intensive level of custodial supervision. This is especially true for inmates suffering from mental illness, as their illness alone may dictate more intensive case management. Inmates who have, for instance, a known history of suicide attempts will not be placed in a room alone. Inmates that are brought in on heavy charges (killing a child or a well-known member of the community, or any other particularly heinous crime) will inevitably be moved up in security level if for no reason other than their own safety.

Essential items in threat assessment:

A Past History of Violence. This is perhaps the most reliable predictor of future violence. A capacity for violence is both innate and learned: the more it is used, the easier it is to use again, and the more likely it will be chosen as a preferred 'problem-solving' activity. This is relevant whether the violence is directed against others or against oneself—in one sense, the only different between suicide and murder is what direction the weapon is pointed. Remember, too, that for many, violence is rewarding: power over others often is the best experience of some inmates' lives.

History of Bullying or Intimidation. This is the psychological counterpart of physical violence. Several different types of inmates tend to 'strong arm' other inmates when placed in a general population unit. Any inmate who is high up in a gang hierarchy will inevitably end up either running a unit, or coming into direct conflict with other 'alpha' inmates, particularly those from other gangs. Some inmates don't need to be in a gang to be natural bullies. As good as intake interviews may be, observation trumps interviews, particularly when evaluating the opportunistic, predatory aggressive individual.

Prior Incarceration. Any incarceration is a heightened risk factor, even if it was for a non-violent crime. The inmate may be terrified or outraged at the idea of being incarcerated again. Furthermore, with the prevalence of physical and sexual assault within correctional institutions, the non-violent arrestee may have come out a very different person than they went in.[4]

Possession of Weapons, Fascination with Weapons, Past History of Using Weapons. A fascination with weaponry, or fantasizing about them in a pathological manner, is very definitely a heightened risk factor. These inmates, if known, usually have an alert code associated with their name.

History of Physical Abuse, or the Witnessing of Physical Abuse and Violence. Beyond a history of personal victimization, it is exceptionally traumatic to have witnessed abuse of a family member. The victim of abuse often hates his own weakness, and begins hating weakness in others as well. Once this occurs, it is a natural move for some people to begin victimizing that which they hate—the weak.[5] The vast majority of women in prison are victims of sexual or physical violence and enormous numbers show symptoms of post-traumatic stress disorder. Many become violent at any sign of aggression from another inmate or even an officer.

Head Injuries. These are associated with impulse control problems. A history of closed head injuries is endemic among violent felons.[6] All too many of our returning military veterans, some of whom may be incarcerated, also suffer from Traumatic Brain Injuries (TBI), the signal injury of the wars in the Middle East. Some proportion of those with TBI may have hair-trigger tempers and difficulty controlling negative emotions. Information that an inmate has suffered a TBI offers advanced warning that he or she may be very explosive. Furthermore, if the inmate actually informs you that he or she has a history of closed head injury, medical staff should be made aware of this fact. They may be in an emergent state or still be in a condition where treatment is needed to alleviate a condition that continues to damage their brain. (NOTE: particularly with inmates with a history of head injury, it is a helpful to ask them: "What sets you off?" Following this, the inmate should be asked, "If you did lose it, what can officers do to help you get control/calm down again?"

A History of Mental Illness. Chronic patterns or symptoms of mental illness may exacerbate an inmate's ability to follow rules and regulations, and in some cases, may precipitate violent outbursts. On the other hand, the illness may leave the inmate vulnerable to predation by his or her peers in prison.

Fear of Attack or Invasion of Personal Space. Paranoid and fearful inmates may lash out in defensive violence. If you are properly 'tracking' the inmate, you should be aware if they become increasingly stressed when in close physical proximity to you or other officers even during the interview process. This is something Transport Officers may have already noticed, so whenever possible, get information from transport about any significant behavior of the inmates they just brought in.

Low Frustration Tolerance, and Inability or Unwillingness to Tolerate Limit Setting. "I want what I want and I want it now—and you'd better not keep me from it." Such an individual may explode from sudden calm: for example, if there is a delay in the lunch line. Officers often observe this during the intake process, with an inmate quickly becoming impatient, physical agitated, snappish, and giving a sense that they are 'wired tight.' Some inmates are already known by officers for low frustration tolerance during past incarcerations, for which they should be flagged in their record.

Recent Stressors and Losses. Bereavement, separation, divorce, job loss, <u>anniversaries of losses,</u> and, of course, incarceration itself can make an inmate more willing to become violent, feeling that they have nothing left to lose. Those personal details will not usually be revealed during intake, but threat assessment is an ongoing process, and if the inmate has a lover or spouse break up with them, if they get more time unexpectedly stacked on, if they are fired from their job while in prison, or any other such stressor, the risk they present to others increases, sometimes exponentially.

A Feeling of Victimization and Grievance. Many, perhaps the majority of inmates, believe themselves to be victimized by society in general, or hold a grudge against 'the system.' They view their current predicament to be always someone else's fault. In many instances the correctional officer becomes the 'face' of the system for the inmate, and then the target of their grievance. This is often revealed during the intake in an unending litany of abuse, complaints, blaming, and verbal aggression. This can often be a sign of paranoia (CHAPTER 21), where the inmate feels under almost perpetual attack from all directions. They store up grievances, and 'appoint' others as their designated enemies.

Almost All Intoxicating Substances Can Be Disinhibiting. Intoxicants tend to 'dissolve' the internal barriers that hold us back from our primitive desires, among them aggression. Intoxicants include alcohol, drugs, industrial chemicals and prescription medications.

Physical Pain or Discomfort (Particularly Chronic). Aside from illness or injury, this also includes withdrawal from drugs and alcohol. Unfortunately, many medications that help mentally ill people can have very nasty side-effects, particularly when the inmate is inadequately monitored. Such side-effects can be maddening. Inmates with any medical condition should have a separate interview and intake process with medical staff.

An Inmate Who Has Already Given Up. Some inmates expect every interaction to be difficult or negative. Their response can be, "What the hell. Nothing will help. If I'm aggressive, at least I can make my mark on the world—or on you." Such 'what the hell does it matter' type of aggression is often symptomatic of depression. Unless the underlying depression is addressed, these inmates will continue to feel hopeless—and maintain an attitude of having nothing left to lose.

Severe Pathological Behaviors.
- Rapid mood swings - such inmates are unpredictable, and can escalate into a rage unexpectedly.
- Boisterousness – a loud, almost aggressive happiness, in which there is no attempt to 'include' others in the laughter or entertainment.
- Hallucinations - particularly auditory command hallucinations that may be telling the inmate to do something terrible.
- Mania - this is a state of excitement, typified by rapid speech, grandiose thinking, very poor judgment, and impulsive behavior. It is a behavior we see in people with bipolar disorder (manic-

depression), intoxication on stimulants such as methamphetamine or cocaine, and not infrequently, alcohol.
- History of predatory or manipulative behaviors - With these individuals, their aggression is planned rather than impulsive. It is typified by sneak attacks ('attacking the corner') rather than a head-on confrontation

Interactional Factors Between the Aggressor and Victim. The aggressor paradoxically views their target as having power over them, views them as being inflexible or controlling, or denying the aggressor his due. In short, the aggressor usually believes himself to be the victim. This dynamic is so obvious that it seems almost unnecessary to include here, but you have surely seen officers who forget that, as far as many inmates are concerned, you are always the enemy. Any officer who ever believes that he or she has a friendship with any inmate will soon find themselves in profoundly dangerous situations. On the other hand, officers who are regarded as tough but fair are actually far less likely to elicit personal hatred from an inmate (never forgetting, however, there are some inmates who regard all correctional officers as enemies or prey).

Religious and Cultural Clashes. Culture is any set of rules and customs that organizes relationships between people.[7] Officers should avoid any religious, political, or cultural debates with inmates. However, correctional officers should try to be aware of the cultural rules and religious practices of their inmates, so they won't *inadvertently* insult them (as long as this caution does not compromise their authority). Be aware that some cultures sanction violence and these cultural rules may be different from one's own mainstream culture.[8]

Tattoos and Gang Affiliation. Gang membership and interaction with other gangs is complex and the best way to handle the intricacies of their interactions is to have a person on staff dedicated to gang management. Inmates may not admit to gang affiliation, but their tattoos will often tell you a different story. They may keep this information to themselves if they want to get close to a rival gang member in prison in order to carry out a 'hit' on them. Many gangs have fight-on-sight orders, meaning that if they see a rival gang member, they must fight or be disciplined by their own gang.

Ongoing Threat Assessment to Reduce Risk
Following the face-to-face interview, the classification officer may find that they need to release an official alert or update to the officers working in the facility. Alerts contain details of how the officers should deal with a certain inmate, particularly with those who are mentally ill. In the latter case, it is not always due to deliberate resistance to authority. They may simply be unable to retain or comprehend complex information. Alerts will specify both procedural matters, such as the requirement to always handcuff an inmate while he or she is being moved, as well as suggestions for the most effective way to communicate with the inmate suffering from mental illness to elicit compliance (for example, "Inmate Hathaway is very paranoid, but it has been observed that if one of the transporting officers talks with him about music, he is less likely to be assaultive"). Alerts should not be posted where other inmates can see them, or discussed with earshot of other inmates.

SECTION II

Core Requirements For De-Escalation And Control Of Inmates Who Are Agitated, Aggressive, And/Or Suffering From Mental Illness

CHAPTER 3

The Development of a Safety Mindset

Correctional work is always dangerous. Officers should never be 'comfortable' in a unit, on a tier, in the recreation yard or anywhere with an inmate. It doesn't matter who or what they are or did—they are a danger to you. Whenever you are in the units or interacting with inmates, be present in the moment. Recognize your body positioning, be aware of your physical environment and pay attention to the signals your body gives you that might indicate that a dangerous situation is developing (CHAPTERS 4 & 5).

> **3.1 From a Veteran Correctional Counselor: A Safety Mindset is NOT paranoia**
> Some officers become over-reactive. Rather than enacting focused threat assessments, they see everything as a threat. This can lead to an officer who is either too timid or too aggressive. With enough time and stress, such an officer may become burned-out, and then numb to potential danger.

Although this book centers on verbal de-escalation skills, we must start at a more basic level, because the contributing causes of many critical incidents can be attributed to a lack of attention to basic safety precautions. This must begin *before* you start your workday. If your mind is unfocused, your ability to notice early warnings signs of potential danger will be impaired. For example, officers cannot allow personal or familial issues to intrude upon their ability to focus on the job at hand.

The development of correctional awareness is based upon the following three fundamental assumptions:
- Being pro-active about safety issues must be a primary concern of all correctional staff: managers, supervisors, line officers and support staff.
- There must be consistency in the application of safety procedures and emergency protocols at all levels of the institution.
- A variety of issues, including overcrowding of cell and dormitory areas, the custody level of the inmates supervised, gang affiliations, physical plant problems, design flaws such as blind spots as well as ever shrinking correctional budgets impact upon the level of risk. Adequate staff safety preparedness and correctional awareness is not a once-and-done training event: ongoing communication is required between all levels of staff. A regular review of safety protocols, operational policies, crisis response processes, physical site safety issues, and ongoing training for all staff is crucial.

Beyond those systemic issues just mentioned, attendance to a number of factors will definitely make a safer worksite.

Solid Boundaries. A predictable and fair set of rules concerning the relationships between inmates and staff, among staff, and among the inmates themselves must be established and enforced. Inmates and staff need absolute clarity regarding what behaviors are permissible and which are not. Inmates need assurance that relationships between inmates and staff will be professional. Staff members must not act in any way amongst each other that will negatively affect the supervision of inmates.

Adaptability. Notwithstanding the necessity for a predictable environment and standardized procedures, correctional staff must on occasion also be flexible. Staffing constraints, logistical problems and disruptive inmates require immense creativity. Standardization must never become inflexible and dogmatic, but rather, adaptable to the changes regularly occurring in a correctional setting. Blind adherence to standardization can particularly impinge on the well-being of inmates suffering from mental illness. <u>Notwithstanding, officers and other staff must never lose sight of their overarching goals: institutional safety and fair, but strict enforcement of the rules must take precedence over anything else.</u>

Presence and Accessibility. The safest agencies are ones where correctional officers and staff have contact with inmates. Boundaries and security concerns must be maintained at a hundred percent levels, but correctional officers can only ensure safety when they are an *active* presence in the lives of the inmates they supervise. In particular, positive interactions with officers offer inmates who suffer from mental illness a pro-social role model to follow, and an opportunity to practice new social interaction skills. This also can promote a modicum of professional trust between inmates and officers, making a volatile environment a little more stable with every positive interaction.

Good Training and Regular Practice. Correctional officers have a professional and moral responsibility to be well-versed and skilled in both de-escalation methods and defensive tactics. While this certainly requires an effort on the part of the individual officer, departmental policy must ensure that de-escalation training is made available and mandatory, and that times are set aside on a *regular* basis to practice these skills. <u>One of the best ways to maintain and enhance skills is to have one defensive tactic/verbal de-escalation drill, taking no more than five-ten minutes at every staff meeting or the beginning of every shift change.</u>

Integrity. Beyond all else, officers must be persons of integrity, who are rightly held to the highest moral and ethical standards. Inmates must be aware that officers are vigilant in maintaining ethical and moral relationships towards the inmates they supervise. Without this, all the de-escalation methods in the world are just empty words.

Staff Meetings Should Always Include a Focus on Safety Concerns

Supervisors and administrators should conduct regular staff meetings to promote, discuss, and build upon existing procedures as well as share information critical to the tasks of the day. This will strengthen the professional bonds necessary for the safe operation of the agency, increase officer morale, and foster staff cohesion throughout the watches. While thoughtful preparation may not prevent a critical incident from occurring, an alert, informed and well-trained staff can reduce the impact of such events through a coordinated planned response.

After Action Reviews (AARs) are particularly important in the wake of a critical incident, in the review of planned actions such as a search of a cell, block of cells, or dormitories, or post incident reports resolving an inmate/staff hostage situation. AARs aren't to be used as finger-pointing exercises, where some look to lay blame for problems or difficulties during an operation. Some things are likely to not go as planned or anticipated in even the most successful operation, and improvement begins with a thoughtful discussion among those involved. Therefore, AAR's must focus solely on what can be done to improve the process and enhance everyone's safety for future operations.

After Action Review Focusing on the Inmate's Actions

Correctional staff must try to learn more about the patterns of behavior that might have preceded a prisoner's aggression, as well as any actions on the officers' part that were either unhelpful or contributory towards an inmate becoming violent. Correctional officers need to note the following:

- What were the circumstances that led to an aggressive encounter?
- What was the *first* sign that indicated that the situation was getting volatile or dangerous?
- Remember what the inmate(s) said and did in the moments just before the incident.
- Generally, people are able to control their verbal signals better than their non-verbal signals, so recall the inmate's body language prior to the incident. Tension can also create a change in the quality of the voice such as rate of speech, pitch, and/or volume.
- What, if anything, do you believe you should have done differently?
- What planning did you do in regard to that inmate subsequent to the incident? How happy are you with that plan?
- Officers are encouraged to report any incident in which they felt threatened in any fashion. Over time, these reports will provide the data for a general representation of the more common threats that officers face when performing their duties, as well has delineating a pattern of escalation that a particular inmate displays. Safety protocols can then be fine-tuned to concentrate on the most common threats.

3.2 Record Keeping Is Crucial to Safety

Good record keeping, be it departmental forms or chronos, is crucial to safe and effective supervision. In fact, poor record keeping or illegible notes in the inmate's file should be considered professional malpractice. Clear and concise documentation is essential to the safety of fellow officers and staff. Critical information should be highlighted, or <u>printed</u> in ink, in the case of hand-written records, so that anyone opening the file is immediately aware of the risk factors involved.

Washoe County, Nevada, uses a method entitled "Confidential Custody Bulletins (CCB). These bulletins highlight individuals about whom staff need to be aware for both safety issues or litigious reasons. Mental health status can also be noted in a CCB, if it poses an unusually high safety risk to staff.

Crisis Response and Intervention

Correctional officers in institutional/prison settings are typically first responders whenever an inmate suffering from mental illness requires assistance up to and including crisis situations such as attempted suicide. As soon as it is reasonably possible, the first responding correctional officer should utilize the institution's radio and designated code call system, and call for back-up. When responding to an apparent suicide/suicide attempt in a cell or when an inmate, mentally ill or not, is assaulting or being assaulted in a cell, the officer shall follow institutional policy regarding the number of staff necessary before a cell door may be opened. Staff safety is paramount in all situations.

Physical Site Safety

A physically secure and well-designed facility will enhance security, while simultaneously leaving the inmate with fewer opportunities to act aggressively. Remember, staff may not only interact with inmates in their cells or in the exercise yard. Spaces such as personal offices and dedicated interview rooms should have a minimum of furniture and no clutter. If possible, you should also position yourself closest to the door in case you need to exit quickly. Although privacy issues may be of concern to the inmate, the author recommends that officers never close their office door when conducting an interview by themselves. Not only will a closed door prevent others from detecting an escalating situation, closing your office doors will simply present a barrier to anyone helping you.

If a closed door cannot be avoided, then the officer (s) should ensure that the area immediate to the office is cleared of other inmates and that any office windows remain unobstructed by blinds or curtains. Finally, the officer (s) should notify other officers and/or supervisors of their intent to conduct an office interview with an inmate. These practices will minimize the possibility of staff harm due to inmate violence in the office setting and also minimize or make unlikely inmate claims of inappropriate or misconduct on the part of the officer(s).

Establishing a secure office may be compromised due to architectural design and/or physical plant limitations, as well as the financial constraints of your institution. For example, the installation of modern security and video surveillance equipment can be prohibitively expensive. However, there are many ways of enhancing security that are relatively free of cost, requiring only that officers and staff be alert to safety issues and communicate with one another. Listed below are just a few of the issues to consider regarding physical site security:

Control ingress and egress to the office proper. As many offices utilized by correctional officers are in the inmate housing or program areas, the control of inmate egress and ingress can be challenging. One way to control the flow of inmates to a staff office is through the use of office schedules for inmate interviews, and adherence to an inmate pass system for non-routine inmate movement (such as office visits). Officers must escort each inmate into and out of the office. Never allow an inmate to wander unescorted through the office. The use of 'out-of-bounds' lines around the office will deter inmates from loitering without a valid pass. Finally, constant communication with other staff about one's whereabouts either through a radio, phone or face-to-face should always be used.

Security doors must remain locked if they are to be effective. Propping a security door open, or leaving the door unlocked to facilitate staff movement negates its intended purpose.

Dedicated interview rooms should be established and used to conduct all inmate interviews. Such rooms can remain free from any extraneous clutter, office equipment, and furniture, leaving the room free of many potential weapons.
- Any object can become a weapon. Keep desks free from pencils, staplers, paper hole-punches, and other office equipment.
- Are picture frames or corkboards secured to the walls? Any item that can be removed from the walls or picked up easily is a potential weapon.
- All necessary office furniture and equipment must be in good condition and in proper working order. Loose chair parts and light furniture can be used as weapons as well. When designing an office, or acquiring new furniture, safety must be considered in addition to comfort and aesthetics. One seasoned correctional officer states, "Being behind a desk provides a slight psychological barrier. It takes slightly more loss of control for an inmate to go over a desk as opposed to come straight at me if I'm standing in front of him."
- Personal photographs of family members and loved ones or any other personal items have no place within a correctional setting where inmates might view them. Photographs and/or personal items may provide sufficient information to identify your home, address, lifestyle, and that of your family members, compromising your family's safety. Finally, personal items also encourage the inmate to talk about *your* family, hobbies, or other interests which is a core tactic in grooming a staff person to let down his or her guard with an inmate.
- Outside your personal office space, consider all hallways, stairwells, staff and public elevators, parking and storage areas, and the reception area if present. Are there adequate sight lines to see who is entering the area? Is the lighting adequate in hallways, stairwells, and parking areas?

- If your department authorizes the use of weapons of any kind, make sure that they are in a locked metal cabinet, lock-box or drawer when not in use.
- In certain settings, it is necessary to use wands to screen for weapons, and requiring inmates to remove bulky overcoats, 'hoodies,' and outerwear and headgear that can easily conceal weapons. Ensure that long, matted or braided hair be scrutinized as a possible location to secure a weapon. Razor blades are often 'cheeked;' be aware that an inmate may be casually speaking with you, but at any moment, they can spit a blade into their hand.[9]
- Emergency numbers should be programmed into the office phone system or posted nearby each telephone extension in the office. Off-hook alarm system should be a part of your telephones' features. An off-hook alarm will notify a central control point of your emergency and location. The *installation* of off-hook alarms or panic buttons is not enough, however. Drills should be conducted regularly to ensure that they actually work, and that designated officers actually respond when an emergency button is pressed.
- Mobile radio units must be compatible with an all-call emergency call system, and the radio should contain site specific and/or incident level specific emergency response calling codes.
- Finally, if you are interviewing high custody, violent inmates such as those found in super-max, maximum security prisons or within administrative segregation, the use of an expanded metal secured holding cage should be utilized to maintain staff and other inmates' safety.

Tactical Response Planning

Even the most secure office site may not prevent an inmate from becoming aggressive. No matter how confident you may be in your skills at verbal de-escalation, situations are best handled by a team. Officers should enlist the help of others whenever possible, rather than trying to resolve a dangerous situation on their own. However, the willingness to assist a fellow officer is not enough. Officers and support staff must know *how* to help if things do go wrong. Therefore, officers and staff <u>together</u> must have a workable tactical response plan. Appropriate responses range from verbal control to actual physical restraint/use of force. Officers and staff must *practice* the requisite techniques so that they can make proper decisions in order to act effectively, with minimal delay. Each officer and staff member must be fully aware of their designated role, and possess the skills and training necessary to carry out their assigned duties.

Correctional facilities should also develop an emergency staff response protocol that identifies on a watch-by-watch, post-by-post basis, response requirements at the levels of first responders, secondary responders and third responders, and radio coded appropriately. This will ensure that staff response levels are sufficient and timely to meet the emergent situation, that <u>only</u> those designated as responders will do so, leaving to other posts the responsibility to maintain control over non-affected areas of the facility. Tactical response will, thereby, not strip staff from other vital areas, given that such incidents can be a diversion from another situation in a different part of the prison.

Individual limitations must be considered when preparing a safety plan, and responsibilities should be assigned accordingly. For instance, some officers should be designated as communications officer, responsible for establishing and maintaining effective communications with emergency responders or other staff. Others may be better suited toward the tactical aspects of the response plan, such as the physical control of aggressive inmates, or the establishment of physical site security.

An effective safety plan must include consistent preparation for violence *before* it occurs. Officers have a professional responsibility to inform fellow officers and staff members that a confrontation may occur when a particular inmate reports to an office or program/housing area. Not all potential emergencies can be foretold, but many can be anticipated, and an appropriate response can be planned. Failure to do this is a guaranteed formula for escalating an otherwise manageable encounter into a critical event. Therefore, never 'surprise' other officers or staff with a last-minute request for assistance *after* the inmate has already been admitted into an unsecure area.

Even the best laid plans will not prevent an emergency from arising, which is why regular practice of the safety plan is a requirement for all concerned. Regular practice will also highlight areas of the response plan that need to be modified and improved, *before* a true emergency occurs.

3.3 Don't Let the Abnormal Become Normal

I cannot underscore how important it is to check out your concerns and intuitions with fellow officers, and other professional staff. Don't only consult others when you are concerned about an individual. **Sometimes, you should consult when you be concerned and aren't.** Some correctional officers become so familiar with pathology that the abnormal becomes normal. The officer no longer reacts in a natural way, tolerating or not noticing covert aggression, boundary trespass, or grooming behavior. Officers can easily become complacent when dealing with familiar inmates. Just because you have not been hurt (yet) does not mean you are doing a good job of keeping yourself safe.

Tactical Concerns

Inmates must be effectively pat searched and pass through metal detectors as they move from one secure area to another. Some officers become far too dependent on the metal detectors and become inefficient or lazy when pat searching inmates. Inmates have access to many heavy-duty plastics items: spoons, mops, mop buckets and other objects. Many of these can be broken and whittled down to make excellent shanks—none of which will register on a metal detector or wand—but are just as deadly when slipped in between your ribs or lodged in your eye socket. Regularly conduct pat search, conduct frequent safety and security checks of each unit and conduct cell inspections on every shift.

Another foundation of safety on the tiers and yards is knowing your population. Much of your 'intel' of an inmate population is acquired when the line officer just observes:
- Which inmates associate with each other?

- Are the inmates separating themselves by race or gang in an open area?
- Are there one or two inmates moving from group to group?
- Are there inmates that don't move around without an entourage of other inmates?
- Are there one or two inmates that appear to be keeping watch for other inmates?

All of these situations could be predictors of an upcoming crisis event (inmates suddenly separating by race or gang can be indicative of an upcoming group altercation) or they could be just an anomaly. Sometimes the only advanced warning is knowledge of your population.

3.4 Individualized Safety Planning: AKA Playing 'What if?'

As officers move throughout their duty stations, they should be acutely aware of their surroundings, while simultaneously, almost automatically, running through every different scenario that could possibly happen as well as what they would do to best handle that situation. Do you want to be the person *wondering* what to do when a mob of inmates is running toward you during a riot scenario? Do you want to be the person trying to figure out where to hide and ditch your keys when the inmates have taken over the prison? In New Mexico, rioting inmates flayed the inmates in protective custody. Do you have a plan to protect such inmates—the job you took an oath to do when you accepted your badge? Every officer should have a plan about where they would go and what they would do if there was a riot, if they were hurt, or if they were taken hostage, in each and every area they work. Make sure you have a plan for every situation you can imagine, because inmates imagine a lot of situations in which you are naked or dead.

CHAPTER 4

Training Your Intuition (Correctional Awareness) to Pick Up Danger

Correctional Awareness

A sense of spatial awareness, of potential escape routes, likely weapons and access to help should become a natural part of the correctional officer's personal and professional life. This routine attentiveness is often referred to as 'correctional awareness.' Some folks (correctional officers and inmates alike) are naturally good at this and others are not. This section offers a method to teach correctional officers and staff to pick up danger on an intuitive level.

Enter a room with a predator's mind and a predator's movements: slowly, gracefully, with calculation. Imagine that you are going to hurt the next person who comes into that room. How would you cut off their escape routes? What could you use as a weapon? Where would you position yourself to attack? How could your victim best escape?

Do the above exercise on an occasional basis. Consider it a refresher course on the mind of a predator. Done over time, you will start to develop the ability to automatically scan any location, as well as switching yourself on to picking up predatory or other dangerous behaviors on the part of inmates.

> **4.1 One Officer's Experience: Scanning Saves Lives**
>
> A correctional officer entered the cell of an elderly inmate, somewhat demented. She had no history of assault in over twenty years of incarceration in various institutions. People took her for granted.
>
> She began screaming at the officer to get out. The cell was not messy, but it was filled with all sorts of small objects, the collection of decades in the prison system. The officer's eyes picked up something on the back of the woman's toothbrush. She'd fixed a razor blade to the back of the brush, but kept the bristles intact, so it might pass a cursory inspection.
>
> As it turned out, she was acutely psychotic. She believed that Satan would come in the cell door to steal her soul, so she planned to back up, grab her shank, and slash the throat of the 'Lord of Darkness.' The correctional officer's habit of scanning, trained through the above exercise, very likely saved him from a very difficult situation.

Intuition: That Small Voice to Which Officers Must Listen

Intuitions, 'gut feelings,' are sometimes vague, but they are often the *first* signs that one is in a dangerous situation. Not only should senior officers be sure to voice their intuitions at staff meetings, but newer officers, too, must not be hesitant to relate their concerns and ask questions:

- Officers should not minimize their gut feelings and intuitions when exchanging information. Don't begin by stating "I know it's nothing, but . . . " In doing so, you may lead others to agree with you: "Yeah, it is nothing . . . "
- Officers should not be hesitant because they don't have 'hard evidence' to support their concern.
- Veteran officers or senior staff members must not belittle others' intuitions. Even the most senior officer has not experienced every possible contingency.
- Differences among officers and other staff must be discussed respectfully, particularly in regard to questions of safety. If one person's intuition is discounted or dismissed, he or she may cease to speak up, and vital information regarding everyone's security will be lost.
- These concerns very definitely apply to non-security and support personnel as well. They must also be trained and aware of intuition and situational awareness. Facility processes should include methods for security and non-security staff to communicate their concerns with mutual respect.

4.2 Author's Experience: Life-Saving Intuition

Once, on a mental health outreach requested by a landlord, some internal sense commanded me not to knock on the resident's door and to retreat to my car. I literally backed down the steps, not taking my eyes from the house. Returning to the office, I wrote in the person's new chart in huge red letters "Something is wrong. Don't go to this house without police back-up."

Thankfully, a co-worker heeded my 'irrational' advice, and several days later, she and the police found an acutely psychotic woman waiting with a gun behind the door. In a previous psychotic episode, she had been attacked by two men intent on raping and murdering her. She held them off with a firearm and was eventually rescued by police. Now, some years later and again in a psychotic state, she was waiting with her gun as I approached the house.

It is probable that only my <u>not</u> knocking on the door saved my life. When my co-worker went to the house with the police (whom the woman viewed as rescuers), she opened the door and willingly turned over the gun. What did I perceive? Was it a stirring of the curtains, or a soft click of the slide of a semi-automatic weapon being pulled back? Was it ESP? To be honest, I do not care. What matters is that I, as well as anyone I work with, respect such intuitive commands.

CHAPTER 5

Honing Your Intuition Through Awareness of Personal Spacing

Communicating with inmates suffering from mental illness is often difficult, particularly when they are becoming agitated. While always remaining ready to respond to any assault, correctional officers must develop the ability to differentiate between true aggression, with the very real possibility of physical attack, as opposed to the inmate who angrily tries to communicate frustration: expressing their upset with the court system, their personal difficulties or treatment issues.

The manifest behaviors of aggressive inmates will be discussed in detail in subsequent chapters. This chapter will focus on developing the ability to *sense* when a potential aggressor is beginning to escalate.

Comfort Zones and Physical Spacing

Agitated people lose the ability to accurately listen to what you are saying, much less maintain a coherent train of thought in their own right. Instead, they track other aspects of communication: your muscular tension, the amount of physical space between you, the positioning of your hands and the quality of your voice. You should be doing the same.

As the inmate becomes more agitated, the correctional officer must take care to remain calm and prepare for the possibility of a physical confrontation, while simultaneously maintaining focus on verbally de-escalating the situation. **Most importantly, the correctional officer should not feed the other's anger, particularly by losing his or her own temper. Most people can't sustain anger for more than a couple of minutes, so if you can keep your composure, many inmates will calm down on their own.**

It is not enough to learn a list of the typical behaviors that aggressive people are likely to display. Although the *basic* emotions are physically expressed in definitive ways, irrespective of culture, non-verbal behaviors can be unique: not only do people often have their own ways of physically expressing their emotions, but they also have their own ways of interpreting (or misinterpreting) yours.

Correctional officers must hone their intuition to detect subtle warning signs that a dangerous situation is developing. The leading edge of intuition is a sense of personal space. This is not just a matter of feet and inches. Simply asserting that you keep an arm's length and a half, or two arms' length apart between you and an inmate is not enough. How much space would you want if the person has a blade, or is twice your size and half your age?

Our attitude can also affect our sense of space. For example, the more relaxed you are in the company of someone you trust, the less personal space you require (something that manipulative aggressors try to take advantage of). When you are uncertain or suspicious of someone, you instinctively move to get more distance from them. If you are having a bad day, you need more space to tolerate anyone's proximity. This is particularly important because some officers, due to training or mindset, are accustomed to try to take control by looming, by entering an inmates personal space. Undeniably, this is sometimes the proper tactic: however, this can really backfire with an agitated or enraged individual in a mental health crisis. Compounding this danger is when one's own life is somewhat out of control (i.e., one comes to work after hearing your kid just got suspended from school for drug use or academic problems), one can try to unconsciously impose control on one's life by controlling an inmate's behavior in a manner that doesn't fit the circumstances.

5.1 Two Cautions Concerning Personal Space
- DON'T step inside someone's personal space, unless you are doing so to establish a clear tactical advantage.
- DON'T accommodate anyone by allowing them to stand too close to you.

You MUST be aware of the physical sensations engendered within you when someone enters your 'zone.' When you set such a limit as "Inmate Tran, I would like to hear what you have to say, but you are standing too close. Move back five feet, and then we will continue to talk."

Whatever reply you get will be excellent threat assessment information. You are dealing with very different individuals when one, told to step back, responds with profuse apologies compared to someone who smirks and says, "What's the matter, are you nervous around men?"
- DON'T step inside someone's personal space, unless you are doing so to establish a clear tactical advantage.
- DON'T accommodate anyone by allowing them to stand too close to you.

The Brain Wants to Survive
There are parts of the brain that are solely concerned with survival. These parts of the brain don't care about being polite, politically correct, or intellectualizing why someone is the way they are. These parts of the brain don't even use words. They perceive by recognizing significant patterns, and signal their recognition through physical sensations and reactions. The survival section of the brain is fast, about half a second faster than the thinking brain. About to step on a squiggly shape, you jerk back your foot even before the rest of your brain thinks, "SNAKE!" You train intuition through becoming more aware of the signals your body sends to you.

Inter-personal space has a kind of 'texture' that we perceive through both physical and emotional reactions. Being mindful of the space between you and others, and the physical sensations it evokes, can give you an early warning system that a situation is becoming potentially explosive. When someone is aggressive, psychotic, excited, depressed, menacing, hateful, or is trying to con you, the survival brain recognizes a pattern in their behaviors, vocal tone and facial expressions and responds with physical reactions. For example, when in proximity to the scared person, perhaps you feel warmth in your chest, but with the con-man, your lips compress and neck tightens. With psychotic people, you feel a sensation of cold in your stomach and your hands and jaw clench with aggressive people. There are no rules to these physical reactions: they are individual to you.

Some of your physical reactions may be unpleasant or unflattering to your own self-image. Because of this, many people get 'skilled' at tuning out those signals, treating them as a kind of unwanted 'noise,' one of the most dangerous things an officer can do. They are literally 'turning off' correctional awareness!

Let us imagine that you get somewhat sick to your stomach with a tingling in your hands and the back of your neck when facing an aggressive person—remember those sensations. When you experience them when facing a quiet relaxed inmate, it is very likely that he or she is hiding violent intentions towards you. How about if you experience a subtle, but real sense of disgust when dealing with someone who is depressed? You don't need to change this reaction—it's a warning system, not a mark of character. Although he is smiling, perhaps talking fast, you know that this physical sensation happens to you very often when dealing with depressed and despairing individuals. You then shift the conversation to assess that, because a sense of hopelessness and helplessness can lead to either suicidal or homicidal thoughts.

If you continue to hone your awareness in this matter, you will develop a form of conscious intuition called **MINDFULNESS**. Mindfulness is the ability to be continuously aware of what is going on 'beneath the surface' in your interactions with other people.

Where these reactions really come in handy is when someone is trying to hide their intentions: smiling, for example, while trying to get close to you to stab you. Let's imagine, in this case, it is an inmate whom you helped when he was at risk of rape from a prison gang. Your thinking mind tells you, "He wouldn't want to hurt me! I saved his life!" But your eyes are tightening and you are getting the same tension in your lower back that you have had on every occasion when someone assaulted you in the past. Don't talk yourself out of it! A very sharp blade is about to hit you right in the gut.

By later taking written notes on your physical reactions, one type of 'after-action review,' you are training yourself to recognize the patterns, consciously, that your survival brain notices unconsciously. Instead of surmising "I was having a lucky day. Something told me not to go to that section of the yard," you say, "I had that feeling in my hands I always get right before a fight. I knew something was going to happen, so I moved to the side and saw him standing behind a screen of inmates with that five-pound weight."

5.2 Don't Label the Message, Associate It With the Situation

It is very easy to train yourself to become more mindful. Carry a small notebook in your pocket. If you encounter an individual who interacts with you in a significant way (aggressive, manipulative, depressed, etc.), note down (later) how your body reacted.

<u>We should be far more concerned with **physical sensations** than what we normally refer to as 'feelings,' our description of emotional states</u>. For example, you have a sensation of high energy, with tension in your stomach. Some would call this 'anxiety,' while others would call this 'anticipation.' If you think that a sense of anxiety does not 'fit' the situation you are in, you will tend to ignore the physical sensation, or talk yourself out of it— "I'm being silly. There's no reason to be 'nervous' here."

If, on the other hand, you merely associate a physical sensation with a situation, i.e., "Every time someone tries to con me, I get a little smile and tension in my neck," you will notice your physical reactions without biasing them based on what you *think* you should feel.

5.3 Author's Experience: When Intuition Was Not Heeded

An individual once thanked me profusely at the end of our meeting. Instead of the warm pride I get when I've helped someone (and I HAD helped him), I had a very strong reaction that I always have when someone overtly threatens me. I mentally brushed it aside, thinking, "I'm being an idiot. The man just complimented me." Sometime later, he poisoned me. I am only alive today because he chose to degrade me by contaminating my food rather than putting something lethal in it. I learned in the ugliest way possible to always pay attention to what my body 'tells' me. The body is linked to structures in the brain that serve to protect us from danger through pattern recognition rather than verbal cognitions. To treat our bodily reactions with disrespect is to disavow that which has kept humanity alive for millennia.

SECTION III

Centering: Standing With Strength In Crisis Situations

CHAPTER 6

Introduction to Centering

Supervising inmates who may suffer from mental illness, drug dependency, be victims of traumatic events, struggle with developmental disabilities, brain injuries, poverty, or a lack of education is an honorable calling. You will be in a position to help, sometimes, some of the most unfortunate members of society. At the same time, some of these people are among the most violent and criminal members of humanity, and you will also be protecting society from them.

Such work can also be terribly demanding. Even more troubling is when you realize that your reactions to an inmate made things worse. Being enraged, frightened, confused or intimidated can be debilitating, and can result in poor decision-making. Internalizing feelings of frustration can lead to burnout, a state of being which could be summed up in the phrase, "I don't want to see any more of this," something that could get you or a fellow officer killed, if you do not pay attention at moments when awareness is most necessary.

Stress Is a Safety Issue

This is surely one of the most stressful jobs in the world. It is a different kind of stress from a war zone, where one tries to survive in the midst of enemy fire. Rather, the correctional officer, by choice, is locked in an environment where hostility is endemic and violent assault by inmates can happen at any time. In other words, it is a world of constant *potential* violence. Such high levels of stress can lead to impaired judgment, substance abuse problems for correctional officers as well as a myriad of medical problems including hypertension, diabetes, etc. Stress can fuel cynicism or anxiety, as well as eliciting feelings of contempt or hatred towards inmates. When the officer's expectations of immediate inmate obedience are unintentionally brought back to his or her family, it can lead to devastating problems in one's home, leading to high rates of divorce and dysfunctional relationships with one's children. Extreme stress also leads to high rates of turnover at correctional facilities, and the constant loss of veteran officers negatively impacts safety issues for remaining staff and inmates.

Solutions towards mitigating stress among correctional officers include structured peer support programs, employee assistance programs (EAP) and supervisor assistance in identifying officers who are overwhelmed, and getting them the help they need.

There is no doubt that good leadership has a profound effect on staff morale and institutional safety. Good leadership supports secure settings by creating a culture of safety, dignity, respect and accountability. There is a certain level of stress, however, that nothing from 'outside' can help. It must be addressed from within.

The strategies in the following chapters of this section revolve around maintaining self-control, even in extreme crisis situations. Mastering methods of self-control is a way for you to model proper behavior to others (both other staff and inmates). This is the ability to adapt to circumstances. Not only will this make you more able to roll with the problems that any inmate presents, but also, it will make you more effective in crisis situations.

> **6.1 A Veteran Correctional Officer's Account: Centering Is for Survival**
> We were called for back-up in our sally-port entrance where a soon-to-be-incarcerated inmate was fighting with the law enforcement officer who had transported him. Correctional officer Number One was already on scene, and Officer Two and I were shoulder-to-shoulder hitting the double security doors to the sally port.
>
> Most law enforcement officers secure their guns in security lockers or the trunk of their vehicle before taking an inmate out of their cruiser. This one didn't. Through the open back seat doors of the cruiser, I saw the police officer and one of our own on the ground, actively fighting with the inmate. In a millisecond, my vision narrowed into tunnel vision. All I could see was the officer's gun, sitting on the front seat of the cruiser, easily within reach of the inmate if he broke free. Officer Two and I didn't need to say a word. I broke right and he broke left, and we started locking and slamming cruiser doors to **secure that gun**! I do not remember clearing the front end of the car after we accomplished that. My next memory is hitting the cement on my knees to pull the inmate's head back, before he could bite my officer. On impact, I automatically drew in a long breath and suddenly, no more tunnel vision. My world opened to the big picture again. I started tactical breathing, as we got the inmate in a restraint chair. I *maintained* tactical breathing when the inmate started seizing, and we (Officer Two and me again) started unlocking and chucking restraints, to get him prone. The Nurse was behind us yelling, 'Hurry! Hurry!" Officer Two and I were talking quietly "Left arm free, you grab that, etc." Our hands were going fast, but my breathing wasn't.
>
> Coincidentally, the Internal Affairs Investigator (I. A.) for our agency, a sergeant, was standing behind us. He had responded to the radio traffic, and had witnessed the entire event. After the crisis event was over I asked him how long it had taken us to get the restraints off the inmate and get him to the floor. I was concerned because the leg irons had been put on the inmate when he was fighting with us, and one key hole was up and the other was down. It had been very difficult to get access, and it took a couple of tries to get that leg iron off. I asked the I.A. Sergeant if it was three minutes or four before we got the inmate to the floor. He said he had timed it. It was only sixteen seconds.
>
> Because I have both trained for this, and been in frequent crisis events, I was able to push through the natural stress reactions would otherwise happen in my body when it is under duress. Tactical breathing allowed me to mitigate those effects, and provide the assistance needed to my fellow officers and to the inmate.

CHAPTER 7

A Fair Witness:
Peer Support Is a Survival Tactic

Feeling helpless or shamed after a physical or emotional assault is one of the worst experiences in the world. This is especially so on our jobs, because if an inmate is verbally or physically violent toward us, our professional pride is also attacked. One often feels isolated when under assault, even with others present. This sense of isolation gets far worse if there is no one with whom we can discuss the event. Some of the things that most powerfully affect correctional officers are so ugly or horrifying that officers are reluctant to discuss them with their spouses or other family members. To do so would be inviting violence or obscenity into their home, and correctional officers don't wish to pass that kind of burden on to a loved one.

In such circumstances, you need *fair witnesses*, people who know you, who respect you, and who are willing to hear you out. Such peer support can include strategizing sessions, (debriefings) or tactical review, but I must underscore that there are times that this is the last thing you need, because the problem is not one of tactics—it is how the incident affected you. The presence of a fair witness informs you, often simply by being there, that you are still a part of the team, and that your negative, even traumatic experience, is not unique to you, but something that any one of your teammates might experience.

> **7.1 Safety Works Both Ways**
> To some of our readers, this chapter may seem far from a discussion on safety, but when we talk about someone 'getting our back,' it does not only mean that they are with us while going through the door. If we don't have an assurance that someone will be there after we come back out, it's a lot harder to go through the doorway in the first place.

Many correctional agencies have formalized the fair witness process through a system of peer support, commonly referred to as Critical Incident Stress Management (CISM), or Critical Incident Stress Debriefing (CISD). A critical incident is an extraordinary event that forces a correctional officer to face vulnerability and mortality during the course of their official duties. These incidents typically occur without warning, and jeopardize one's physical safety and/or emotional well-being. Incidents such as being victimized in an assault or engaging an inmate in a lethal force encounter can overwhelm the correctional officer's stress capacity. A prompt and structured departmental response can reduce the negative consequences of such incidents and help restore the affected officer's physical and mental health.

CISD members are fellow officers who are trained to respond to critical events, and provide the affected correctional officer with assistance. In the event of an emergency, CISD members report to the scene as soon as possible where they will assess the correctional officer's physical and mental well-being, request that emergency medical services be dispatched to the scene if necessary, or serve as a liaison to other first responders already present. The CISD member will also accompany the affected correctional officer to the hospital, if necessary, and attend to any number of related duties, such as contacting his or her family. A prime responsibility is to hear out the officer so that he or she can safely talk through the incident with an assurance of absolute confidentiality, if they feel the need to speak about their experience. <u>Please note that some individuals do far better by working things out on their own, at least for a time: not everyone needs, and no one should be required, to speak.</u>

Following the incident, the CISD member will consult regularly with the affected officer's immediate supervisor and recommend services (counseling, for example) for the individual as deemed necessary and appropriate. They will also assist with any necessary paperwork that must be completed by the affected officer. Typically, the CISD member will contact the affected officer once a week for at least one month following the incident, and remain in contact with them until they are confident that the affected officer's physical and emotional needs have been addressed.

7.2 The Debate Concerning Documentation in CISD

Some CISD protocols recommend submitting a critical incident report to the administrative unit for the purpose of collecting information necessary to provide short and long-term assistance to the affected officer and to document activities, services and progress.

A potential problem can be that, although this report is not intended to be used as an investigative tool, it can be. As an official record, it may also be subpoenaed in a lawsuit or other legal proceeding. Therefore, many CISD protocols recommend, and I concur, that nothing should be put in writing. This helps the affected officer feel like he or she can talk more freely. Written records should be confined to formal after-action reviews.

In many states, the right of the privacy for the peer support system is upheld by state law. The law is written similarly to the privacy protections afforded to clients of therapists—unless there is a crime reported or harm threatened to another, the peer support client and provider cannot be compelled to reveal what is talked about during the peer support interactions.

CHAPTER 8

It's Not Personal Unless You Make It So

Retaliation towards an inmate on a personal or emotional level, no matter what the provocation, will cloud an officer's judgment, while distracting him or her from legitimate safety concerns.

At any rate, although their attacks on you might *seem* personal, that is only true if you make them so. If the attack is invalid, what is there to be upset about? And if what the inmate said is valid, you knew it anyway, so what are you upset about?

- They call you fat? Well, you knew that already, didn't you?
- They called you a Nazi? Well, you aren't, so why are you taking it personally? As one person wrote: "My first day working in a prison mental health unit, I was told 'Never take anything personally, even if beyond a shadow of a doubt it's directed personally." And I once said, talking of my partner with whom I did a lot of restraints of aggressive patient-inmates, 'If I wasn't short and you weren't fat, they wouldn't know what to say.'"

Correctional officers must also remember that personal feelings of revenge, of 'getting even,' are unacceptable in the true professional, and your actions must be the result of unbiased decision-making, based on the facts at hand. Inmates must not be violated simply because of a personal vendetta or hurt feelings. Consider obscenity:

- Some inmates use obscenity and verbal violation to get you focused on what they are saying rather than what they are doing.
- Others are just spewing verbal garbage, and suddenly realize that you have lost focus, upset at what they just said, and are open to attack.
- Still others suddenly perceive, in your response to what they said, that *you* are infuriated, and they 'attack you back first,' because they believe you are about to react. Paranoid inmates, in particular, use a 'defense mechanism' called 'projection'—they are afraid that you will react towards them as they would towards you in similar circumstances, so that's what they accuse you of.
- Others challenge you by trying to offend you or by making you explain yourself. In this case, provocative challenges are for the purpose of getting psychological leverage on you.
- Lastly, your reaction is a form of information-gathering for the inmate. If, for example, you react when an inmate calls you fat—he now knows what sets you off, and he and probably every other inmate in the institution will use this at every opportunity.

> **8.1 One Officer's Experience: Creating a Win-Win Situation in Response to Those Who May Push Your Buttons**
>
> It is a given that in a crisis situation, your protocols must be followed. In non-crisis situations, however, creating win-win situations with inmates allows the officer to meet whatever objective is at hand (making the inmate lock down for instance) and allows the inmate to feel alright about how the situation ended for them.
>
> For example, an inmate suffering from mental illness was housed in a single cell in a segregation unit. A movie was being played for the inmates. They could watch by standing at their door and looking through the window. During my segregation check, I noticed that this particular inmate was naked below the waist. Although she was housed alone, this is a violation of facility rules, and it is a rule we enforce to impose a sense of normality for the inmates. By the 'book,' I could have closed the cover on her window and denied her the movie. Instead, I asked why she did not have her pants on. She told me that the underwear 'bite.' We compromised that she did not have to wear the underwear, but the pants were required. I waited until she put her pants on (to ensure that she actually followed through), and let her continue to watch the movie. Perhaps some may find this a trivial example, but these small win-win situations, with the rules still enforced, accumulate as positive interactions which create the possibility of the inmate gradually becoming more compliant in future interactions.

No One Will Own Me

The verbal aggressor is trying to 'push your buttons,' often in an attempt to elicit an unprofessional or off-centered reaction. Remember, the brain is organized to respond to danger through pattern-recognition: a large object moving rapidly towards us, a sudden pain, or a violent grab initiates a cascade of responses—fight/flight/freeze/faint/flinch—that are geared to keep us alive in the worst of circumstances. At lower levels of danger, particularly that presented by another human being, we are provoked into posturing—dominance/submission displays—that serve to maintain or enhance our position within a social structure.

The curse of being human, however, is that these survival responses are precipitated by any noxious stimuli, particularly those that shock or surprise us. When someone unexpectedly violates our sense of right and wrong or verbally assaults us, we often respond by automatically shifting into those responses, even when survival is not truly an issue. **When our buttons are pushed, we physically (and then emotionally) react as if we are threatened with bodily harm.**

Taking Inventory

Anything that pushes our buttons and sets us off-balance, puts us at risk. A technique called *bracketing* makes it harder if not impossible for others to even get to our buttons. Bracketing is a technique that entails facing your vulnerabilities head on, and making them 'bulletproof.'

Not surprisingly, we are most likely to lose our temper (our flexibility, our edge and our strength) when we are blind-sided. Sudden emotional shock elicits the same responses in the nervous system as a physical attack. For example, if someone suddenly insults your race, religion, or gender, it is very likely that you will shift into a response using the more primitive parts of your brain (the limbic system) that express raw emotions. The limbic system is not concerned about the truth, about negotiation, or how to make peace. Instead, it views the world as one at war, with the other person trying to destroy one's position of strength.

Here is a worksheet that can help you name and bracket your own hot buttons. (You may photocopy it to work on.) Once you work it through, keep those hot buttons conscious in your head. Keep or throw away the worksheet as you choose.

Some example statements may include:
- I can't stand it when someone attacks or demeans _____ , because that's something I love and treasure.
- I feel outraged when someone demeans _____ , because it is something I believe to be unquestionably right and good.
- People get me defensive when they say or point out _____ , because, to tell the truth, I hate it in myself.
- When people say or do _____ , I lose it because it's as if they are taking control of me or disrespecting me.
- They better not say _____. That's the one word I won't take from anyone.
- I cannot believe that this inmate is acting this way, when I went the extra mile for them (we expect to be rewarded or appreciated when we do the right thing).

Statement	Why Does this Get to Me?
EXAMPLE: When people say or do _____ , I lose it because it's as if they are disrespecting me.	

Taking inventory is the equivalent of checking your kit before going out into the unit. Every morning, upon waking, and maybe a few times during the day, you run a mental inventory as if flipping through a set of cards, and call to mind each of your emotional hot buttons. By bringing them to consciousness, you prepare yourself for the possibility that someone may try to set you off. This is merely the equivalent of checking your mirrors before backing out of your driveway. When (not 'if'), an inmate tries to push one of your buttons, you are not surprised or caught off guard. If you take inventory, you center yourself for another day, ready for the worst without it tearing you down.

If you are able to accurately take this inventory and implement it into your day-to-day mental activities, then you have a good handle on who you are and what is important to you. <u>Before walking into the prison, before putting on your stab vest or your less-lethal weaponry, before you gear up for a cell entry, you had better know yourself to the core, and that core needs to be rock-solid. If it isn't, inmates will see right through you.</u> You can't carry any issues on your sleeve, even good issues such as military service. The moment they catch on, they already know too much about you. Once you are aware of your buttons, you should have responses already prepared in case they try to blindside you. Those responses should roll off your tongue as if they were the most natural response in the world.

> ### 8.2 A Veteran Officer's Response: How Can You Get Mad When It's True?
> While working in the Disciplinary Segregation Unit, the unit sergeant and I were performing a routine tier check. As we reached one particular cell, the inmate jumped off his bunk and screamed at the sergeant, with just the cell bars separating them, "Hey! Your wife looks like Harry Potter on crack!" I was expecting the sergeant to blow up, but he paused for a second and said with a calm voice and straight face, "You're right, she does." The inmate was dumbfounded, and remained quiet for the rest of the shift.
>
> Side note: We returned to the officers' area and busted up laughing. Because it was true.

You must establish a steady infallible core, both for yourself and for the people around you. You are obligated to the other members of your team to refrain from escalating a situation, even when the inmate nails you with some sudden insight or 'tell' that they read in you. You must present yourself as the embodiment of strength and calm, both for yourself and your team, when you are involved in crisis events, especially when your teammates are scared or otherwise off-balance.

8.3 One Officer's Experience: On not Being 'Owned'

Our correctional facility was host to a somewhat notorious serial killer. The inmate was infamous for escape attempts, manipulative behavior (above the norm) and rapid escalation into violence. Staff were directed to observe this inmate continuously when he was out of his hardened cell in the dayroom during his out-time. We were also directed to limit conversation with him, because he had a history of getting information about staff, and using it to his advantage. I often sat watch on him when he was out of his cell. Although uneducated, he was both very intelligent and a fabulous storyteller. Just as leopards are beautiful, human predators can be very charming.

Even though I observed him from outside the unit, my body was on high alert. The inmate tried to get information from me *(I call this a 'bump.' Sharks bump objects or people with their nose or take a small sample bite before going into an all-out kill. Some inmates do the same thing.)* He tried to find out if I was ex-military. When I told him that was personal information and therefore none of his business, he first tried to convince me that being in the military was not personal. When I told him that I was the one that got to decide what was personal for me, he exploded, going from laughing and affable to screaming and throwing objects in the room. I remained quiet with a blank expression. When he did not get the reaction he wanted, he started calling me obscenities, starting with "bitch." The only response I gave him was to quietly say, "Lock down." As I expected, the next word out of his mouth was that which usually sends female officers into outer-space (starts with a 'c'). All he got for the effort was a monotone, "lockdown." Officers were piling up behind me—nothing angers officers more than an inmate calling their boss foul names. I wouldn't let them in the unit.

This inmate expected and craved the fight, All he kept getting was that same word: "Lockdown." He sort of 'popped a mental clutch' because he didn't get the outcome he wanted. He finally went into his room and slammed the door shut—lockdown. I looked at my teammates, told them thanks for the support, but their safety was much more important than me being called a few ugly names.

I felt the assault coming long before it started—while he was still friendly. With such advanced warning, I stayed calm and non-reactive, giving him literally 'nothing,' and kept my staff away from a useless bout of violence from a killer who desired only that.

CHAPTER 9

Circular Breathing: Be the Eye in the Center of the Hurricane

Aggression and violence can smash through a previously peaceful day with the suddenness and force of a hurricane. Chaos doesn't only take over the day; it may also overtake you. However, when you can respond by stepping coolly into the worst of situations, you embody the eye of the hurricane, with all the chaos coalescing and revolving around you. The root of this skill lies in breath control. Using a method called 'circular breathing,' you regain control of your physical self. When you control your body, you control your life. Then you are in a position to take control of the crisis as well as the person causing it.

Circular breathing—a form of 'tactical breathing'—is derived from East Asian martial traditions and was used to keep warriors calm on the battlefield. There are two variations. Try both, alternating between them, until you know which one works best for you. From that point on, exclusively practice the one you prefer. *If you train regularly, it will kick in automatically, rather than being something you must think about.*

9.1 Clarification – Not Meditation, Not Blissing Out

Lest there be any confusion, this is NOT a 'time-out' where you take a few deep breaths and then return to the problem, refreshed. Rather, you are training your body and mind to immediately go into this breathing as a *response* to danger and stress. It is a trained response that should be instantaneous. And remember: you can still be moving very fast while breathing very slowly.

As someone who has practiced the following technique for over thirty years, I can assert that it has become automatic. Unlike my younger days when the adrenaline would hit and I'd start breathing fast and high in the chest, my breathing usually slows down in emergency situations. You develop a 'pseudo-instinct'—a trained response so bone-deep that you don't even have to think about it, any more than you have to tell yourself to yank your hand from a hot stove.

TWO VARIATIONS
Circular Breathing Method #1: Initial Practice Method

- Sit with your feet on the floor, hands in your lap.
- Sit relaxed, but upright. Don't slump or twist your posture.
- Keep your eyes open. (**As you practice, so you will do.** If you practice with your eyes closed, your newly trained nervous system will send an impulse to close your eyes in emergency situations. If you want to use a breathing method for closed-eye guided imagery or relaxation—to get *away* from your problems—use another method altogether.)
- Breathe in through the nose.
- Imagine the air traveling in a line down the front of your body to a point two inches below the navel.
- Momentarily pause, letting the breath remain in a dynamic equilibrium.
- As you exhale, imagine the air looping around your lower body, between your legs and up through the base of your spine.
- Continue to exhale, imagine the air going up your spine and around your head and then out of your nose.

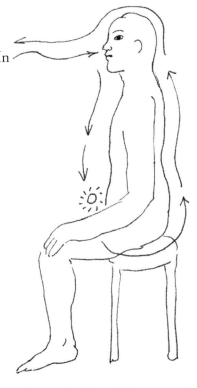

Circular Breathing Method #2: Initial Practice Method

- Sit with your feet on the floor, hands in your lap.
- Sit relaxed, but upright. Don't slump or twist your posture.
- Keep your eyes open. (**As you practice, so you will do.** If you practice with your eyes closed, your newly trained nervous system will send an impulse to close your eyes in emergency situations. If you want to use a breathing method for closed-eye guided imagery or relaxation—to get *away* from your problems—use another method altogether.)
- Breathe in through the nose.
- Imagine the air going up around your head, looping down the back, falling down each vertebra, continuing down past the base of the spine to the perineum, and looping again, this time up the front of the body to a point two inches below the navel.
- Momentarily pause, letting the breath remain in a dynamic equilibrium.
- As you exhale, imagine the air ascending up the centerline of your body and out your nose.

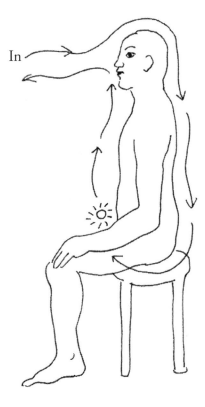

How to Practice Circular Breathing

First of all, you have to select which method, #1 or #2 suits you. Even though the air going in a circle around your body is not anatomically correct—the air never leaves your lungs, except out your mouth and nose—one way will work better for you than the other.

Secondly, some people do 'belly breathing'—letting the belly expand a little on the inhale and drop back under the rib cage on the exhale. Others do 'reverse' breathing—drawing the belly inwards on the inhale and relaxing it on the exhale. Breathe the way you always do—the technique starts with the imagined visualization of the circulation of breath, not a particular way of moving your pneumo-thorax.

Some people find that imagining their breath has light or color is helpful. Others take a finger or object to trace a line down and around the centerline of the body to help focus their attention. Again, choose which of the variations works better for you.

First practice this method while seated. Once you develop some skill, try circular breathing standing, leaning, or even while driving. Most people find that after a short period of time they don't need to visualize the circulation of the breath. You begin to feel balanced and ready for anything.

<u>In a short period of time, you will literally will feel it, a ring of energy running through your body.</u> This is a sign that you've mastered the basics of the technique. Now, experiment with it in slightly stressful circumstances, like being caught in traffic, or sitting through a meeting as a supervisor drones on about new paperwork requirements. Of course, if this helps you get through these circumstances more calmly, all the better. <u>The real purpose is to train your brain to associate stress with</u> *slower, deeper* breathing.

When this becomes an automatic response, you will also naturally shift to this type of breathing in emergency situations. If you have practiced enough, it kicks in by itself. There will no longer be a need to tell yourself to 'do' circular breathing. It will become automatic, replacing old patterns of breathing that actually increased anxiety or anger within you.

Remember, this is a skill to be used during emergencies. You are enhancing your ability to do whatever is needed: to fight, to dodge, to leave, to think strategically—whatever is required for the situation at hand.

When to Use Circular Breathing

The way you organize physically affects your thinking. For example, if you let your body slump, breathe shallowly and start sighing, after a while you will actually start to feel depressed. If you clenched your fists, and start glaring around you with a lot of tension in your body, you will start to feel angry. (You have probably observed a number of inmates working themselves up from anger through rage into an attack in just this way.) Similarly, circular breathing creates its own mindset; one adaptable and ready for anything, equally prepared for an easy conversation and for a fight, yet fixed on neither.

This method of breathing is very helpful when you are anticipating a potentially dangerous situation, anything from walking down the tiers towards a disturbance, or preparing to supervise a parole hearing with an often-volatile inmate. This breathing activates the entire nervous system in a way that enhances both creativity and the ability to survive.

Even in the middle of a confrontation, particularly a verbal one, there are many times when this breathing will have a very powerful effect, on both yourself and others. People tend to template their mood to the most powerful individual close by. Not only do we get more stressed or upset in the presence of an upset person, but we also become more peaceful in the presence of a calm one. We are sure that you know officers who, when they walk onto a scene, often calm it down before they have said a word. You have probably seen the opposite as well, officers who just flame everyone up without saying a word. Using this breathing method is a vital tool in making you the former type, a correctional officer of quiet power.

Use this method of breathing after the crisis as well. You need to regroup to go on with the rest of your shift. Circular breathing will bring you back to a calm and relaxed state, prepared to handle the next crisis, should one occur.

If we bring feelings from a crisis situation back home, we carry violence back to our family. Therefore, before entering your home, sit quietly in your car or even in the yard, and practice this breathing for a moment or two. The only thing that should come home is 'you,' not the crises you have weathered.

Circular Breathing to Ward Off or Even Heal From Trauma
Post-Traumatic Stress Disorder (PTSD) is not defined by how horrible the event sounds in description. It is defined by the individual's response to the event. PTSD is not exactly a problem of memory; it is a problem because the event has not fully *become* a memory, and instead, is still experienced as if it is happening in present time. When an event is fully a memory, it is experienced as something in the past, over and done with. Another way to think of it is a scar, it may not be pretty, and it certainly is a sign that something significant happened, but it no longer hurts. A trauma, on the other hand, is an open-wound. <u>A trauma is a current experience</u>. It is not in the past, and in fact, may be affecting every moment of the person's life, or emerge suddenly, when evoked by something that elicits a sense that the event is happening again.

In PTSD the person's nervous system is set to react as if there is an emergency whenever the trauma is recalled. This can be anything from an explicit memory to a small reminder. For example, although he does not consciously know why, a correctional officer gets anxious every time someone coughs. This is because one of his team coughed right before a riot went off.

9.2 The Value of Circular Breathing to Help Deal with Trauma

What is particularly valuable to many correctional officers who use circular breathing imagery is that it allows one to take power back on one's own. There is no doubt that counseling, sometimes, is invaluable. However, it is sometimes hard to find a good counselor who understands a correctional officer's situation.

Furthermore, ongoing litigation, in which confidentiality can be threatened by subpoena or court order, can sometimes force correctional officers to forego counseling that they might really need. This particular breathing method offers an option when counseling is either not an option, or something that the correctional officer does not want.

Furthermore, if you can, on a daily basis, 'inoculate' yourself against stressful, even potentially traumatic experiences, life will continue to be enjoyable, or will become enjoyable once again, even as you continue to work in a highly stressful environment. You will begin to develop something author David Grossman calls a 'bulletproof mind.' The goal is not trying to restore some kind of mythic 'innocence,' that one had "pre-trauma." The goal is to relegate the experience to its proper place—something ugly that happened sometime in the past.

Image-associated breathing techniques, which affect the brain as a whole, can assist people in realizing that the event is over, no longer part of one's current life. The following should be helpful in handing PTSD:
- Recall something very upsetting that has happened to you, either recently or in the past.
- Whenever you think about it (or it forcibly intrudes into your consciousness), your body tenses or twists in various ways. Your breathing pattern often changes. If you physically organize (with your breath, muscular tension, posture, etc.) *as if* something is happening, the brain believes that it truly is occurring right now. At an extreme level, that is PTSD.
- If this is your situation, go someplace where you won't be disturbed for a while. Make the mental image of that trauma as vivid as you can tolerate. This takes some courage, because most of us simultaneously 'avoid-as-we-remember.' If only for a moment or two, meet it head on. Notice, in fine detail, how you physically and emotionally react. As difficult as this may be, it is important to establish for yourself what your baseline response is to the trauma. You must clearly experience what it 'does' to you when you recollect it.
- Now take a couple of deep sighs. Sighing breaks up patterns of muscular tension and respiration. This is like rebooting your computer when the program is corrupt.
- Mentally say to the ugly experience: "Move right over there to my right (or left). I'll get to you in a minute." For some people, it is even helpful to make a physical gesture, 'pushing' the experience off to the side. You won't be able to *force* yourself to stop thinking about an experience if it has psychological power. Instead, move it aside, as if you are guiding a wounded person to a waiting room, while you organize yourself to properly deal with it.

- Now initiate your preferred method of circular breathing.
- As the memory creeps back in (and it will), just breathe and center yourself, again placing the memory off to the side. Once again say, "I'll get to you in a minute." You can't fight it, so don't try. Just ease it aside until you are ready.
- When your breathing is smooth and your body is centered, you will be relaxed like an athlete, ready to move but with no wasted effort.
- Now, deliberately bring that ugly memory or trauma into your thoughts and imagination. As you again find yourself reacting, continue circular breathing, trying to bring yourself back to physical balance as you focus on the traumatic memory.
- Bit by bit, in either one session or a few, you will notice that you are increasingly able to hold the image with a relaxed body and a balanced posture. You are now able to re-experience the memory without the same painful, tense, or distorted response you had in the past. You are, metaphorically speaking, turning the open wound into scar tissue. You are not wiping the slate of memory clean. Rather, you are placing it in a proper context—something that happened to you, but does not define you.

9.3 A Veteran Correctional Officer's Experience: Flash Images Versus Traumatic Images

It is very common for correctional officers to walk past a room in their facility and see a flash image of an event that happened in that particular area. The most common of these images seems to be the re-occurring image of an inmate hanging in a room when an officer had to either cut the inmate down or helped during the event. The first time this happens can be very startling. It is important in our high-stress field to distinguish what is a common bi-product of an event (seeing a momentary image of a previous crisis/traumatic event) and what is more severe, such as seeing that image everywhere and feeling imprisoned by it.

"How Can I Help?" – Your Loved One Can Get Your Back

A career as a correctional officer can be extremely stressful, even corrosive to a relationship. You come home and your spouse tells you about an unpleasant incident at work—one of his or her co-workers was rude during a political discussion. They ask, "How was your day," and you think about the inmate, cheek slashed open from the corner of her mouth to her ear, and you honorably don't want to burden your partner with that. So you grunt, "Ok," and by the way, you might not have been listening to their complaint about their co-worker, thanks to the memory of that mutilated young woman, and they press, out of honest concern, or maybe because they are hurt that you seem to shut them out, be silent, etc. And maybe, you are seriously struggling with something that it is difficult to talk about because you believe you'll end up having to take care of your spouse if you talk about it. Even if you asked them to sit with you, as you tried to do circular breathing, they would see the look on your face and you would see the look on theirs. They'd want to help and not know how. You'd never get to center.

One technique is to breathe back-to-back. Explain to your partner that you have things that you do not want to talk about, because you do not want to hurt or scare them, or disgust them either. But you have learned a method to work things through, and that it's hard to do alone. What you do is sit back-to-back on the floor with your legs out, leaning very slightly into each other. This way, you physically support each other. There is no doubt that your partner has your back, because if they move, you fall over. You feel them breathe as they feel you. You begin to work through the event, using circular breathing as described above. If it gets difficult, you can always reach back and hold each other's hand. But because there is no eye contact, you don't have to talk, you don't have to feel that you need to take care of the other person.

I have gotten a number of positive reports from officers who use this method. And in particular, I have heard, several times, "I'm not sure how much this helps me. But I know it helps my wife (or husband). I've been shutting down and they feel helpless. I really do feel better after this breathing. Sometimes I work things through. Always, they feel like they've helped and that we are a team. That's worth a lot."

Numbered Breathing: Another Form of Tactical Breathing

It should be noted that the mere fact of consciously breathing in a particular pattern can break you out of 'automatic responses. An alternative method is 'numbered breathing.'[10] After experimenting with this type of breathing, the author has found that it does help focus the mind in crisis, and helps people achieve calm. However, it does not seem to foster the same level of mental agility, consistent over the entire crisis situation, as the previously described circular breathing method. Nonetheless, it is a 'tried and true' strategy that has proved itself useful to many people.

- Inhale, hold briefly, and exhale.
- Do so at the most comfortable pace for you.
- Next, count as you inhale, hold and exhale. Perhaps you will do a 4-4-4 breath, but maybe it's a 5-3-9. Whatever works for you. Whenever you are in a situation of potential stress or danger, initiate numbered breathing to get control of your physical state—and through that, your mind.

Matching Breaths

One rather popular technique is to try to 'get in sync' with the other person by matching your breathing pattern to his or hers. This can be effective, but I view it as potentially problematic. Some people are acutely sensitive to any kind of manipulation—and they can be among the most dangerous people you face. They may be seasoned enough in interpersonal conflict to be aware that you are applying a technique to them. Others do not realize this consciously, but on an unconscious level, begin to feel controlled by the other person, even though they don't know why they feel this. The authors have found that one can achieve all the benefits of deliberately 'matching breaths' by simply slowing and controlling one's own breathing patterns. Your powerful calm influences the other like planetary gravity pulls errant comets into an orbit. The agitated person will more likely perceive you to be a calming presence due to you controlling yourself rather than controlling them. You influence them rather than manipulate them.

One place where 'matching breaths' is invaluable is with people in a state of high anxiety or even terror, someone who may be breathing rapidly, shallowly or even hyperventilating. In this situation, the Coordinator, in a calm, commanding manner, orders the anxious person, "Breathe with me." He or she then begins breathing slightly slower than the other person. As the anxious individual matches breathes with the Coordinator, the latter very slightly slows his or her breathing down a little more. The Coordinator raises and lowers his or her hand slightly in time with breathing. The Coordinator commands again, "Breathe with me," and perhaps also includes any statements that will further serve to calm and de-escalate the other person (see CHAPTER 50). As this process is repeated, the anxious person, breathing in sync with the Coordinator, will unconsciously become more bonded and dependent upon the Coordinator for a sense of safety.

Team Breathing

Different situations need different techniques. Team breathing is a method to unify a team before, for example, a cell extraction or room entry. At "Breathe!" all officers take a deep breath, whoosh it out in unison, and then GO. Ken Good, a world-class trainer on tactical entry and low-light tactics, states that this helps coordinate the team into one focused entity.[11]

CHAPTER 10

The Intoxication and Joy of Righteous Anger

Most people consider anger to be a harmful emotion, one that upsets the angry person as well as the recipient. This is not true for everyone. Some people, certainly including some correctional officers, don't mind fighting, particularly when they believe their cause is just. These individuals go off-center in an interesting way, becoming calm, even happy, when someone offends them. As a boxer once stated in regards to an opponent, "When he gets hurt, he wants the round to be over. When I get hurt, I get happy." Such people, when functioning in a professional capacity, have an especially difficult task, because when they feel *good*, they are in danger of becoming part of the problem. Instead of imposing calm, they escalate the situation—not minding it in the least.

Circular breathing (CHAPTER 9), for those who are anxious, stressed, or frightened provides a real sense of peace and relief. However, if confrontation feels good to you, such calming breathing feels like the last thing you would like to do. You think, "Center myself? Hell, no. I'm right where I want to be." The righteously angry correctional officer may be known among his or her peers for this type of reaction, but he or she is the one most likely to *not* recognize this, and *not* believe they need to do anything to rectify it. If this description fits, your task is to recognize the special joy that comes with righteous anger, and act to center yourself to a calm state of mind, even though in the heat of the moment, it feels like a loss rather than a gain.

This is not about becoming some sort of sage: never angered, never off-balance. There are times when you should be angry—it may even help keep you alive. However, the real issue here is the correctional officer who reacts angrily to even the slightest provocation, or worse, one who treats every inmate, in every situation, with anger. Such officers simply serve to escalate minor situations into serious ones, heightening the chances for a physical altercation with the inmate, placing everyone involved in danger unnecessarily.

Protecting Your Family From What You Otherwise Would Bring Home

Another type of righteous anger is that evoked when someone does something so clearly evil that one feels annihilation of the perpetrator is the only justifiable response. Returning to the subject of the last chapter, this is a particularly important example of how such breathing can protect your family. For example, I have had the experience of feeling totally contaminated by being in the presence of the perpetrators of child abuse or sexual assault. Having done my job well, so that, for example, I got a confession, evidence to make a case, or have helped ensure that a molester never had access to the child again, I have left the room feeling a failure because I did not take their throat between my hands and squeeze the life out of them.

I made sure, however, that I never brought this feeling home. I would sit in my car, running the breath around my body, maybe going to a quiet place in the house or yard and working through the images in my brains so that when I walked into the presence of my wife and children, the only thing I ever brought home was myself. No child molester or other evildoer will ever walk into the house with me.

SECTION IV

Dealing With Those Who Have
Unusual Or Intense
Communication Styles

CHAPTER 11

Overview of Section IV

This book focuses on behavior, not on illness. Correctional officers should not feel it incumbent upon themselves to diagnose what an inmate may be suffering from, even in the most general way. If someone behaves in a way that makes it difficult to communicate with them, or even more problematically, enacts disruptive behaviors, then the correctional officer (you) should be prepared with several skills:
- The ability to recognize a set of behaviors as showing a pattern.
- The knowledge of best practice communication strategies to respond to a person who is displaying said pattern, whatever the cause of the behavior may be.

Not everyone who needs to be calmed or de-escalated is aggressive. However, those who display unusual or eccentric patterns of behavior are more difficult to communicate with, and when the ability of people to communicate breaks down, the risk of aggression increases.

IMPORTANT NOTE: a mentally ill or eccentric inmate may display more than one of the behaviors described in subsequent sections. Respond to whatever behavior is most prominent.

11.1 A Veteran Officer States: Don't Get Stuck in the "Everlasting Why"

It is easy to get frustrated in dealing with the same problematic behaviors day in and day out, especially if those behaviors deviate from to what most human beings finds normative, As a correctional professional, it is easy to fall into the trap of the 'Everlasting Why.' The Everlasting Why is what correctional officers try to answer when inmates do unexplainable and often harmful things. When an inmate smears his own feces all over his room or body, or even eats it, or acts in disruptive or violent ways when they could, with a little calmer attitude, accumulate enough 'good time' and actually get released, it is easy to fall into the trap of trying to understand these behaviors. It is the normal human condition to try to make sense of things, to place things in order—even on a basic level, our brains seek to find the patterns in wallpaper or shapes within the clouds.

If you fall into the trap of trying to answer the Everlasting Why when it comes to inmates suffering from mentally illness, you will find yourself in a constant state of frustration and anger. You may be lucky enough to figure out that certain words or actions on your part evoke certain behaviors from an inmate, or that there are warning signs that an inmate will act out; beyond that there will be an entire host of inmates that have behaviors that are not even understandable to themselves.

Don't try to figure out the 'Why.' Instead try to figure out the best ways to communicate in order to manage the behaviors. Any other approach is a hard lesson in futility.

CHAPTER 12

Rigid Personality: High-Functioning Autism and Other Similar Disorders

Despite what can be formidable intellectual abilities, often sectored in one area of knowledge, inmates with rigid personalities often have tremendous difficulty in negotiating social interactions. They find other people to be confusing and/or threatening, and to make matters worse for them, they find it very difficult to know from facial expressions, body posture, and vocal tone, what others are feeling or thinking. The diagnostic term for extreme levels of this used to be called Asperger's Syndrome—now it is called 'high functioning autism.'

People with high functioning autism are frequently socially withdrawn, often very intelligent outcasts, who may live their lives mostly in an online environment. Such individuals are becoming more involved in computer crimes, particularly hacking, and they may commit a sexual offense, sometimes due to their extreme difficulty understanding social cues and norms. They are not suited for life within the confines of prison, and therefore, are often placed in protective custody. Other inmates, particularly some inmates with schizophrenia, often show a similar combination of 'cluelessness' and rigidity in communicating with others.

People with such rigid personalities become stuck on their own preoccupations, and may imagine that everyone else shares them too. As one inmate with high functioning autism said, when asked what the other inmate who beat him up was thinking, "Oh, he was thinking of high energy physics." When asked with astonishment why he would be thinking of that, the inmate replied, "What else could he be thinking about? Quantum mechanics is the greatest scientific discovery…." It was a good ten minutes before the correctional officer could get him off the subject. Such rigid individuals can also be very literal (concrete), and can get 'stuck' on certain thoughts and behaviors (obsessive). Others are simply not interested in or aware of other people's feelings, which can lead them to be very blunt or brutally honest.

> **12.1 Two Examples of Socially Clueless Statements by an Inmate Displaying Rigid Personality Traits**
> - "What is the bump on your face? It's quite ugly. You know, it could be a melanoma, which could cause your face to simply rot away, or it could infect your brain and then you'd die. I've seen photos of tumors that have actually eaten right through a person's cheek and you can see their teeth and tongue out the side of their face."
> - "You've gained a lot of weight in the last year. I don't mind, but many men don't think that is attractive."
>
> There is no malevolent intent here. Other people's feelings—unimaginable and incomprehensible—are simply not a relevant bit of data for such a person. Instead, they see themselves as giving you the equivalent of a public service announcement.

Such a person usually seems stiff and socially awkward. Their voice may be too loud, and they may sound odd. Their eye contact may be 'off,' or non-existent, and they are sometimes physically uncoordinated. They do not pay attention to the effect that their actions or appearance might have on others. They are frequently insensitive to body spacing. Because they find people unpredictable and unreadable, they frequently experience high anxiety. As a result, they use self-soothing movements like flapping their hands or rhythmically tapping an object and/or body part to help distract themselves from what stresses them out. Although these inmates do not normally pose a threat to other inmates (other than giving offense in one way or another), they may be victimized due to their odd behaviors and blunt responses. Inmates in general population have little tolerance for oddities. If he or she is fortunate, one of the inmates will tell the correctional officer: "Get this guy outta here before he gets hurt."

<u>If you are dealing with an inmate with a rigid personality, stating or reiterating the rules is the first method of intervention.</u> If an inmate had difficulty figuring out what an officer wants him to do, and the officer's body language, tone of voice, and facial expression are incomprehensible, the rules, clearly stated, will be very reassuring. On the other hand, 'tactical paraphrasing' (CHAPTER 46), also known as 'active listening,' which is so often recommended as the best tactic to deal with angry inmates, will often result in the inmate becoming confused or upset. Instead, state each rule in a matter-of-fact way, as if simply providing information. State the obvious. Follow this up with a logical sequence of steps to resolve their problem:
- In a matter of fact tone, explain the rules. She says, "Why should I lower my voice? I am angry!" The reply should be, "Because it is the rule to speak about grievances with a quiet voice." "That's a stupid rule," she replies. "Nonetheless," you say, "it is the rule."
- Give them a logical alternative way to follow-up on their grievance.
- Even more than with other individuals, try to avoid physical contact unless it is tactically required. Many folks with rigid personality traits detest touch, and can react violently. Only touch them when you are taking physical control (defensive tactics).

- If they continue to be non-compliant, you may have to physically require them to comply with your order, but take the extra time by repeating the rules over and over. The message is that "the rule is the rule." Again, although this can be very aggravating for most people, it can be reassuring for the person with a rigid personality, because it gives some structure and predictability to the exchange.
- Another trait that you will sometimes observe with a person displaying a rigid personality is *echolalia*. They echo what you say, usually word for word. You must be able to distinguish between the provocative inmate who mocks you, trying to aggravate or distract you (that should be obvious from the smirk on their face or other manifestation of attitude), from the individual with the rigid personality who simply repeats what you say in a flat tone of voice, usually with no eye contact. In the latter case, the individual is probably so overwhelmed that they cannot organize their mind to verbally respond to what you are requesting or ordering. Seeking to somehow stay out of trouble in what is, to them, a chaotic situation, they simply repeat your words—it *must* be important because, after all, you said it. In many such circumstances, you may have to 'physically guide' them to where you want them to go. Often, the inmate will remain passive. Hold their limbs firmly, but not forcibly or harshly, if they are not combative. Nonetheless, such individuals, if they are startled or fearful, may start flailing their arms or lash out in trying to defend themselves. Be ready for that—whatever the motivation, it is still a violent act—and that flailing limb can knock you out.
- If they are displaying a physically repetitive movement, such as flapping their hands, understand that it is for the purpose of calming themselves down. Nonetheless, if the movement (hand flapping near the waist or chest) could resemble a move towards a weapon, order them to stop, by telling them that it is, for example, "against the rules to wave your hands near your waist while standing near a correctional officer." When they ask why, simply repeat that it is against the rules. When they ask if it's OK while speaking on the phone or alone in their cell, say that it is alright in that circumstance, but not face-to-face. Understand that their incessant questions are an attempt to try to figure out just what they can and cannot do. It is not game-playing. However, they often feel the need to cover all possibilities. ("What happens if a giant Asiatic hornet somehow flies between us. Can I flap my hands then?") Sometimes, after a few too many questions, you should take over and give a general policy that, hopefully, will cover all variations.

12.2 PROPS—A More Universally Applicable Technique for Anyone Displaying Rigid Behaviors & Decision Making

A veteran correctional officer notes that the matter-of-fact technique described in this chapter is similar to a method called PROPS. When dealing with an individual who is rigid, but not at the extreme level described above, the officer: **P**resents a statement that demonstrates he or she understands and takes the individuals concerns seriously; **R**efers to law, policy or standards; **O**ffers the individual a choice (both of which are equally acceptable to the officer and institutional policy; **P**resent a mutually desirable outcome. If necessary, the officer repeats this, over and over, to indicate that these are the only available options, doing so without showing irritation or condescension.

12.3 Example: De-escalation of Someone With Rigid Personality Traits

Pavel. "I can't go to my disciplinary hearing tomorrow. I saw seven spiders in my cell, and that is bad destiny."

CORRECTIONAL OFFICER. "Pavel, you are required to go to the hearing, no matter the number of spiders you have seen."

Pavel. But this could mean a disaster for someone. Seven spiders are terrible.

CORRECTIONAL OFFICER. "The rule is that inmates must appear in such hearings when ordered, and this applies even when the inmate believes that there are unlucky signs."

Pavel. "Destiny, officer, not bad luck."

CORRECTIONAL OFFICER. "It is still the rule, destiny or not. The rule has no deviation."

Pavel. "How about if a meteor hits the prison?"

CORRECTIONAL OFFICER. "Pavel, the rule is ironclad. If you are scheduled to appear at the hearing, you must appear, unless I call you and inform you that court is cancelled."

Pavel. Something bad will happen—it's destiny."

CORRECTIONAL OFFICER. "Nonetheless, you will be there at 10:00 A.M. It is the rule."

12.4 Review: Dealing With Rigid Personality

You will recognize the inmate with a rigid personality because they get stuck on subjects that seem rather odd in the circumstances. They seem unaware of their effect on others. Their emotions, if they are even displaying any, are not those you would expect in the given situation. Recalling your school days, they often act like the kind of person who was, unkindly, called a 'nerd.' To deal with this type of individual do the following:

1. State the rules in a matter-of-fact way, as if simply providing information.
2. Follow this up with a logical sequence of steps to solve their problem.
3. Discussion about their feelings will be counter-production. Tactical paraphrasing (CHAPTER 46) or other ordinary tactics to deal with an angry person tend to make things worse.
4. No physical contact unless it is part of defensive tactics or physical control.
5. Don't get deflected from your task. Like a parody of a lawyer, they may bring up possible exceptions to your order. 'Step through' the objections and simply state that they are required to follow the rule.
6. When the rigid person repeats what you say (echolalia), they are not giving you attitude or mocking you. They truly cannot think of anything else to do. Yelling at them or ordering them to stop will most likely not succeed. They will simply repeat your order in a flat tone of voice. <u>It's not personal so don't take it personally.</u>
7. Use this type of strategy only when it is clear that this is the type of inmate you are trying to interact with: rigid, stiff, concrete, and socially out-of-sync. They will be either coldly logical (like Spock or Data, from Star Trek), or frustrated, and out of control. In the latter case, as always, control based on the mode of rage (SECTION X) they are displaying.

CHAPTER 13

Tell It Like It Is: Communication With Concrete Thinkers

Concrete thinkers have a lot of difficulty, or even a complete inability, to understand metaphors, slang, or imagery. Instead, they take everything you say literally.

> **13.1 Example: How Concrete Thinking Caused Problems for an Inmate**
>
> We had a minimum-security inmate working in our laundry room. Inmates manufactured the jeans worn by all the other inmates, and it was the laundry room worker's job to wash, dry, and fold them into organized piles for distribution. Our laundry worker was doing a fantastic job until he encountered jeans that were not previously labeled as to their size. He was given a permanent marker, and told to label the jeans clearly so they were easily identifiable. Most any other person would have written the size on the inside of the back waistband. Our intrepid worker took the 'easily identifiable' part to heart and labeled the jeans small medium and large accordingly. However, since he had already folded the jeans, the part that was at the front (and therefore 'easily identifiable') was the seam down the front of the jeans from the waistband to the groin, it was here that he wrote "small," "medium" or "large" in large block letters in permanent ink. For about six months after this, none of the male inmates would wear small or medium pants for fear that the label bore some sort of personal reflection on their anatomy, rather than their pants size.

When communicating with concrete thinkers, correctional officers should use short, clear sentences, using simple language that is easy to understand. Remember, they only understand what you say in a very literal manner: they will comply with the specific directive, while not even understanding the general principal. Speak in a firm manner, and refrain from showing too much frustration. It's not personal: if you become angry or frustrated the inmate will react to your emotions, not your instructions.

13.2 Example: A Non-emergent Dialogue Between a Correctional Officer and an Inmate Showing Concrete Thinking

CORRECTIONAL OFFICER. "Okay. So you don't have to worry anymore."

Inmate. "I wasn't worried. I was upset."

CORRECTIONAL OFFICER. "Oh, okay, you were upset. Anyway, the nurse is coming, and will be here shortly. I want you to sit tight."

Inmate. "How do I sit tight? Should I wrap myself in a blanket?"

CORRECTIONAL OFFICER. <Sigh> "No, you don't have to wrap yourself up. I meant you should sit quietly and…."

Inmate. "You mean I shouldn't talk?"

CORRECTIONAL OFFICER. "<Aghhhhhh> No, you can talk! I want you to talk! It's a figure of speech!"

You get the idea. In the last example, what might be a better way to accomplish the task? Imagine this just from the CORRECTIONAL OFFICER'S side:
- The nurse is coming.
- Sit in the chair right here.
- Yes, sit where you are right now and keep talking to me.

13.3 Review: Concrete Thinkers

You will recognize **Concrete Thinkers** because they take what you say literally. Therefore:
- Use clear, short sentences, with a firm, calm voice.
- Give directions using simple words that are easy to understand.
- Show a minimum of emotion. Don't get irritated when the inmate does not immediately understand you. They respond much more to your tone of voice than to what you say.

CHAPTER 14

Information Processing and Retention: Consolidating Gains

Many inmates with mental illness develop the ability to 'fake normal' People around them may do frightening things, but they don't show their fear. Other people may anger them, but they smile and pretend everything is all right. Conversations and ideas may be too complex, too fast, or irrelevant to what is going on inside them, but they have learned to pick up the rhythm of other people's speech, nod at the right moments, and smile or laugh when needed.[12] Never assume that an inmate with mental illness understands what you have told them just because they nod their head at the right moment. You need to verify that they understood you.

In dealings with the mentally ill the following points have been proven helpful:

Least Effective Method. The least effective method is to repeat using other words. If they have either tuned you out or did not understand you the first time, they may fake understanding again. This is different from the repetition you must do with the disorganized inmate (CHAPTER 27), when you DO repeat yourself when giving instructions, as a form of behavioral management. In that instance, your repetition is to 'get through' the confusion. Repeating yourself and assuming the inmate understood what you said often fails.

Repetition by Inmate. Have the inmate repeat your instructions. However, some inmates with mental illness may echo what you say, so this, too, does not prove that they actually understand or will follow through.

Open Sentences. A better method is open sentences. For example, "So, Inmate Hussain, if I've got it right, I will call the doctor tomorrow and explain the problem. And you will...." Of course, you expect (hope) that the inmate will complete the sentence.

Write Down Important Points. Write down the most important points. Many people with mental illness don't assimilate a lot of information that they hear, no matter how hard they listen. The correctional officer may find that writing the most important points of the conversation or agreement on a 3 x 5 card is quite helpful. Remind the inmate to check the card if they have any difficulty remembering what they are supposed to do. (I am aware that there are many circumstances where this strategy would be out of the question, but when safety concerns and policy issues are addressed, it can be very useful.)

CHAPTER 15

Coping With Stubborn Refusals

There are many occasions when inmates refuse to comply with directives, sanctions notwithstanding. Of course, if you have been bossing them around, patronizing them, or treating them with disrespect, (beyond, of course, your professional responsibility to maintain order and control, which will, of course, be primarily in the form of direct orders), it should not be surprising if they resist you. All people, mentally ill or not, have pride, and no one likes another person talking down to them or controlling their lives. If it is not your approach that is creating the problem, what, if anything, can correctional officers do to elicit compliance, without having to resort to the violation process?

Focus on the Task. Correctional officers should never take personally the non-compliance of an inmate suffering from serious pervasive mental illness. (Note the words 'serious pervasive mental illness.' Many individuals who do have a mental health diagnosis or substance abuse issues are, nonetheless, quite manipulative and strategic in their interactions with correctional officers).

Clarify the Message. Correctional officers must be clear on what the inmate is required to do regarding their immediate supervision plan. Don't bring up previous examples of their non-compliance, such as "the last time this happened," or "you always," or "remember when you." Stay here-and-now.

Deflection. Get them to focus on something else that they feel comfortable with. This is related to the 'island of sanity' tactic (CHAPTER 31).

15.1 Veteran Correctional Officer's Experience: The Tactic of Deflection

In dealing with one very large and frequently aggressive mentally ill female inmate who would rarely keep her pants on, I found out that she could sing fairly well. When medical, classification or our mental health team would come to see her, I would ask her to get dressed and she would refuse, often charging the door. Her use of profanity was legendary. Usually (not always) I could get her to keep her pants on if I asked her to perform a song for whoever was there to see her. She would sing (surprisingly well!) and dance a bit. The outcome was that she was happier and, at times, would comply with the interview process. The unexpected outcome was that the other divisions that dealt with her got to see her in an entirely different light, and they began to interact more with her. With less of a sense of social isolation, her dysfunctional behaviors decreased.

Control the Interview. Stay on topic and don't allow the person to divert your attention to unrelated issues, as inmates suffering from mental illness will naturally do.

Use a Strong and Calm Voice. Keep your tone of voice strong, but not demanding or aggressive.

De-personalize Your Role. Remind the inmate that you are enforcing the policies of the correctional facility, and that any sanctions are the result of the inmate's behavior, not anything personal.

State the Consequences. Correctional officers should be very clear in explaining to the inmate the consequences and possible sanctions that may be imposed for non-compliance. This should be provided as 'information,' rather than threat, the same way you tell your kid on a cold winter day, "If you stick your tongue on that metal pole, you are going to get stuck." Such consequences include placement in a treatment facility, loss of various privileges, being placed on 'confined to quarters' status or housed in a temporary segregated unit for non-compliance with established rule and policies.

Place the Power in the Inmate's Hands. Without handing over one iota of your authority, allow the inmate to be the decision maker, and clarify their role in complying, or not complying with an order. Say something along the lines of "It looks like you've got something to decide. You have a couple of choices. You CAN comply with my order. Or, you can refuse, and be taken before the classification committee and tell them why you don't feel like complying with the facility's programs. And we will place you in administration segregation pending that meeting." Correctional officers must never threaten anything that cannot be backed up with action. Simply state the facts of the consequences for non-compliance. Based on their response, follow through with the appropriate action.

You can also point out the benefits of following through with what you are directing them to do. You needn't offer any rewards or promise anything, but you can point out the obvious, such as, "You know classification does their interviews on Mondays, and that it sure would help with your request to get moved if they came in and saw how clean your room was…." In this instance you are not offering anything more to this inmate than any other inmate: just helping them realize how they can help themselves. **However, when people are acutely agitated, they can't handle options; rather, they should be given simple directions.**

CHAPTER 16

Stuck: Coping with Repetitive Demands, Questions and Obsessions

Sometimes inmates will make repetitive demands for information, or for permission to deviate from their supervision and treatment plans. Some try to impose their own conditions for their supervision, such as, 'program hopping' in order to find something that is to their liking, or 'shopping' for the right officer to get what they want after being told "no" by several others

- Some inmates become 'stuck' with an obsessive thought or idea. No matter how many times you answer their question, they have to ask it again. This is often a sign of Obsessive-Compulsive Disorder (OCD), which is frequently missed by evaluators, because people become skilled in covering up such a humiliating problem. Those with Rigid Personalities (CHAPTER 12) also show this trait. Such people experience unbearable anxiety when they don't give in to the obsession or compulsion. The correctional officer may be the first to really notice OCD behaviors when an inmate gets stuck on things and can't 'let go.' The officer should refer the inmate to psychiatric services for further evaluation and/or treatment of this specific disorder.[13]
- An inmate may obsess as part of another disorder like schizophrenia, developmental disability, or other serious impairments. Their repetitive questions or obsessing on a single point may be due to information processing errors (CHAPTER 14)—in other words, they misunderstand what they are being told, and can't understand the correction or explanation you give.
- Sometimes an inmate repeats a question *intending* to be irritating or challenging. In a bland tone of voice, simply say, "You already know the answer to that," or otherwise calmly point out that they already have the information, and *move on*. By disengaging, you are saying, "I'm not participating in the game."
- Inmates with serious mental illness sometimes *perseverate*, meaning they are stuck on a subject and feel like they have to talk about it, often at length. This behavior is slightly different from the almost automatic kind of locked-in quality of the OCD inmate. These inmates simply get stuck. This is often a particular problem with inmates in mental health units. In this case, the correctional officer may say something like, "I know this is very important to you, and you want to talk about this and ask me questions. But you also know I have a lot of work to do, so I will make you a deal. Sometime between the hour of ten and eleven in the morning, we can talk about this for three minutes and thirty seconds, and no longer. It's your job to think carefully about what you need me to know about the subject each day, because when the time limit is reached, that is it. Any further information will have to wait until our next contact." Note that the reason for the 'odd' number of minutes is that it sounds important, as if you have calculated it down to the second.

16.1 Coping With Obsessive Questions and Demands

1. If the problem seems to be OCD (a mental disorder that is involuntary) refer to psychiatric services.
2. If it is due to information processing errors (usually because of a serious mental disorder), refer to the information in CHAPTER 14.
3. If it is game-playing, disengage.
4. For the inmate who just gets stuck on things, give them a brief, time-limited interaction, once a day, to voice their concerns.

CHAPTER 17

The Need for Reassurance

Some people are quite anxious by nature or circumstances. For others, intolerable anxiety is either their primary illness, or one of the most troublesome symptoms of their mental disorder. Anxiety is living as if something that you are afraid *might* happen, **is happening right now**.

Imagine an inmate who has been traumatized, either before they were incarcerated, or as too often happens, during their period of imprisonment. Despite what sympathy that you may have, don't treat them like they are weak: that will support the weakest aspect of their personality. They may think that something awful is going to happen and that is why you are talking in such careful tones. At the same time, don't affect a cheerful, "ain't no big thing" tone of voice. This kind of falsity will make the person either uneasy or irritated. Instead, speak in a matter-of-fact tone. Take their unease into account, but speak with an expectation that they are strong enough to manage their anxiety.

> **17.1 Veteran Correctional Officer's Experience: The Power of Reassurance in Inmate Management**
> One inmate was terrified that he was going to be transferred to a Supermax facility, even though there were no grounds for that occurring. While such a pattern of behavior was, at times, quite frustrating to the correctional officer, the few moments she spent talking to the inmate, reiterating that such transfers were based on infractions of behavior, not at random, were met with extreme gratitude, and this inmate was otherwise compliant with the rules of the prison.

CHAPTER 18

Dealing With Mood Swings

Such inmates can be very difficult to communicate with, much less de-escalate, because just as progress is made with their current mood, they shift into another. They can be verbally abusive, provocative, complaining, passive-aggressive, blaming, apologetic, ingratiating and friendly all in the space of an hour or less. They often try to get control of others even when they have no control over themselves.

Coping With Mood Swings

Rather than getting frustrated by the inmate's mood swings, something that will be reflected in your own body language or words, remain balanced and emotionally non-reactive. **A correctional officer can influence others by being exactly what they are not.** The more the correctional officer is unaffected by an inmate's emotional storms, the more likely that the inmate will calm down (SECTION III).

> **18.1 Review: Mood Swings**
>
> Inmates with mood swings shift emotions rapidly with no relationship to the situation they are in. Remember:
> - Don't mirror the individual's emotional state or lose control of your own emotions.
> - Control them through controlling your own emotions. Remain powerfully calm.
> - Speak in a firm, yet calm and controlled manner.
> - Because they display any emotion you can imagine, use general de-escalation tactics, as described throughout this book, as needed.

CHAPTER 19

They Aren't Moving: What to Do?

Sometimes you tell an inmate to do something and all they do is stare at you vacantly, voice a million questions, express misgivings or anxiety, or drift off into mumbling about something completely different.

Others seem to lack motivation; they just won't do what we think is good for them. I am referring here to the inmate whose mental illness impedes their ability to accomplish the things they are required to do, not the defiant inmate.

The correctional officer must assess the inmate's actual ability to comply, and use their discretion when determining what constitutes an acceptable level of compliance, or at least a concerted effort at compliance on the inmate's part.

If the inmate is actually defiant, the correctional officer should initiate the official violation process and bring the inmate back before the classification or treatment committee for a violation hearing, or possible modification to program. The violation process may be incredibly motivating for some inmates. Correctional officers should not be reluctant to document a violation report against an inmate with mental illness or overlook their non-compliance because of their illness. On the other hand, this may serve as the evidence to establish that a modification of their treatment plan is necessary.

> **19.1 Using One's Genuine Mental Illness as Manipulation**
> Some inmates have learned to use their mental illness as an excuse for their failure to comply with even the most basic rules and regulations. Mental illness becomes their 'fallback' position for their non–compliance, so that they never accept any personal responsibility. If correctional officers are assisting an inmate who suffers from mental illness, they should never do things for the inmate that they could do for themselves, other than perhaps scheduling certain appointments (and this is done primarily so the correctional officer knows the appointment was indeed scheduled), or helping them navigate some institutional bureaucracy.

Inmates with mental illness must be held accountable for their actions, and safety concerns certainly outweigh any exigent circumstances related to the inmate's mental capacities. Beyond the issue of basic accountability, correctional officers, as part of an interdisciplinary team, have a responsibility to document facets of inmate behavior indicative of treatment program compliance or non-compliance.

Correctional officers should also be mindful of how they attempt to motivate the inmate. Are you overly threatening? Or conversely, are you pleading with them? Correctional officers must retain their dignity when trying to motivate inmates. Give directions in a firm tone of voice. When you are dignified, the inmate will respect you more, sometimes in spite of himself or herself. Inmates are far more likely to be compliant for correctional officers who are perceived as fair and equitable in their approaches, and who maintain a high level of integrity and professionalism when interacting with inmates.

> **19.2 They Aren't Moving—What to Do?**
> - Don't do for them what they can do for themselves.
> - Don't require them to do things that they are incapable of doing.
> - If they are truly non-compliant, use the violation process for motivation (or sanction if they continue to refuse).
> - Act with dignity. Don't try to 'cheerlead' them into compliance, berate them, complain, or any one of a number of actions that compromise your integrity in the interests of getting them moving.

CHAPTER 20

Should a Correctional Officer Ever Apologize?

Some inmates store up grievances, allowing feelings of persecution and perceived personal slights to affect their entire worldview. With inmates suffering from mental illness, these feelings can be more problematic, because their memories may be distorted or even delusional. Frequent complaints about old history can become a significant barrier to an inmate's compliance with their supervision and treatment plans, not to mention being extremely aggravating to the correctional officer who must continually turn the inmate's attention to immediate issues.

As a correctional officer, you represent the last stop along the inmate's journey through the criminal justice system. Feelings of animosity toward the arresting police officer(s) and other correctional officers, perceptions of civil rights infractions, dissatisfaction with their legal representation, and bitterness toward the sentencing judge—all of these resentments are now directed toward you, one more authority figure who is intruding into their life, and telling them what they can and can't do.

As already described, correctional officers must refrain from reacting emotionally to the inmate's inability to move beyond the past, even as you try to redirect their attention to the present situation. Above all, don't personalize the inmate's complaints or their feelings of prior injustices. Correctional officers can hardly be expected to bear the emotional burden for the entire criminal justice system, nor should they feel responsible for any actual mistreatment or improprieties surrounding an inmate's case that occurred previous to their incarceration, or in another institution.

Acknowledge Their Concerns. Quite often inmates merely need to express their frustrations or feelings of helplessness regarding their case, and they view the correctional officer as the only available outlet to do so. Sometimes, permitting the inmate to express their feelings (as long as they do so in a brief and appropriate manner), may be enough to alleviate their anger. Don't agree or disagree with them, or otherwise reinforce their feelings of persecution, just recognize their complaints and then move forward. **Do not, however, allow the inmate to revisit the issue at every encounter.**

Apologize. If the inmates complaints do, in fact, concern your actions, think about it quickly, but carefully. Perhaps, in this instance, you were wrong. If so, apologize. In some situations, this is enough. However, the author cannot stress strongly enough that officers should be wary of apologizing to an inmate as a means of moving them off of a specific subject or grievance. An apology may lead the inmate to believe they are now in control of the relationship, and that the correctional officer will act cautiously

<u>so as not to upset them in the future.</u> By acting ethically and professionally at all times, and staying calm and in control, a correctional officer is much less likely to say or do anything for which they would ever need to apologize.

If an Apology Is Not Enough. Correctional officers may say to the inmate, "You are still upset about this. You want to talk about it again, don't you?" Notice that you don't ask the inmate; you merely state your understanding. This gives them the opportunity to correct or adjust your understanding so that if their complaint is legitimate, you are able to effectively put it to rest.

Complaints as Their Own Reward. Certain inmates are never satisfied, because the complaint becomes a 'rewarding' activity in itself. Others bear a pervasive resentment toward their correctional officers, an institution, or even life itself. For them, complaints are merely a way to express hostility or an attempt to control you by insisting on talking about things on their agenda. In these cases, simply take the issue off the table, forever. Remind the inmate that you have already addressed their complaint, so that there is nothing more to discuss. Terminate the contact if they continue.

> **20.1 Review: Should a Correctional Officer Ever Apologize?**
> - If they have a general grievance towards their situation and the criminal justice system, acknowledge their complaints in a 'one-and-done' manner, as long as you neither apologize for things that are not your fault or responsibility and you don't compromise your authority.
> - If you have wronged the inmate, <u>if it does not put you in danger and if it, thereby, **enhances** your authority</u>, then you should apologize. Example: "Anderson. That was my bad. I promised to notify you that the new church group was starting and I forgot. I've talked to the group leader and you can start next week."
> - If the inmate is stuck on the issue, say, "You are still upset about that," or something similar, giving them an opportunity to clarify why it is still a problem for them. Then, after you hear them out, it should be finish.
> - If the inmate is using the grievance or complaint to get control of the exchange, distract you, or simply complain for the sake of complaining, shut it down. Call them on their game and don't allow it to continue.

CHAPTER 21

Useful Tactics for Dealing with Symptoms of Paranoia and Persecution

21.1 This Chapter Focuses on the Paranoid Attitude

This chapter focuses on tactics specific to paranoia. Rather than the delusional state (CHAPTERS 30 & 31), we are here discussing an attitude, with the following characteristics: a sense of being persecuted, blame of others for any problem, and a hair-trigger sensitivity to being vulnerable. We are here talking about something much more common than the fixed false beliefs and hallucinations of the inmate suffering from paranoid psychosis. Paranoia is, in this case, a character trait, one that, by the way, is held by the vast majority of inmates in any correctional institution. If they didn't already have it going into the penitentiary, the majority develop it once they are institutionalized.

The inmate with the paranoid attitude has a motto of life: "If there is a problem here, that would be your fault." The paranoid world is one of dominance and submission: they try to dominate the people in their life, and are terrified or enraged at being forced to submit.

I am not only referring to a psychotic or delusional state, but also the far more common paranoid character, in which the inmate (without delusions) has a consistent *attitude* of blame, resentment of authority, fear of vulnerability, and an expectation of being betrayed by people he or she trust. Stimulant users, notably those using methamphetamine, cocaine, and cathinones ('bath salts'), frequently display these behaviors. It is also a very common 'solution' that criminals arrive at to excuse any failure. Many such inmates are essentially terrified that they will be made vulnerable, but they cover it up through aggression towards whomever they are afraid. One helpful image is an angry porcupine, all quills, with a soft underbelly, hunched over, ready to strike in hair-trigger reaction. Character traits and behavior patterns of inmates with the paranoid attitude include:

They Interpret Relaxation as Vulnerability. Therefore, they become *more* paranoid when you, their correctional officer, begin to establish rapport with them. Friendship means letting your guard down. Don't be surprised if inmates with a paranoid attitude suddenly flare up with suspicion or accusations during times that are uneventful or even, within professional limits, friendly.

Being Mistaken Or Wrong Is Another Form of Vulnerability. Rather than admitting wrongdoing or mistakes, inmates with a paranoid attitude reflexively ***project*** negative feelings on the other person. If they feel hate, they believe, "You hate me." If they neglected to leave the yard for a medical appointment, they will claim, "You set me up. You knew I couldn't get there on that day."

Inmates with the Paranoid Attitude Live Like Detectives. They continually search for evidence to prove what they already know is true. They have ***ideas of reference***, in which they believe that other conversations, glances, or actions are directed at them. They assume that others are conspiring about them, talking about them, laughing at them. Ironically, their reactions, in response to their own paranoia, frequently cause others to act in exactly the way the paranoid person expects.

Inmates with a Paranoid Attitude Make Others Uncomfortable Or Afraid. Because of their aggressive, brooding or standoffish behavior, they can make other people uncomfortable or afraid. If they sense fear in you, they expect you to attack, and they "attack you back first," fear driving their own aggression.

Try to Let Them Know What Is Going On
Because these inmates are so suspicious, they will often question your actions and instructions. Clearly and explicitly explain the rules and regulations of their supervision plan. Correctional officers should also make clear their expectations of compliance, and explain the violation process, as well as the potential consequences of non–compliance. Even if you must perform a cell extraction, put them in solitary confinement or protective custody, explain what you are doing and why, once they are secure. If they have a sense that you treated them in good faith, despite requisite severity, things are more likely to go well next time. However, you should not accept being quizzed incessantly. You are not required to explain every action. It might be a tactic to throw you off guard or distract you, or simply control a few moments of your day.

Personal Space: Physical and Psychological With the Paranoid Inmate
Many inmates with paranoid attitudes are preoccupied, even obsessed, with fears that they will be invaded, violated, or controlled in some fashion. The more severely psychotic may be afraid that they will be sexually violated, even in situations where that is not a possibility. Some of the following are, of course, relevant when dealing with any inmate, but they are doubly important when an inmate is paranoid.

Maintain the Angle. Whether standing or sitting, turn your body at a slight angle (blade/staggered stance), so that physical 'confrontation' is a choice on their part rather than a requirement. If you directly face a paranoid inmate ('square up'), you *force* them to turn away if they do not want to face you. Paradoxically, the stance that is safer for you makes them feel safer in turn.

Mindfulness. Never let your own guard. You are in an avalanche zone, and anything could set off another slide. NOTE: You are safest in an avalanche zone when you are aware and relaxed, moving smoothly with confidence—just like an officer who has mastered the skills necessary to survive.

Differentiate. Inmates with a paranoid attitude feel safest when you differentiate yourself from them, so that they don't feel—emotionally—that you got under their guard. It is better to be somewhat emotionally distant rather than too warm and friendly.

Too Friendly. Be aware when things are getting too relaxed. It is not only about you maintaining awareness. If they relax, they may suddenly startle, realizing that for a brief moment, they let their guard down. They may respond by exploding to make sure you do not 'take them over.'

Cover Your Triggers. Inmates with the paranoid attitude will try to provoke you. If you lose your temper, they will feel justified in whatever they do to you, and it may just as well key into their terror-based aggression. A slang expression for this is 'fear biters.' They bark and snarl and when you react, they attack as if you attacked first.

Is There a Specific Paranoid Rage or Violence?

There is no specific 'paranoid rage.' Instead, paranoia is an 'engine' that drives rage in all its various forms. De-escalate the inmate using tactics specific to the mode of rage they are exhibiting (SECTION X), rather than de-escalating 'paranoia' itself. Paranoid inmates can exhibit traits of fear, frustration, intimidation, and manipulation. With their focus, however, they are rarely disorganized. Even so, some disorganized inmates can experience an 'omni-directional dread,' a pervasive terror that is inescapable. Unlike paranoia, however, this pervasive sense of terror has no target.

21.2 Review: Paranoia and Persecution

The inmate with paranoid traits has an attitude that if anything is wrong it is another person's fault. Whether delusional or not, they see others as conspiring against them or persecuting them.

- De-escalate based on the behavior, not the paranoia.
- Let them know what's going on.
- Speak in formal tones. Do not be too friendly.
- They will try to provoke you so they can 'hit you back first.'
- Be aware of both physical and emotional spacing. Maintain a correct distancing, neither too close nor too far.
- Differentiate by not being too friendly, and if they are delusional, clearly separate yourself from their paranoid ideas without arguing (CHAPTERS 30 & 31).
- Maintain your calm: the paranoid inmate is usually assaultive when they feel under attack, when they perceive you as controlling, or when they perceive that you are afraid.
- If you do place them in custody or otherwise control them, let them know what is going on and why. Such inmates are most likely to become dangerous when they base their actions on their imagination rather than on reality.

CHAPTER 22

Feces Smearing ... and Worse

When I have interviewed officers, inmates smearing and devouring feces is often raised as the most troubling aspect of their job, more so than the threat of violence. Aside from the disgusting smell and sight, it is horrifying to see a human being so degraded.

One of the most important insights about this behavior is the obvious—it is very rare to ever see it on the 'outside' among adults, where it is almost entirely a behavior of imprisoned individuals, who are either suffering from profound mental illness, dementia or severe personality disorders.[14]

Why would people to this? Perhaps the two major reasons are:

Social isolation associated with profound disability (mental illness and cognitive impairment). Human beings need human contact—social interaction, even human touch. Many inmates suffering from mental illness or developmental disabilities are put in isolation, because they are either a danger to others, or more likely, others are a danger to themselves. But isolation almost always causes further deterioration of their mental state, and their actions reflect this deterioration. In addition, some inmates experience profound psychological breakdowns when *held* in isolation. This segregation may have been enacted for legitimate safety reasons, but that does not change the fact that as a result, some inmates lose all sense of psychological stability.

Power and control – It can be, in essence, a statement: "You control my life, you control my freedom, when and where I move, eat and sleep. This is the one control I have left, and through it, I take away your comfort and ease in controlling me. I change your work day and your mood. And if you have to clean my cell, at least for a few moments, you work for me."

No Easy Answers

If, at this point, the reader is hoping I will offer some magical solution to make this problem go away—regrettably, I do not. I truly wish that I would have an easy answer for this problem. The truth is that there are probably millions of hours of brain power devoted to this subject—and no one has a truly good answer. This behavior is, unfortunately, relatively frequent among children, particularly those suffering from autistic disorders, and there are a number of websites devoted to helping these children and their parents. Even with an understanding that one has to create an optimal environment, find distracting behaviors, wear special clothing, attend to delusions, sensory motor disabilities and the like, this behavior is incredibly difficult to alleviate, even with loving parents and fully involved caregivers. Is it any surprise that we are so often at a loss when it comes to adults within a prison environment? Finally, any solutions are on the level of program and policy change (i.e., creating specific programs and environments for inmates with serious mental illness that are clinically driven, effectively treating their illness on a long-term basis). Officers are put in a position of suffering other people's suffering.

Two Distinct Drivers of these Behaviors

In general, inmates who enact these behaviors fall into two categories: those who are desperately ill and those who are engaging in the behaviors for tactical reasons.

The seriously ill are using the behavior as a kind of desperate communication. As one man, desperately ill with AIDS-related dementia, put it to me, "I just want my outsides to be the same as my insides." These people, generally speaking, are terribly ill and they need psychiatric care and psychological support. This includes medication, counseling and case management. Of course, this is NOT meant in any way to minimize the fact that some such inmates are profoundly dangerous and all safety precautions to protect medical and counseling staff, correctional officers and inmates much be maintained.

Those who enact these behaviors as a kind of assault on the institution and the officers who work there are different, similar to the young man I worked with who would hack open his wrists when officers passed his cell, trying to spray them in the face with his blood. This could be referred to as 'weaponizing body fluids,' Two famous examples of using feces and other body fluids as an act of rebellion are the so-called 'Dirty Protest' by the Irish Republican Army against their British captors,[15] and currently, some of the captives at Guantanamo Bay.[16] When feces, urine and blood are weaponized, they are frequently stored up and flung on officers, rather than simply smeared or devoured.

Is There Anything that the Correctional Officer Can Do?

Perhaps the only power that officers have in this situation, beyond maintain their own integrity, dignity and professionalism, is *observation* and *documentation*. Correctional officers' detailed records may help establish that the individual in question is smearing/devouring feces as a manifestation of a desperate illness, and that his or her current environment only makes them more ill. As stated, these individuals need psychiatric care and case management of their illness—it may well be the officers direct observations that make that possible. To have successfully proven through observation and documentation that the inmate needs care, and then receives it, is both an act of humanity in getting them help, and power, because, through this observation, you have protected the morale and well-being of both officers and inmates alike.

On the other hand, when officers' observations establish that the repulsive behavior is assaultive and manipulative, the prison can better respond through a behavioral plan rather than placing them in (unnecessary) psychiatric care, where such inmates may spend their time victimizing genuinely ill patients.

SECTION V

Recognizing The Strategies Of
Opportunistic And Manipulative Inmates

CHAPTER 23

Divide and Confuse:
Borderline Personality Disorder and Splitting

23.1 Author's Note
Individuals with borderline traits frequently display suicidal and para-suicidal behaviors, which will be discussed in detail in SECTION VII.

Personality disorders are habitual patterns of behavior that sometimes cause an inmate, and almost always, others associated with them, considerable problems. Most types of personality disorders, however, do not cause behaviors that significantly affect safety. Several, however, are often associated with dangerous behavior: paranoid personality (CHAPTER 21), anti-social personality, with its most intense manifestation, psychopathy/sociopathy (CHAPTERS 25 & 26), and a third type called borderline personality disorder. An inmate with borderline traits believes that whatever feeling they are having right now is their only possible reality. For example, an inmate is accidentally bumped in the lunch line. Instead of brushing it off, he explodes. This is a borderline reaction. On the flip side, he meets his new attorney's assistant, and within five seconds, he knows that she is the love of his life.

Any of us can be overcome by feelings that seem beyond our control and make emotional decisions that are not in our own best interest, such as falling in love with the 'wrong' person. We are sometimes impulsive, and sometimes we get angry, even enraged. For us, however, such experiences are rare, while for the inmate with borderline personality disorder, they are an everyday occurrence.

Those on the mild end of the spectrum will be quite emotional, over-reacting to things that others could take in stride. With those whose disorder is more severe, it is as if their nervous system, at least that part which regulates emotion, lacks any protective sheathing. Imagine trying to live your daily life with two layers of skin peeled off. That is borderline existence on an emotional level. Whatever one feels is inescapable. The borderline person lives with the intensity and the lack of emotional resilience of a toddler. They experience the world and the people in it as good and bad, perfect and foul. They are frequently arrested for domestic violence, road rage, and impulsive fights ("What are you looking at!").

23.2 Movie Portrayals of People With Borderline Personality Traits

The two main characters in the movie, *Monster,* starring Charlize Theron and Christina Ricci, are portrayals of women with two types of extreme borderline personality disorders. Theron plays Alicia Wournos, a woman who came from a horrendously abusive background, drifted into prostitution and then murdered six 'johns.' She had the emotional stability of a toddler, shifting from sweetness and trust to hair-trigger rage. Whatever she felt at that moment was her only reality. Some of her murders, at least, were based on the threat and abuse she *felt* she was experiencing from the johns.

The Ricci character was a woman of almost no character at all. She templated to whomever she was with at the time. Rather than 'active,' like Wournos, she was passive. Like Wournos, however, all her actions, too, are based on feelings alone, not on any rational evaluation on what was good for her, in this case—bonding with a dominant, violent individual, and then, later, betraying her to her law enforcement interrogators.

Because of this combination of character traits, inmates with borderline personality disorder frequently find themselves in various crises. Among them are genuine suicide attempts as well as para-suicidal acts—self-mutilating behaviors or repeat suicide 'gestures' staged for discovery and attention (SECTION VII), *impulsive* acts of assault, and brief psychotic episodes (CHAPTERS 30 & 31).

Typically, other correctional officers, case managers, lawyers, psychologists, and nurses disagree how to respond to an inmate showing these borderline traits, even to the point of arguing about whom is at fault for their current crisis. In particular, those involved in a therapeutic relationship with the inmate, often lean to 'contextualizing'—explaining away or excusing their behavior, especially when the inmate has a previous history of trauma or abuse. When the team associated with an inmate with borderline traits get tangled up in intense disputes about what is best for them, this type of conflict is called *splitting*.

Splitting doesn't happen in a vacuum. The inmate, although not really conscious of what they are doing, presents different facets of their personality to each person with whom they interact. This is different from conscious, strategic manipulation—instead, the individual reacts to different people based on how those people make them feel. These feelings can be reality based, or simply elicited because an officer has the same hairstyle as their abusive mother. Whether the inmate is aware of it or not, this is strategic, a 'divide and confuse' tactic, one that might have served them well growing up in an abusive environment. If people are arguing or confused about you, they can't gang up on you.

DIVIDE AND CONFUSE: BORDERLINE PERSONALITY DISORDER AND SPLITTING

Such inmates are quite reactive to other people's emotional reactions. In their world, if you elicit a feeling, you 'made' them feel it. If they are happy, then they are sure you love them. If you anger them, then you are scum, trash or evil. Like a toddler, whatever they feel, they become. It is not surprising, really, that an inmate will appear quite different to a counselor trying to build a supportive relationship, as opposed to a case manager trying to help them negotiate their way through the prison system with a minimum of conflict, and to the correctional officer who is responsible for the establishment of order and safety within the prison.

Not only is there 'splitting,' in the sense of the inmate expressing different emotions and thoughts with different people, but the inmate splits with individuals as well. Based on their feelings—which may actually have nothing to do with you—the inmate may interact with you quite differently on different days, or within a single hour.

The correctional officer can, of course, unilaterally decide to place the inmate into a higher custody setting, based on concerns of correctional safety. However, if all members of the team responsible for the inmate remain at odds, the 'victory' by the officer will be short-lived. You will be working with the same people on other cases, and you will most likely continue to work 'at odds together' regarding this inmate. Thus, whenever a team gets intensely at odds regarding a single inmate, suggest the possibility of splitting, and see if you can, by comparing observations, figure out if the inmate's interactions with various people have created the adversarial situation in which you find yourselves.

In general, the attitude of the correctional officer should be someone who wishes the inmate well, yet undeviatingly enforces the rules. By maintaining a type of 'warm emotional distance' (a subset of firm, but <u>Such inmates are, not surprisingly, quite reactive to other people's emotional reactions</u>. In their world, if you elicit a feeling, you 'made' them feel it. If they are happy, then they are sure you love them. If you anger them, then you are scum, trash or evil. Like a toddler, whatever they feel, they become. fair), you won't get emotionally worked up over things, and the inmate will find less to react to as well.

23.3 Not Multiple Personality Disorder (AKA Dissociative Identity Disorder - DID)

Inmates with borderline traits—whose way of relating to themselves and other people can be summed up in the phrase: "What I feel is what I am'—are relatively common. Many have a background of abuse, and many have also abused alcohol and other drugs (which almost always make their symptoms and their lives far worse). Their shifts in mood and action can be so sudden that a correctional officer might quite reasonably wonder if they 'have' multiple personality disorder.

More commonly called Dissociative Identity Disorder, this is a rare and quite controversial diagnosis, which seems to 'appear' far more often when individuals are involved in particular types of therapy. Whatever the cause, individuals who display DID symptoms do not just have mood swings: they show changes in posture, facial expression, use of language: they even claim different names associated with each 'personality.'

If correctional officers are responsible for the safety of an individual displaying these behaviors, they need guidance—a specific plan on how to interact with the person.

I will emphasize, this is a very rare phenomenon, and the vast majority of inmates with unstable behaviors are not suffering from Dissociative Identity Disorder; rather, they are people who are over-reactive to both positive and negative experiences, who identify themselves with whatever emotion or feeling they are currently experiencing.

CHAPTER 24

Bad Intentions: Recognizing the Strategies of Opportunistic and Manipulative Inmates

All humans manipulate our environment, other people and ourselves ('impression management') to get what we want. For most of us, our intentions are benign, simply helping us negotiate social interactions. For many inmates, it is how they survive, striving to manipulate situations to stay out of trouble, or not draw attention from predatory inmates or correctional staff.

Beyond this, however, some inmates, in order to satisfy their need for instant gratification, attempt to manipulate nearly everyone with whom they come into contact. Some use manipulation as a means of furthering criminal actions. A few live for hate and destruction, and delight most in duping people so that they don't even know how 'dirty they were done.' Some manipulative inmates lie in a way that no one can pin them down, using a 'divide and disappear' strategy so that the more powerful beings in their life argue about them, instead of focusing directly on what they are really doing.

Manipulative Strategies

Manipulative strategies can result from a variety of emotions and intentions, such as those born of revenge, malice, desperation, laziness, guilt, or as the result of drug and alcohol use.[17]

Correctional officers should be wary of inmates who appear to be overly compliant, especially those inmates who have committed serious offenses, such as sex crimes or offenses involving the use of weapons or violence. Quite often, some of the most dangerous individuals will be apparently, agreeable, low-risk inmates, complying with any requirements in their custodial setting. Their motives are hardly altruistic. This seemingly compliant behavior may in fact be nothing more than an attempt to manipulate and control *your* behavior. <u>Require proper verification of any information given by the inmate.</u> Remember, inmates realize how busy and overworked you are, and they certainly pick up if you are stressed in any way. What the compliant inmate is likely trying to accomplish is to manipulate you so that you do not see what they are up to. After all, why would an already stressed out correctional officer bother to focus much attention on a truly compliant inmate!

Inmates sometimes use stories to overload you with information to keep your attention away from what they are doing. They try to charm you so that you actually look forward to contact with them, yet remain unaware of what is really going on.

Manipulative inmates ask correctional officers for personal information, such as marital status, children, in which part of town the correctional officer resides, and so forth. These questions appear innocent enough. What the manipulative inmate is doing, however, is gathering information, something that they can use either for themselves or as a medium of exchange with other inmates. Redirect any questions that touch on personal matters back toward your professional duties.

Inmates are also masters at quietly hanging around officers' conversations, harvesting revealing personal information. This is the easiest way to find out who could be vulnerable to manipulation whether it is through love ("My husband and I are having troubles"), money ("I had to take out a loan to make my house payment") or any other information that could be used for leverage in the future. How many officers talk about their kids at work? Are there any inmates hanging around while you talk?
- "I took my boy hunting last week."
- "She scored three goals."
- "Yeah, he's doing better now. The doc says he'll be off chemo in three months."

Manipulative inmates are also quite adept at reading body language. Remember, they virtually have nothing to do but observe others' behavior, including that of officers. They are particularly interested in potential victims, those who are easily intimidated or frightened, including both inmates and staff. They are also intrigued by those who put up any kind of a front, including an attempt to appear tough. All the manipulative inmate has to do is challenge him or her, and the 'fronting' correctional officer begins reacting like a yo-yo on a string, trying to keep up appearances, to an inmate who has already read them inside and out.

Manipulative inmates are also likely to blame others for both their failures and their behaviors. Nothing is ever their fault: they were simply in the wrong place at the wrong time; they didn't know their 'cellie' had a shank under the mattress; it is the correctional officer's fault for them losing their 'good time.'

Another means of manipulation is that of flirtation and sexuality, which can manifest in any gender configuration, including same sex. All correctional officers must address flirtatious behaviors or sexual innuendo immediately, and the officer must follow through with appropriate written documentation on the inmate's behavior. While this may be embarrassing, it is the only way an officer can let their administration know, formally, that the inmate's behavior was addressed and boundaries were enforced. Firm limits must be set as to the professional nature of the relationship, and what constitutes acceptable conversation. If this issue is not addressed instantly, the inmate will view it as implied acceptance, which may lead to further advances or even attempted blackmail. It may also lead others, both inmates and co-workers, to assume that something is actually going on. By following through with written documentation, this allows the officer's supervisor to take further action if the inmate's behavior continues. Some inmate's security classification should be enhanced, if they show a pattern of trying to flirt or 'come on' to staff. This is yet another of the many reasons that correctional officers should not be isolated while interviewing inmates, regardless of gender.

Manipulative inmates view relationships as transactions, with an eye toward gaining an advantage or placing the other individual in their debt. The manipulative inmate will sometimes deliberately make things difficult, only to then suddenly 'give in,' or become compliant. The likely purpose for their newfound compliance is to engender a sense of gratitude within the unwary correctional officer, or at least a lessening of frustration, toward the inmate. Along with a sense of gratitude however, can come a lessening of supervision or investigation. Officers should always be wary and always be thinking about what an inmate has to gain from any interaction not only with correctional officers, but also with non-security personnel, such as rec specialist, officer and educational staff.

> **24.1 Comments of a Veteran Officer: Strategies Used to Keep Officers Away**
>
> Inmates sometimes find a 'theme' that either gets them out of trouble or is threatening enough that officers either chose not to deal with them or excuse their behavior. Female inmates that continually accuse officers of raping them or touching them inappropriately generally cause male officers to shy away from them, refuse to deal with them, or pass the inmate's bad behavior off to another officer. This creates dissention among the officers and reduces those dealing with them to only women officers. Think of the sense of power this engenders in the inmate— "All male officers are afraid of me!"
>
> Other inmates tell officers that they are HIV positive when they are not. This is especially effective for the inmate in use-of-force situations as officers do not want to be exposed to bodily fluids. Inmates using this theme will often attempt to spit on officers. Because inmate's medical records are not available to officers, no one wants to deal with this inmate's bad behavior as their HIV status cannot be verified. Inmates cannot be compelled to take an HIV test without a court order. Officers will sometimes let these inmates get away with much more than they would tolerate from any other inmate.

CHAPTER 25

Tactical and Safety Considerations Related to the Supervision of the Sociopathic Inmate

25.1 Author's Note: Sociopaths Stand Alone

There is considerable overlap in this chapter with the safety recommendations made throughout this book, particularly in the last chapter on manipulative behavior. In SECTION X, I will discuss what to do when facing someone presenting with Hot, Predatory, or Aggressive-Manipulative Rage—all modes that the sociopathic inmate can manifest when they become dangerously aggressive. Here, the author is highlighting the most salient point's specific to sociopathic individuals. I believe that this information is so important to officer safety that it must be presented as a stand-alone chapter for easy reference.

The terms psychopath and sociopath are interchangeable. I have chosen to use the latter term so that the reader will not confuse two similar sounding terms—psychotic and psychopathic—that are profoundly different (psychosis will be discussed in later chapters). Sociopaths evoke very strong reactions. Estimates are that 1-3 percent of any population, and perhaps 40 percent of the prison population is sociopathic. A small percentage of inmates commit most of the crimes in any society. Many theories are formulated about criminogenic societies or families, and yes, social factors very often factor into criminal behavior. Nonetheless, the sociopath, to a remarkable degree, seems independent of social factors. They are born in all kinds of homes, with all kinds of parents.

The entertainment media as well as sensationalized news accounts of horrendously violent killers and rapists have introduced an image of the malevolent criminal mastermind and the sadistic predator into the public's consciousness. Without a doubt, violent sociopaths do exist, but they are often rather mundane in appearance, blending in with their surroundings without attracting any undue attention.

> **25.2 Examples of Sociopaths in the Movies**
>
> Instead of thinking of some movie monster such as Hannibal Lector, a much more useful image would be Johnny Depp's character in *Pirates of the Caribbean*. In his role as Captain Jack Sparrow, Depp plays an aggressive narcissist; he is attractive and likeable, but also utterly selfish and quite willing to violate social norms. A second image would be the Matt Damon character in *The Talented Mr. Ripley*, an inoffensive chameleon-like con-man, who has no particular desire to kill anyone (it even appears to 'stress him out,') but when circumstances 'require' it, he does so without hesitation.

Although sociopathic inmates can be charming and ingratiating, they can also be violent, provocative, dishonest, arrogant, and quite willing to break any rule. Although some are remarkably talented, even brilliantly creative, the only thing they truly care about is themselves. The sociopath presents problems far beyond what you will experience with the 'ordinary' criminal inmate, however manipulative (CHAPTER 25) the latter may be.

Just as a leopard or a cougar is known to attack whenever a prey animal exposes its neck, sociopathic inmates feed off vulnerability. Because of their manipulative charm, they can easily get under the defenses of others. They will gravitate to the most vulnerable people on your team. They study everyone with whom they come into contact, making note of any apparent weaknesses and developing new strategies of manipulation and control, either as a direct point of attack ("When I raise my voice, Officer Grohl flinches."), or as a new weapon to use against others ("When Officer Gibbs tilts her head and smiles while I'm talking, I find myself relaxing a little. I can use this the next time I'm trying to get close to that kid in D Block.") Not only do they lack a sense of remorse at the harm inflicted upon their victims, they often take delight in it.

They view themselves as utterly unique and special (grandiose narcissism), and therefore, do not view themselves as being incarcerated for the purpose of rehabilitation. They view the entire criminal justice system—from correctional officers to treatment programs—with contempt.

Because such inmates are easily bored, they deliberately flame up other inmates so that they come into conflict either amongst themselves or with correctional officers. Many, parasitic rather than violent, revel in the instigation of emotional drama or conflict through the use of lies, rumors, and/or intimidation. Another purpose of these 'set ups,' is to create a unit chaotic enough that they are able to accomplish their own deeds unseen, with officers preoccupied with other inmates.

Without a doubt, the most dangerous are the sexually violent sociopaths, who use their guile to groom others for exploitation, prior to enacting sexual assaults. Although common sense would dictate against a correctional officer ever fostering a personal relationship with an inmate, it happens all too often. A sociopathic inmate may attempt to groom and seduce a correctional officer, just for the thrill of destroying their career, or for the purposes of blackmail or privilege.

Such inmates owe their allegiance to no one, although they may form quasi-sentimental attachments or gang affiliations that last until a stronger interest or desire pushes them onwards to something else. This loyalty is on the level of, "Who do you think you are, patting my dog without my permission!"

As with many criminal inmates, sociopaths are often impulsive, and their sense of invincibility often leads them to ignore consequences. Their impulsivity and sense of entitlement can also result in explosive violence if they don't get what they want. Other sociopaths are 'instrumentally violent,' using it as a tool: 'just business,' so to speak. For others, the violent act itself is gratifying; they are sadistically violent. In sum, sociopathic inmates' propensity for physical and emotional violence, coupled with their charming manipulativeness and the fact that there are **NO** therapeutic interventions that can 'cure' them, means that correctional officers must remain observant and wary at all times when dealing with them. <u>In fact, pointing out characteristics of their behavior (a frequent therapeutic intervention) only allows them to better mask it, making them more dangerous. In a sense, a therapist can provide a kind of 'instruction manual' on how to behave in a way that appears non-threatening or otherwise 'normal.'</u>

When supervising and interacting with the sociopathic inmate, correctional officers need to remain conscious of the fact that these individuals are quite skilled in reading other people, in light of how strong they are, their susceptibility to manipulation, and most significantly, what danger they represent to the inmate. Quite simply, they are out to destroy you by one means or another. The author recommends Robert Hare's illuminating work, *Without Conscience: The disturbing world of the psychopath* for a detailed discussion of this subgroup of inmates.[18]

25.3 Substance Abusers May Present as Sociopaths
Substance abusers often act like psychopaths while using. Addicts in remission who *truly* are engaged in treatment usually begin to abandon manipulative and strategic behaviors. Sociopaths, on the other hand, don't fundamentally change. They may use different strategies when they are sober, but they will never abandon a tactical, manipulative approach.

Tactical and Safety Considerations
You will be attacked through your 'best' and your 'worst' points. Of course, the sociopathic inmate will attack your weak points. If you are insecure about your personal appearance, the sociopath will either make you feel more insecure, or in a more sophisticated tactic, reassure you that he or she, at least,

finds you very attractive. What is harder to notice is when you are attacked through your best points. For example, if you appear to be physically fit, they will try to consult with you about your exercise regimen, or ask where and when you work out. If you love children, they will find a way to ask your advice on an alleged phone call from their ex-wife about putting their child on medications. They might really have a child who needs medication. But they are asking you in order to gain some traction, not to get your help. For such an individual, anything can be leverage. Remember, they don't even have to lie. The truth is an even better tool!

Notice when others start making excuses for the inmate. When manipulated, people often find a way to rationalize what the sociopath is doing. For example, after a near assault during his substance abuse treatment group, a counselor says, "You have to understand. He was brought up that way. When you threatened him with a violation, it was like a flashback to the way his father treated him." Don't allow others to sway your opinion or prevent you from attending to your professional duties.

Track any manipulative strategies, document them well, and alert all other members of your team to the tactics an inmate is using. Consult and consult again. Don't discount the observations of other officers. They are often very important, especially those of correctional officers, who interact most directly with the inmate in question. Consult yet again. Remember, it is certainly a warning sign when others agree with you about the danger a particular inmate presents; it can be an even more serious warning sign when officers *do not* agree.

You may be intimidated. The most obvious manifestation of intimidation is fear. <u>There is always a reason when you experience fear</u>. If you are frightened of an inmate, consult with your fellow officers or supervisors immediately. What is more difficult to recognize is an unconscious attempt to avoid being frightened by giving in to the demands of the sociopath. Ironically, the intimidated officer may sometimes claim that they have a working relationship or special rapport with the inmate, when, in fact, all they are doing is giving the predator exactly what he wants.

Be aware of grooming behaviors. The 'grooming cycle' is a pattern of behavior designed to alleviate the intended victim's fears and apprehensions, all the while targeting them for attack. The inmate will make their target feel a little off-balance, making them anxious, scared, or flattered. Then they lessen the pressure while making a request that the correctional officer would have granted anyway. The inmate begins to 'train' the correctional officer to experience a sense of relief when granting a request.

TACTICAL AND SAFETY CONSIDERATIONS RELATED TO THE SUPERVISION OF THE SOCIOPATHIC INMATE

> **25.4 An Example of Grooming**
>
> The inmate stands too close to you (slightly, not enough to require you to issue a command that they back up). Then, simultaneous to moving back to a more comfortable distance, he asks permission to get a drink of water. His goal is to cause you to associate granting a request with a release of tension. Hard eye-contact, shifting to friendliness, is another common grooming tactic.
>
> If successful, the inmate will make requests that get closer and closer to a moral or ethical line. Once he can get you to do something *over* the line, however, slightly, you are now compromised: an object of blackmail or worse. An example of this would be, once groomed, you let the inmate have 'just one minute' on the phone, past curfew, to say goodnight to his kid. Once you start bending the rules, breaking them isn't so far off.

Guard all personal information. As discussed previously, personal information can be used in a variety of ways. The sociopath can use such information to determine points of leverage against you. They can talk publicly about you, apparently displaying intimate knowledge of your life. In the worst case, such information can be used to track you down outside of your professional life, or make you fear for the safety of your friends and family.

Don't get beyond the horizon line. <u>Don't meet sociopaths alone!</u> Don't close your office door when interviewing them, and either have back-up present or in immediate contact. You are vulnerable to false accusations. You are vulnerable to manipulation when no one is present to witness and monitor the interaction with the inmate. You may not even perceive manipulation is happening. You are also vulnerable to physical attack at any time the sociopathic inmate believes that it is to their advantage, if their rage is triggered, or simply because it would be enjoyable.

Detecting calculated splitting. The sociopathic inmate uses gossip, rumors, misdirection, and blatant lying to set all the stakeholders involved in their supervision and treatment against each other. Regular communication and consultation with the various members of the treatment team is the best way to detect and confront splitting.

[See CHAPTER 52 concerning verbal control of individuals displaying 'predatory rage,' the most typical manifestation of violence by the sociopathic individual]

SECTION VI

Communication With Inmates That Have Severe Mental Illness Or Other Conditions That Cause Severe Disability

CHAPTER 26

Overview of Section VI

This section offers detailed descriptions of the most significant *behaviors* that inmates suffering from severe mentally illness may display. Along with each description will be suggestions on optimal communication strategies. Some are generally applicable, therefore overlapping among various sections, while others are specific to only one type of behavior/symptom. Just because you might be reading about paranoia for example, doesn't mean that paranoid inmate is not also disorganized, delusional, or manic. What you are trying to develop is a range of communication tactics that cover as many situations as possible.

It is a common misunderstanding that all individuals with mental illness are extremely impaired individuals who manifest severely disordered or unusual behaviors. That is not necessarily so. Even those with severe mentally illness can have many periods throughout the day where their illness is not predominant. Furthermore, most contacts with inmates are not emergencies, whatever their psychological difficulties. Nonetheless, the basic principles of communication presented here will serve you just as well with those who are manifesting a mild level of disorder, as well as those who are on the extreme end of the spectrum.

As the establishment of safety and the de-escalation of aggression are the primary purposes of this book, we focus on general patterns of inmate behavior, **regardless of the cause**. Mental illness, in this vein, does not refer only to such disorders as schizophrenia, bipolar disorder or depression. For example, intoxication can be considered a time-limited, substance-induced mental disorder. Beyond any medical condition, people, otherwise normal, can display acute, 'out of character' behaviors, due to problems or stressors in their lives, and prison itself is certainly stressful (referred to in CHAPTER 2 as the 'crisis inmate.') Thus, for the sake of this discussion, substance abuse, distinct neurological disorders, so-called character or mood disorders, as well as atypical episodes brought on by stress or other factors, all function as mental illness, sometimes of 'time-limited' duration. The cause may be relevant if making appropriate referrals for treatment; the correctional officer, however, should most emphatically focus on the behaviors, whatever the cause.

Speak to the Person, Not the Illness
You are walking outside on an icy winter day. You slip suddenly and spin toward the pavement. You thrust out an arm that breaks your fall. It also breaks your right wrist. Your life, for a few weeks or months, is different. Even the simplest tasks are difficult and may require assistance. Still, even though you are inconvenienced, and the injury probably changes your mood quite a bit, you are still 'you,' the

same person as before. Your injuries will eventually heal, the accident forgotten, as you continue through life. Such is not the case with mental illness.

Severe mental illness can cause mental and emotional disturbances far more profound than the temporary inconveniences brought on by physical injury. One's ability to think is distorted, and with delusions, reality is skewed. Perceptions may be bizarre, even hallucinatory. Emotions swing from high to low, or shift into realms at odds with one's immediate circumstances. Even so, as bad as such an illness may be, **there is a still a person behind the symptoms.** The inmates under your supervision aren't simply bundles of raw emotions or distorted cognitions. There exists an essential part of each of them untouched by their mental illness. We can choose to speak to the illness, or speak to the *human being* who is ill. For both humane and tactical reasons, it is that core part of his or her psyche that we are trying to reach. In short, decency, kindness and respect are great tactics (as long as they are supported by proper correctional awareness).

CHAPTER 27

Struggling in a Fog: Dealing With the Symptoms of Disorganization

> **27.1 Author's Note**
> See CHAPTER 49 for a detailed discussion of de-escalation of disorganized inmates in a state of chaotic rage. See CHAPTER 53 for information concerning agitated developmentally disabled inmates.

Understanding Disorganization

Disorganization is a general term used to describe what it is like when a person can't adequately organize their thinking, perceptions, behaviors and/or emotions so that they can function well in the real world. This can include those who are developmentally delayed, profoundly psychotic, head injured, those suffering from any kind of dementia or delirium, as well as those who are severely intoxicated (chemically induced disorganization).

Due to their cognitive limitations, inmates with developmental disabilities are not skilled at problem-solving situations. Furthermore, they often lack the maturity to manage complex or frustrating situations, and prison is nothing if not frustrating, confusing, intimidating, frightening, etc.

Inmates with psychotic disorders also become disorganized when they deteriorate. In fact, their delusions may have served them as an organizing principle, helping them to stay stable. For example, if you believe yourself to be surrounded by enemies, or are on a mission to save the world, you have to concentrate, because of your mission, as delusional as it may be. When one becomes disorganized, even delusions break down into chaotic thoughts, which are often manifested in incoherent speech and disorderly behavior. This noted, remember that heavily medicated inmates are sometimes slow to respond to your directions, and this can be misinterpreted as either noncompliance or disorganization.

27.2 The Near Impossibility of Communication

You will know you are dealing with a disorganized inmate because they are incoherent, or it is otherwise nearly impossible to communicate with them. They may seem to shift from one emotion to another, for no logical reason, and it is very hard, if not impossible, to hold their attention. Disorganization is an 'over-arching' category, including aspects of almost every syndrome described in other chapters. A disorganized person can be latent and/or concrete, have mood swings, paranoia, anxiety, extreme agitation, confusion, delusions, hallucinations, and information processing problems, to name only a few traits that are discussed elsewhere in the book. This chapter is concerned with the overall phenomenon of disorganization.

Small Bits at a Time

To better communicate with disorganized inmates, officers should divide tasks and instructions into small bits. Make sure that you are very specific concerning what you expect them to do. There is no point in being irritable with them. That just makes things more difficult and confusing because they usually don't know why you are upset.

Be realistic about what they can do. Correctional officers should not expect severely disorganized inmates to do something that is beyond their individual skill level, or their current mental status. Of course, the inmate should still be held to a high standard; just don't make it an impossible one. Such inmates need a program plan including work, academics/vocational training, and therapy-medical needs, all within their cognitive abilities.

Creating Room for Success

Although supervising disorganized inmates can be frustrating, inmates should be rewarded for positive behaviors, not just punished for negative ones. Indeed, your positive feedback may be the first they have ever received, and it will often help them adjust to incarceration in a positive manner.

27.3 A Note on False Confessions by Individuals with Developmental Disabilities

Important: Research on false admissions to crimes reveals that a large number of such confessions are made by developmentally disabled individuals. The developmentally disabled inmate may do something similar, when feeling emotionally pressured or if they are trying to impress or please you. During investigations with developmentally disabled inmates, you will get the most accurate information when they are calm and feel safe.

Over-stimulation

Loud noises, the presence of many people (particularly if more than one is talking), too much background noise or even bright fluorescent lights, will both distract and further agitate the disorganized person. Given the conditions in most prisons, it is hard, if not impossible to address this problem, but whenever possible, move the individual to a less stimulating environment. **Whenever you are trying to elicit compliance, it is particularly important with disorganized inmates that only one person speaks to them at a time.**

Keep It Simple

The disorganized inmate pays far more attention to non-verbal communication. Self-control is particularly important when de-escalating disorganized inmates. Your sentences should be short and each should only have one 'packet' of information. Keep the emotion out of your voice, and limit your physical gestures.

Let Me Repeat Myself

When we are not understood, our usual impulse is to elaborate. We use different words, expressive hand and facial gestures, and the emotional tone of our communication intensifies. This makes things worse for disorganized inmates. **Rather, simply repeat the same statement or question word-for-word, with the same gesture and facial expression**. When their disorganization is profound, you may need to repeat information and statements several times. The aim is not to browbeat them. You should not shout at them to 'get through.' <u>Repetition can be a touchstone of stability</u>. However, if you change your vocal tone or get irritated, you will defeat the purpose of the repetition. Rolling your eyes, making side-long glances of amusement at your back-up, sighing, raising your voice, pointing, standing close to them to get their attention, snapping your fingers or suddenly clapping your hands in front of their face, to name only a few, undermine safety, whether you are repeating the same words or not.

By repeating yourself several times, with a clear measured tone of voice, telling the inmate exactly what you want them to do, you provide a verbal lifeline that they can focus on rather than the chaos that is otherwise overwhelming them.

Magical Thinking

'Magical thinking' (mentioned in CHAPTER 1 as 'speaking into being') is telling stories which you then believe. It is most common among small children, adults with dementia, and individuals with developmental disabilities. Inmates displaying magical thinking don't show the same 'locked in' quality of delusional inmates (CHAPTERS 30 & 31), where a fundamental truth is suddenly revealed and then locked into place in their mind. Rather, the disorganized inmate verbalizes his fantasies, repeats them, and then believes them to be reality.

You will usually observe magical thinking in an inmate with developmental disabilities, often as a kind of fable making, the kinds of stories told by very young people, either young in age or young in mind.

Once you have established that a claim or statement is not true, there is little to be gained by arguing with the inmate about it. Sometimes just let it go. Other times, you can say, even with a little tiredness in your voice, "I've heard that story before. You don't have to tell me again." Then, simply move on to the next topic at hand and shift the inmate's focus toward the actual issues of concern regarding their supervision plan.

27.4 Dealing With a Disorganized Inmate

You will know you are dealing with a disorganized inmate when he or she is:
- Nearly incoherent, or otherwise impossible to communicate with.
- Shifting from one emotion to another with no logical reason.
- Distracted and you cannot hold their attention.
- Acting in a bizarre or chaotic manner.

When responding to a disorganized inmate you should:
- Divide tasks into small bits.
- Give simple, specific instructions.
- Be realistic about what the person can and can't do.
- Repeat your instructions rather than elaborate on them and don't change your vocal tone.
- Don't argue with magical thinking—redirect them to discussing what, if anything is emergent.
- Allow only one person to speak to the disorganized inmate.
- Particularly in crisis situations, minimize environmental distractions when possible, such as the TV in the background, other people talking, and bright lights, etc.

CHAPTER 28

Latency: The Unresponsive Inmate

Latency is a behavior in which individuals respond in a much-delayed manner to directions, commands or even simple attempts at dialogue. It is often a manifestation of disorganization, but because of its confusing nature, I have chosen to discuss it as an entity of its own. With latent inmates:

- You ask a question, and they talk to themselves quietly as they puzzle out what you might be saying.
- They may not even make eye-contact, or engage in odd movements in the air.
- Some latent inmates may simply stare away, a vacuous look on their faces.

28.1 How to Recognize Latency

You will recognize latency when the inmate to whom you are speaking not only delays his or her answers for a long time, but also when they do reply, their communication is somewhat odd and disjointed. You will notice that they do not really respond to the questions asked. This is different from being silent or defying you. You get the sense that they are not 'there,' that it is about something going on inside of them, not about you at all.

> **28.2 Example of Latency**
>
> The correctional officer comes upon an inmate, tying himself to the bars of his cell with his shirt:
>
> - **CORRECTIONAL OFFICER.** "Why are you tying yourself to the bars?" *(**30** seconds pass with the latent man standing and staring at the ground, frozen.)*
> - **CORRECTIONAL OFFICER.** "Why are you tying yourself to the bars?"
> - **Inmate.** *(The mentally ill man slowly raises his head, and his eyes vacant, slowly speaks.)* "Uh, bar fly." *(He then resumes his tying himself to the railing with thin string.)*
> - **CORRECTIONAL OFFICER.** "I can call for help so you can go to the clinic. I know there is someone there that is able to help you."
> - **Inmate.** *(The inmate suffering from mental illness stops tying himself, his hands still holding the string in mid-knot. His lips move as if he is talking to himself. He raises his eyes, lowers them, and raises them again. He speaks.)* "Don't take me steal me." *(He then resumes his activity without eye contact.)*
>
> Note the CORRECTIONAL Officer's exemplary patience. This contact is not a failure. The officer has ascertained that the individual is so profoundly ill that he is unable to communicate. That the officer is calm probably keeps the inmate from becoming fearful or combative in response.
>
> Note also that the officer did not try to analyze this, for example, asking the inmate if he is afraid he will fly away, and that's why he's tying himself to the bars. Given how impaired the inmate is, figuring things out is unnecessary.

Coping with Latency: Keep Things Simple

Although communicating with a latent inmate can be frustrating, as well as time consuming, the correctional officer should remain calm. Indeed, any frustration or anger you display will only further confuse them. Keep your sentences and instructions short and direct. Minimize the use of qualifiers, such as "you might" "maybe" "kind of," etc., that you ordinarily put in your sentences. Officers should also minimize the use of hand gestures or changing facial expressions. Don't speak robotically; simplicity is best.

It is useless to try to 'get through to them' by yelling. All this does is drive them further into the latent state, as they get more frightened, overwhelmed, or confused by the irate officer yelling incomprehensible things at them.

Latent inmates usually don't need things explained in further detail; they just don't 'get it' the first time. Say the same thing again and again, with a slow measured pace.

28.3 How to Speak and Respond to an Inmate Manifesting Latent Behaviors
- Keep your sentences short.
- Don't change your vocal tone.
- Repeat the instructions using the same words and the same tone of voice.
- Pause between sentences, giving the inmate time to process what you have said.
- Try to get the inmate to repeat back your instructions (No guarantees on this item!)
- Contact medical. Changes in mental states may indicate the recurrence or onset of serious mental illness.

CHAPTER 29

Withdrawal from Intoxicating Substances

29.1 Author's Note: The Question of Dual Diagnosis
Given all the attention usually paid to this subject, the reader may question why I have not devoted a large section specifically to the behaviors of inmates with dual diagnoses (those with both substance abuse and mental health issues) as a separate concern. There is no doubt whatsoever, that dual diagnosis can profoundly affect every aspect of an inmate's life, including their success or failure in a corrections setting. Substance abuse makes it much harder to heal from or even manage mental illness, and mental illness makes it much harder to recover from substance abuse. And both affect their ability to maintain themselves in general population.

This book, however, is concerned with the issues of safety and de-escalation from extreme states. Imagine all the pages that would be necessary to distinguish between, for example, a solvent-inhaling inmate with bipolar disorder, a marijuana-smoking inmate with social phobia, and a schizophrenic who shoots up a mixture of cocaine and heroin. To be sure, each and all of these concerns are relevant when it comes to treatment, but whatever substances they may have ingested, whatever illness or syndrome they may be suffering from, we are concerned with the behaviors that they are displaying. Deal with the behavior, not the cause.

Many inmates with mental illness actively use or are addicted to drugs and/or alcohol. These inmates are 'dual diagnosed;' that is, they have been diagnosed as having a mental health disorder as well as substance abuse issues. The abuse of drugs and/or alcohol not only complicates their recovery, but also can be life threatening if the inmate suffering from mental illness experiences a severe reaction brought on by mixing drugs and/or alcohol with their prescribed medications. Others develop conditions (amphetamine psychosis, for one example) that function exactly like mental illness, although the primary cause (the drugs) of their illness is different. Many of these substance-induced disorders continue long after they have discontinued use of the drug, due to damage to their neurological system.

Many inmates suffering from mental illness have been abusing drugs and/or alcohol for years before they were even diagnosed with a mental health disorder. Having started from such a young age means that they never learned to deal with even normal, day-to-day anxiety without being high. Breaking the cycle of addiction for long-term drug users, while attempting to get them to address their underlying mental health issues, can be a Sisyphean task,[19] where you work like that mythic figure, pushing the inmate up the slope of addiction treatment only to have him or her fall down the slope of decompensation into mental illness, and then when you push them back up *that* slope so that their mental illness is under some control, they relapse again on drugs.

Unfortunately, certain inmates enjoy the effects of combining illicit substances with their prescribed medications, such as opiate abusers enhancing their 'high' by taking the prescription medication Klonopin. Other inmates may be too addled by drug and alcohol use to remember to take prescribed medications, while others simply prefer the drug-induced state of consciousness to that of being properly medicated. In any event, correctional officers are encouraged to not only obtain a working knowledge of the various psychotropic medications that their inmate's may be prescribed, but also to familiarize themselves with the wide array of illicit substances and prescription medications used (and abused) within the prison. Being familiar with the symptoms of drug use, either independently or in conjunction with prescription medications, will better prepare the officer to de-escalate an inmate who is going through withdrawal. Officers should also note that some inmates go through withdrawal or other drug-related crises not because they have been abusing illicit drugs, but because they have been 'cheeking,' or otherwise intentionally skipping their medications. This can cause either a re-occurrence of their illness, or withdrawal symptoms caused by stopping prescription medications.

Another important factor is that medical staff may decide to change the inmate's medications: either decreasing or increasing the dosage, or changing to different medications entirely. The inmate may have an extreme reaction to the change, which can range from radical changes in mood and thought patterns, to actual medical emergencies. Ideally, correctional staff should be made aware when medication regimen have changed so that they can assist medical staff in monitoring if the change is, in fact, beneficial for the inmate, and also enable the officers to be more than usually alert/aware of this inmate's behavior, so that no one—the individual, staff or other inmates—are hurt.

Withdrawal Is a Medical Emergency

First and foremost, alcohol and drug withdrawal are medical emergencies. There is no specific 'withdrawal rage.' Use whatever tactics necessary to de-escalate and control them, <u>based on their behavior</u>, as described in the latter sections of this book (SECTION X). The correctional officer should summon medical attention immediately, and then focus on keeping the inmate calm while waiting for medical assistance.

Inmates in withdrawal are often in pain or feeling quite ill. They are also frightened or irritable, and very much focused on one thing: getting their needs met. This may include a high level of resistance to seeking medical attention, or assurances by the inmate that they are well enough to be left alone (sometimes this is in hopes that if correctional officers ignore him or her, they'll be able to secure more drugs and get out of withdrawal). The signs of withdrawal can include:

Unstable Coordination. Try to get inmate to sit or lie down for their safety.

Restlessness and Agitation. Try to reduce any stimulating input.

Unpredictable and Sudden Actions. Keep your movements calm and slow so that you don't elicit a startle reflex on their part, which can easily turn into an attack.

Slurred or Incoherent Speech. Speak to them in a calm, quiet voice and make an extra effort to understand what they are saying. Provide short explanations.

Abnormally Rigid Muscles. It is hard to sort this out from a pre-assault indicator. Be on guard for an attack.

Being Argumentative and Demanding. Try to redirect them or de-escalate depending on the mode of anger or rage they exhibit.

Extreme Difficulty in Understanding What You Are Saying. Take your time, avoid being frustrated yourself, and repeat simple phrases in a calm tone of voice.

29.2 Calming Inmates in Withdrawal

Be calm and firm. Redirect them when they get very demanding. Reassure them that help is on the way. You are simply trying to delay things until the ambulance and/or back-up arrives. To reiterate, this is a medical emergency. A person in withdrawal—at least from some drugs—may die without help.

There is no specific withdrawal rage. They will display terrified, chaotic, hot, cold, or predatory rage (SECTION X). Use the tactics that best fit the mode of rage they are experiencing.

CHAPTER 30

Psychosis: Delusions and Hallucinations

Whatever the diagnosis (i.e., schizophrenia, bipolar disorder, trauma-induced, depression, drug induced), the syndrome of psychosis is typified by delusions and/or hallucinations. A **delusion** is first and foremost a belief that does not fit reality. A **hallucination** is an unreal perception through any of the senses.

What Is a Delusion?
A delusion is actually a lot more than a belief that does not conform to reality. People from different cultures have different beliefs. Shared cultural beliefs, however, are not delusional, even if you can't conceive how others could see the world as they do. Why? Because such cultural beliefs a) do not cause a deterioration of the person's functioning over time b) do not cause the person to be alienated from their own family or society c) Actually serve social goals, serving to bind people together.

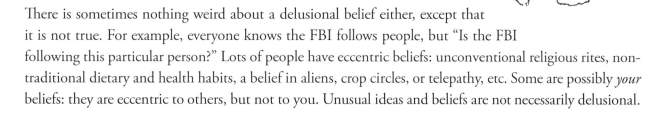

There is sometimes nothing weird about a delusional belief either, except that it is not true. For example, everyone knows the FBI follows people, but "Is the FBI following this particular person?" Lots of people have eccentric beliefs: unconventional religious rites, non-traditional dietary and health habits, a belief in aliens, crop circles, or telepathy, etc. Some are possibly *your* beliefs: they are eccentric to others, but not to you. Unusual ideas and beliefs are not necessarily delusional.

A delusion is a <u>fixed</u> belief that is not reality based. Having a delusion is like being a member of a one-person cult. All the confusing thoughts the person may have had, all their worries, prayers, fantasies, or ideas suddenly coalesce into **BELIEF**. Such beliefs are unshakable, inarguable, and unaltered by conflicting evidence. The difference between a cult and a delusion is that cult beliefs are externally imposed: even confirmed cult members can, in a single moment, realize the beliefs are false and abandon the cult. Delusions, however, are internally generated. One cannot simply stop being delusional when presented with an alternative belief system.

Types of Delusions
The following is a list of the different types of delusions:

Grandiose. A belief that they have been appointed to a special mission, that they have extraordinary or unusual powers, or are special, remarkable beings.

Religious. Often linked with grandiose delusions, an inordinate preoccupation with religion, focusing all their attention on their beliefs, which may be self-made or associated with mainstream doctrines. To reiterate a previous point, it is not the religious belief itself that makes it delusional, because religion is based on faith, not knowledge. It is the locked-in quality of the belief. In a religious delusion, one is locked into the belief by one's own mind, just as, in a cult, one is locked into an unshakeable group belief.

Jealous. A belief, against all evidence, that their partner is unfaithful to them. Jealous delusions surpass the almost always irrational nature of ordinary jealousy. The inmate with jealous delusions concocts infidelity out of the slightest glance, a change in clothing, or a five-minute delay in meeting when promised, etc. Perpetrators of domestic violence, particularly those with a paranoid (CHAPTER 21) or borderline character structure (CHAPTER 24), often manifest this type of delusional psychosis in periods of stress. Some of your inmates will display such delusions focusing on someone on the outside; others will display it towards another inmate.

Delusional Stalking (Erotomania). A belief that another person is in love with them, is married to them, or has been somehow designated as theirs, whether they know it or not. Special requirements for communicating with those who display erotomaniac stalking behaviors will be discussed below.

Persecutory (Paranoia). A fixed belief that people, institutions or other powers have hostile intentions toward them or have committed evil actions against them, that others are sending energy toward them, thinking about them, talking about them, or looking at them with malevolent intent. In addition to general strategies for managing any inmate with psychosis, there are specific strategies for communicating with a paranoid inmate (CHAPTER 21). The paranoid delusion the person fee like a 'special victim,' singled out for persecution by powers beyond them.

What Are Hallucinations?
Hallucinations are false perceptions through any of the senses. Hallucinations are often, but not always, accompanied by delusions. It is possible to perceive a hallucination, but be neither delusional nor psychotic. For example, people suffering from several days of jet-lag may complain of hearing voices. However, they are quite aware that the voices are caused by sleep-deprivation, and pay them no more heed than people do when they have a song 'stuck' in their head. However, most of your inmates who experience hallucinations will be psychotic.

Types of Hallucinations
The following is a list of the different types of hallucinations:

Auditory. There are two levels of hallucinations perceived through hearing. The first level is **_auditory distortion_** (this is, strictly speaking, an illusion rather than a pure hallucination). One mishears what is said, something that is frequently part of persecutory delusions. For example, a paranoid inmate is sitting near someone who says, "I like chicken and ribs." They hear, "I'd like to get this chicken in the ribs."

The second level is true **auditory hallucinations**. In this case, the voices are as real to them as the voice of your coworker or spouse is to you. Brain scans reveal that the neurons of a person experiencing auditory hallucinations are 'firing' just as those of a healthy person do when they actually hear something. The person actually *hears* the voices. That is why you can't simply say, "The voice isn't real:" that makes as much sense to them as someone saying to you that your foot isn't real.

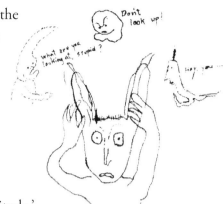

Inmates experiencing paranoid ideas often display a 'listening attitude.' They enter a situation that evokes their paranoia, and expect to be victimized, accused, talked about, and/or assaulted. They then either mishear people, based on what they expect to hear, or in more severe cases, actually hear hallucinatory voices uttering just what they expected or feared.[20]

Visual. Psychotic individuals may experience **visual distortions**. The distorted visual image appears to move, melt, emerge toward them, or even speak. Think of a Salvador Dali painting in which the objects melt and flow. The second level is true **visual hallucinations,** in which objects or beings appear that no one else can see.

Olfactory. This is sometimes a result or symptom of brain injury, as the part of the brain that detects odor(s) is at the front of the head, a frequent target of injury. If a previously non-psychotic inmate complains of hallucinatory smells, get them immediately checked medically. This is often an emergent situation that, if not addressed, can result in permanent brain damage, something particularly important with incarcerated active military and veterans. Other inmates, without head injuries and purely psychotic, can get focused on their own body smells, and believe, for example, that they are rotting away. Others believe they can smell poison gas seeping through the walls.

Tactile. These are sensations felt within the body. Formication, the sensation of bugs crawling under the skin, is a frequent side effect of such drugs as methamphetamine or cocaine. Tactile hallucinations can also be a side effect of the inmate's psychiatric medication. A medical doctor should always check this symptom, because individuals with tactile hallucinations are frequently very irritable or aggressive. Be especially on your guard when dealing with them.

The Torment of Hallucinations
Hallucinations torment their victims in a variety of ways:

For unknown reasons, hallucinated voices are almost always cruel. Inmates can be ordered to do degrading things, or they may simply hear awful sounds and demeaning words. Visual hallucinations can be as haunting as ghosts. Olfactory hallucinations are often foul, and tactile hallucinations are almost always very unpleasant sensations.

Inmates try to tell others what they perceive, but their experience is denied over and over again. They can be teased or laughed at. Ironically, the people they tell often torment them in ways similar to the torment of the hallucinations. For example, the author was acquainted with one man who suffered from persecutory delusions. His 'friends' would notice when he was hyper-vigilant while they were walking from one bar to another, and one of them would say, "I think someone is following us," causing the man to pull out a knife and go on the hunt for his stalker. They could keep him at it for hours, and they found the dangerous confrontations he got into with innocent people to be funny.[21]

Inmates suffering from psychotic disorders find that their worldview is called into question every day. They don't know what is real and what is not. Imagine reaching to pick up your coffee, and not knowing if the liquid will disappear from the cup, or if the handle will suddenly twine around your finger like a little snake. Imagine this is true of every object in your life. Imagine that every time you relax with a friend, they suddenly blindside you with a vicious attack; further imagine that they do nothing of the sort, but you are absolutely convinced that they will. In such circumstances, the you would find it very difficult to trust anything at all. In this, the inmate is not different thrown you.

CHAPTER 31

Communication with Inmates Experiencing Delusions/Hallucinations

Disengage

It can be very draining to talk with an inmate who is delusional. Like a cultist trying to convert you to their group, the inmate may try to convince you that what they believe is real. They may insist that you accept their beliefs, or even more problematic, insist that you *do* believe, but simply won't admit it. They become focused on debating your resistance, or furious that you deny what is, to them, absolutely true.

There is often no good reason to continue such a discussion. Delusions are not like some sort of backed-up fluid that you vent and drain away. The more the inmate talks about his or her delusions, the more preoccupied he or she becomes, and more agitated as well. While inmates with delusions may feel locked in their inner world and desperate to communicate what they are experiencing, discussion and argument seem to cement the delusions even further.

> ### 31.1 Rule 1: Disengage
> There are many occasions when nothing at all can be accomplished by talking about delusions or hallucinations. There is no emergency, and no need for investigation or information gathering. In such cases, disengage.

Islands of Sanity

Imagine being dropped overboard into the ocean. It is cold and rough among the waves, and there are all sorts of sea-life that demand your attention, everything from sharks to sea snakes. There seems to be no way to escape, and it is so overwhelming that you can't take your mind off of it.

Even in the ocean, however, there are islands. If you can only get to them, you can put your feet on solid ground. For inmates with psychotic disorders, too, there are 'islands of sanity,' areas of their lives where they are not delusional. They may be convinced, for example, that someone is poisoning their food, or that someone is beaming messages directly into their brain. However, when you bring up the subject of football, and the two of you begin talking about how the Pittsburgh Steelers' destroyed yet another opponent, the inmate takes his mind off his delusions, and for a brief moment, has a moment of peace.

Remember, you and other will deal with the same, profoundly psychotic inmate on a frequent basis. If you have a means of deflecting them out of their delusional rut and into discussing something where they can feel solid, they will begin to associate correctional officers as beings who stabilize them rather than stress them. This, alone, is a significant factor in risk reduction. Therefore, try to ensure that other correctional officers are aware of what the particular island of sanity is for a potentially dangerous psychotic person. Finally, sometimes officers are able to establish a relationship with an inmate where there is some non-aggressive back-and-forth, joking a bit, etc. <u>The island of sanity should be considered off-limits for any joking around.</u> If the inmate believes that he or she has to 'protect' that island of sanity from officers, it will no longer be available as a tool to help calm the inmate down in a crisis situation.

31.2 Rule 2: Move to the Island of Sanity

Other than threat assessment, it does not benefit the inmate to talk about his or her delusions or hallucinations. Rather, try to divert the inmate to areas of discussion where they are not delusional. Speak with them about these subjects, even for just a few minutes. Through doing this, the inmate feels saner at the end of the conversation than they did at the beginning. If the inmate gets stuck within his/ her delusions, you may find that changing the subject requires real finesse. Nonetheless, do so whenever you can, because talking about delusions makes it worse.

The goal is that they begin to associate correctional officers as 'agents of sanity.' For this reason, for tactical as well as common humanity, no officer should ever tease the inmate about their 'island of sanity.'

Warning: Do not 'light them UP': One person's island of sanity may be funny-sounding, eccentric, or perhaps, at variance with your own beliefs or interests. (For example, they love a football team that you hate—or they are obsessed with earthworms). No one on your team should ever tease or provoke the individual about that island of sanity. Aside from the lack of human decency that entails, you will undermine the safety of all officers. If the person now associates correctional officers with people who make fun of something they believe to be special, you will no longer have something stable or sane to shift their thoughts towards when they become agitated or delusional.

These islands of sanity are not necessarily 'nice' subjects. The author worked with a very dangerous man for nine months and the only subjects that he wasn't floridly psychotic were bar fights and motorcycles. It was safer talking about the sound of a cue ball impacting on someone's skull than what he had for dinner or what his childhood was like.

Threat Assessment: When *Should* You Talk About Delusions Or Hallucinations?

With some of the more dangerous inmates, it is necessary to do a brief threat assessment every time you see them. Imagine a delusional inmate who is sure that he is the Archangel Michael. If you recall this biblical story, Michael, the righteous sword of the Lord, casts Satan out of Heaven. Furthermore, imagine that this man believes he perceives Satan's work in the behavior of other inmates. Based on his past history, you must intervene when he gets preoccupied with his delusions, because some time ago, seeing evidence of Satan's corruption within his cellmate, he tried to cut out his heart with a shank. The cellmate managed to fight him off, long enough for correctional officers to arrive and stop the assault.

Therefore, whenever this inmate begins to talk about God, angels, Satan, or anything similar, it is a good idea to ask questions about that which he is preoccupied. Some questions you could ask him follow:
- "Inmate Hampton, are you telling me that you have seen Satan?"
- "Where?"
- "How do you know that this is Satan's work?"
- "Do you think you should do anything about this?"
- "What do you think you should do?"

If the inmate's answers are bland and not aggressive, change the subject to an 'island of sanity.' If, however, he was to say, "Don't call me Demon-spawn Hampton! I'm Michael, the Lord's most beloved angel. Satan will have no place on this earth when I take my righteous blade in my strong right arm!" You need to act immediately to protect everyone. Dangerous answers require the correctional officer to alert other officers, and conduct a search of his cell/dorm area for weapons, or perhaps ensure he gets a psychiatric evaluation. He may have to have his medications adjusted, or need to stay in a crisis care unit or treatment facility for an extended period of time. Whatever the appropriate response, you must intervene when such an inmate is acting or thinking dangerously. And consider this, the mightiest angel in Heaven is likely to object when you try to take him into secure custody. Be very alert to danger! (And once you have him under control and are waiting for medical to arrive, once again, shift and talk about an island of sanity if you can).

31.3 Rule 3: Talk About the Delusions to Assess Risk

Talk about the delusions as a means of threat assessment. Ask direct questions, particularly in regard to the person's intention to hurt him/ herself or others. When contacting such an individual bring up the issue of concern yourself, if they don't do so on their own, just to see if they have become seriously delusional again. For example, "The last time we talked, you told me about the Angel Michael and Satan. Are you worried about the Devil today?" Remember, the distinction between this rule and the previous two is that in this case, you are assessing risk, not just indulging in a conversation about inmate's preoccupations.

Don't Agree: At Least Most of the Time

It might seem to be easiest to take the line of least resistance: simply agree with the delusions, or pretend that you, too, perceive the hallucinations rather than get caught in arguments with an inmate suffering from mental illness about reality. However, there are a number of problems in doing so:

- Agreement with delusions and/or hallucinations will entrench them even more deeply into the inmate's belief system.
- Agreement can also lead to the correctional officer being *incorporated* into the delusions and hallucinations. Sometimes this can be merely wearying, as the inmate wants to talk incessantly about their delusions with the only person who seems to share their point of view.
- This can also become dangerous if the inmate decides that you are in collusion with their perceived enemies, or they may perceive you as either scamming them or making fun of them. In almost all circumstances, don't agree with the delusions.

31.4 Rule 4: Don't Agree With the Delusions

In almost all circumstances, don't agree with the delusions. At most, if you have a consensus that it is worth the risk, passively accept their perception in the interest of their complying with something that will keep everyone safer.

31.5 Example: An Exception to the Rule of Agreeing with Delusions—Tacit Acceptance

Sometimes the inmate will incorporate their correctional officer into their delusions in a positive way. For example, an inmate believes he has a secret team of advisors who tell him what to do. Recently, he announced that one correctional officer was on the team, and he had therefore decided to listen to what she said and follow her advice. Don't try to 'prime the pump' by claiming a positive role in their delusions, or simply accept it if the inmate so 'appoints' you. Rather, consider this development from all sides. It may be worth consulting with the treatment team or a mental health professional. You have to assess if there is any risk that the delusion might 'mutate' in a dangerous way. If, in your considered judgment it does make tactical sense, at *most* that you tacitly accept this information. In the example above, you might reply, "Well, all I know is that if the doctors think you should take your medications, then I think that's a very good idea."

In another example, let's say an inmate is convinced that demons will try to enter his cell to harm him. If you find out that he is, in his own way, a Christian, there is nothing wrong with suggesting, "if you are concerned about that, it's okay to put a crucifix on your wall."

However, don't assume that a delusional person is suggestible, and anything you tell them will work. This author recently spoke to some police officers who had detained a psychotic naked woman who was convinced that bugs were crawling in her clothes. After some struggle, they got her under control and then with the help of EMS, strapped onto a gurney. She was still naked, however, and began screaming and fighting when an EMT tried to put a blanket over her. Trying to be slick, he said, "Don't worry, it's a Jesus blanket." The woman stopped screaming, looked him dead in the eye and said, "What the fuck are you talking about, that's the stupidest thing I ever heard," and then began screaming again to get the blanket off her.

Don't Disagree: At Least Most of the Time

The problem with arguing with delusional or hallucinating people is that you are telling them that their perceptions are lying to them. If they had any trust in you before, it is unlikely that telling them that the world as they see it is not real will improve that rapport.

Sometimes, however, a delusional inmate may ask, or even plead with you for disagreement because they don't want to believe what their delusions seem to tell them. At other times, a hallucinating inmate can make a tenuous distinction between real perceptions and hallucinations and will ask if you think something hallucinated is real. In these cases, *when you have been invited*, you may state that not only do you not perceive or believe the hallucination or delusion, but you also don't think it is real.

31.6 Rule 5: Don't Disagree—At Least Most of the Time

Don't engage in arguments about whether the psychotic inmate's perceptions are real. However, if they <u>ask</u> you for a 'reality check,' then you can state that you don't believe that the delusional belief is correct or the hallucination is real. In this case, you are helping the inmate understand that what he or she perceives is not the 'rule' of the world.

Important Exception to the "Do not Disagree" Rule: Delusional Stalking

Stalking delusions (clinically referred to as 'erotomania') are dangerous because they involve another person as the victim.[22] The inmate is often possessed of an absolutely entitled sense of their right to approach or harass the victim. Such advances may be criminal in nature, and the inmate must be confronted about their behavior immediately. It is very likely that the psychotic stalker in a prison is incarcerated *for* stalking or felony harassment. Correctional officers have an important responsibility to make sure that nothing they say could possibly be construed as support for the inmate's delusions. This would put the victim at greater risk.

If the inmate has succeeded in contacting a celebrity or other public figure, or verbally fantasizes about this, correctional officers must flatly, but directly, inform the inmate that the subject of their delusions is not destined for, in love with, or otherwise involved with them. Calmly and directly tell the inmate they have no right to the victim they stalk.

For inmates convicted of stalking, harassment, domestic violence, sexual assault, or similar offenses, their supervision plan will likely include a 'no victim contact' stipulation, giving the correctional officer a solid legal basis for any necessary violation proceedings, including temporary segregation and/or crisis care placement of the inmate. Other times, criminal charges can be filed. Public, institutional, staff and inmate safety, including that of the victim, is the correctional officer's paramount concern.

Particularly if the object of the inmate's delusion or obsession is another inmate or prison staff, and if the inmate threatens or hints at committing an act of violence against the subject of their delusions, correctional officers should conduct a search of their cell or dorm to locate weapons or other contraband. In addition, the correctional officer should contact the other members of the treatment team to alert them of the inmate's delusional thoughts and behaviors. In the event that the correctional officer becomes the subject of an inmate's delusions, suitable safety precautions must be taken, including, in many cases, moving the inmate to another unit: such delusional ideation or other types of stalking must be regarded as a high-risk factor in assault on correctional officers.

> **31.7 Rule 6: Exception—Disagree with the Delusion of Erotomania**
> Calmly and directly tell the delusional inmate they have no right to the victim they stalk. Define to them that what they are doing is stalking. Do whatever you can to ensure the safety of the victim, whether they are a correctional officer, another staff person, an inmate, or someone outside the prison.

Differentiation: Distinguish Between Your World and Theirs
Delusional beliefs are nearly inescapable. When an inmate experiencing psychotic symptoms attempts to talk about their delusions, they are often brushed off, minimized, or even ridiculed. If you should neither agree nor disagree with their delusions, how can you respond in an effective way to the inmate's delusional thinking, while also trying to get them to recognize the distinction between your world and theirs?

<u>Differentiate yourself from them</u>. To differentiate is to perceive or express a difference. While also informing them that you don't share their perceptions or beliefs, you are not arguing about them. You are, however, attempting to help the inmate grasp that other viewpoints do exist. Here are some examples:
- Alice, I see the bunk and the bars, your picture on the wall, and the books on the floor, just like you do. But I don't see a basket of puppies in the corner of the room. No, I'm not saying you don't see it. I believe you do. I'm just saying that it is something you see that I don't. I don't know why, but that's the way it is.
- Sal, I only hear two voices in this room, yours and mine. I don't hear a woman's voice at all. What do you hear her say?
- Jamey, I know about the Democrats and the Republicans. I've never heard of the Illuminated Ones. I'm not arguing with you. I'm just saying that I've never heard of them, so I'm not the person to talk about them.

Remember, the point here is not to convince the inmate that their delusions are not real, or even that they are wrong. Differentiation simply helps you keep the lines of communication open. Think of two people from different cultures, trying to explain what it is like to live in their respective worlds, or even two beings from different planets. If the inmate finds himself or herself shut-down or discounted when s/he tries to talk about perceptions or beliefs, it is very unlikely that he or she will be open about any other area of concern to the correctional officer, like if he is planning an assault because of what the voices are telling him. In some circumstances, you can act in concert with their belief without endorsing it. For example, "I can't see the laser beams, but I know lasers don't pass through solid objects. Maybe you will feel safer in that room (crisis unit, for example) instead of sitting out here in the yard."[23]

31.8 Rule 7: Differentiate

Give the inmate the 'right' to their own perceptions and beliefs. Inform them that while you don't perceive what they do, you are not arguing with them about what *they* see or believe. In some cases, take their delusions into account without agreeing with them. Example: "I don't see any razor blades on the bars in inmate Jackson's cell, but if I did, I wouldn't walk over there. I'd stay in my own cell area, over here." Please note that, in this case, and others like it, this may be a symbolic attempt to inform you of some real danger (for example, Jackson is so scary, it is as if he has razor blades all around him), so view such communications from several perspectives. He may have been trying to warn you of danger and you didn't get the message.

Steam Valve: Take the Time to Save Some Time

Some inmates, either psychotic or manic (CHAPTER 32) are so full of things to say, think or feel that they seem like they are going to explode from the pressure. Their speech can become pressured as well. Words burst out of them like a waterfall. Sometimes they make sense, but they totally dominate the 'air time' in the room, talking over other people. Even if there is a task to be done, they can't focus and they make it nearly impossible for you to focus as well. Other times, they make no sense whatsoever. Their words may sound like poetry as they link words by sound, not by meaning. They may jump from idea to idea, in what are called 'loose associations,' or 'tangential thinking.'

You can't allow the inmate to dominate the air, even if they are ill. The correctional officer must regain control of the interview. Sometimes the officer simply has to say, "You have talked enough for a while. We need to move on to ____." For some inmates this works quite well; it is honest, it is direct, and it sets a limit.

At other times, particularly when the inmate is more pressured or intense, one needs to let out a little pressure like opening a valve in a steam pipe. Then you take over saying one portion of what you have to say:
- Let them speak for a little while about their preoccupations. In the process, they let out a little pressure, like a steam valve.
- Put out a hand, palm down, fingers curved at waist level to interrupt them. If they do not perceive it, put up both hands, using a little drama in your facial expression, to get their attention and interrupt.
- Sum up what they said in a sentence or two. Put a little energy in your voice to prove that you are really 'with' them. Then, ask or say something, getting either some compliance or a bit of information. "That is serious. Politics right now are terrible! You HAVE to tell me more about the left-wing conspiracy, but before you do, did you take your pill last night?"
- In return, let them return to their cascade of ideas, allowing a little more pressure to be released.

- Once again, firmly interrupt, sum up in a phase what they are saying now, and ask the next question or get agreement on the next item on your list.

In essence, you sum up what they said to prove you were listening, and *then* ask your question or make your statement. 'Steam-valving' is for the purpose of letting the inmate say enough of what is pressuring him or her internally so that he or she does not fight you for the conversational floor.

31.9 Example of the Steam-valve Technique

Inmate. "I was looking outside my window at the thistles, and they were covered with gold finches. The lemony yellow just burned my eyes so badly I closed my eyes. My eyes were burned by the fiery birds."

CORRECTIONAL OFFICER. *(Interrupting firmly)* "Charley, I want to hear more about those birds. I haven't seen any goldfinches this year. But first, have you been taking your meds."

Inmate. "Yes, I did, behind my closed eyes, where the birds couldn't burn my eyes out. I talked to a very nice nurse about my meds last week. They have a sound that is piercing to the brain, and a single glance can burn your eyes to a crisp—the birds, not the nurses."

CORRECTIONAL OFFICER. "I can see you are worried about your eyes. That's why you have your hands on your face, huh? I want you to tell me how your eyes feel, but first, when do you see the nurse again?"

Inmate. "It's on a Thursday, but I don't know when, or what time. I'm burning among the birds, you see, with their lemony scalding flame."

As you can see, the correctional officer was able to get the information that the inmate actually did talk to the nurse, but it's obvious he's getting worse, and his next appointment is not until Thursday, three days away. At this point the officer would contact medical staff so that the inmate can be assessed more immediately

31.10 Rule 8: Steam-valve

This is useful with inmates whose speech is a cascade of words and ideas that are either all over the place (zigzag) or delusional. Listen and then interrupt. Sum up what they said, and tell them you want to hear more, but before they do, you have a question (or instruction) for them. Then let them return to their cascade of words. Listen a bit more, and then interrupt again. Sum up what they just said. Continue with multiple sequences of release of pressure, interruptions, and questions until you get the information you need.

Physical Space, Physical Contact, and the Use of the Eyes With Psychotic Inmates

Concerns about eye contact and physical contact are incredibly important in regard to inmates with psychosis. Even more than in ordinary circumstances, be aware when you are inadvertently 'pressuring' the inmate by standing or sitting too close to them, looming over them. Consider this *your* responsibility. Don't expect them to necessarily tell you. The first sign that you are too close, if you are not paying attention, may be an attack because the inmate believes they must protect themselves from your 'invasion.'

Other inmates suffering from psychosis are not aware of personal space and stand or sit too close to you. Firmly, without aggression or heat, tell them to move back. "Inmate McDougal, I really want to hear what you are saying. But you are standing too close to me. Take four big steps back and tell me more." After all, officer safety is the primary goal here, whether the interview is conducted in the office, inmate prison mainline or housing area. In the office setting, correctional officers can control spacing issues more easily with proper furniture placement and other physical site safety procedures. While conducting interviews in the prison mainline or housing area, correctional officers have to remain alert to their surroundings in this regard. Do not allow yourself to be maneuvered into an enclosed area or otherwise cut off from an escape route.

For many inmates with psychosis, direct, sustained eye contact seems to pierce them to the brain. It's as if you can read their thoughts. Other such inmates can misinterpret direct eye contact as aggressive, threatening, or seductive. Therefore, if they are uncomfortable with being looked at directly (you will know it), occasionally 'touch base' by making brief eye contact, and then shift off to the side of their face, where you can still see their hands, feet, and facial expression.

Ease your eyes away and back again, smoothly. **Of course, never take your eyes away from the inmate so that you are unaware of any precursors to assault. Furthermore, in the event of aggressive behavior, you MUST make direct eye contact, whether they are psychotic or not.**

31.11 Rule 9: Body Spacing, Body Contact, and Eye Contact

Be aware of physical spacing—don't stand too close, and don't accept the inmate standing too close to you. Most inmates with psychotic symptoms are made anxious by direct eye contact, experiencing it as either a threat or a challenge. Limit direct eye contact unless the situation is emergent. If it is, then you will hold direct eye contact, no matter what their diagnosis, because you must establish control through command presence.

CHAPTER 32

Welcome to the Rollercoaster: Tactics for Dealing with Symptoms of Mania

Mania is a state of high energy. Inmates in manic states need little sleep, and can be excited, grandiose, agitated, or irritable. They often have flights of ideas, which can be either creative or completely irrational. Their speech is often pressured. Not only is it rapid, but there is a sense that there is more to say than they can get out.

They are usually extremely confident, even to the degree of believing themselves to be invulnerable. Inmates experiencing mania feel wonderful, and their own needs and desires are the only things that matter. Their judgment can be extremely poor and impulsive, and they engage in behaviors that can put them or others at risk.

The manic state is associated most commonly with bipolar disorder (manic-depression), in which periods of mania are one-half of a cycle in which the other is periods of depression. Some drugs can also cause manic episodes (particularly stimulant drugs such as amphetamine, cocaine or 'bath salts'), and not infrequently, mania can also be a side effect of psychiatric medications.

> ### 32.1 Extreme Manic State Becomes Delirium
> Inmates with different brain malfunctions can have periods of agitation that may look very much like mania, but this kind of delirium is usually more extreme than the classic manic state. Such inmates are usually quite confused and disorganized. On the other hand, some inmates in manic states can get so agitated, called 'manic excitement,' that they shift into a delirium state. All such individuals are de-escalated and controlled using the strategies for Chaotic Rage (CHAPTER 49).

Such inmates are particularly vulnerable because they are most susceptible to making harmful decisions when they feel wonderful. Imagine the best spring day of your life. You wake up and literally jump out of bed, and you have so much energy that it feels like there is champagne in your veins. You know you will make some new friends today, so you are going to go to the park, the club, the bar, whatever, and just hook up! You've got a new idea, a chain-saw on an extendable baton—think how that will make tree trimming easier! Imagine that feeling day-after-day, multiplied by ten or twentyfold. Can you see how easy it would be to make unwise choices, how your confidence could lead you, for example, to hijack that freight train because you always wanted to be an engineer?[24]

When you feel this good, it seems like a good idea to feel *even better*. Thus, inmates experiencing mania very often want to party. Drugs and alcohol are always available, and in a corrections setting, they can easily get into debt to one or another prison gang and then into terrible trouble. Their energy can turn sexual, and the person gets involved with people who may be inappropriate for them or even dangerous, or if they are also aggressive, turn to sexual assault. On the flip side, some inmates in manic states—stimulant drug users or not—sometimes try to calm themselves with other drugs: barbiturates, heroin, and alcohol. Alcohol can have a 'paradoxical effect' on some manic individuals, further exciting rather than sedating them.[25]

Such inmates often talk in rapid cascades of words, a waterfall of ideas leaping from one area to another. Sometimes you can follow their thoughts, although they are speaking very rapidly, but at other times, they leap and zigzag, making connections that have little or no meaning to you. In extreme manic states, inmates can become psychotic, displaying, in addition to their mania, some or all of the symptoms of grandiose, persecutory, paranoid, and religious delusions that any other psychotic inmate might.

Some inmates in manic states become very irritable. They can have hair-trigger tempers, and may also be provocative. Rather than merely being reactive, some will aggressively tease and taunt other people. It may seem to be in good fun, at first, but it goes too far—way too far. Others may simply try to pick a fight, or explode into rage and violence.

Brittle Grandiosity

Inmates experiencing mania can act as if they don't have a care in the world. They spin ideas, one after another, and expect both agreement and admiration. They seem utterly self-confident. However, truly self-confident individuals are resilient; unfair criticisms seem to bounce off them. Think of manic grandiosity, however, as a fragile structure, like a tower made of spun sugar. It glitters, it glows, and it is huge! But tap the wrong strut or beam and the entire tower falls down in shards. It is **brittle**!

- If you bluntly criticize inmates who are manic, they can experience your criticism as a personal attack, and from giddy happiness, they suddenly turn on you in rage.
- If you tease them about their somewhat irrational ideas, try to joke around with them, or laugh at something funny that they said, they easily misinterpret these, too, as an attack, thinking you are making fun of them.

WARNING! Boisterousness Is Not Happy

One of the warning signs of impending assault, particularly with individuals in manic states, is a loud happiness—boisterousness, where the inmate is the only one who thinks things are funny. They make their own fun, and violence can easily be part of it, because in the boisterous manic state, you are just something to mess with. Such people make life like an "Itchy and Scratchy" cartoon (see the Simpsons TV show). No one gets 'really' hurt in a cartoon—or at least, that's the way they see it at the time.

Watch Out! Mania Can Be Infectious

Although manic inmates can present themselves as brilliant conversationalists, witty, sexy, provocative, entertaining, correctional officers must be wary of being seduced by their overt friendliness or entertaining demeanor. Don't allow an inmate's apparent personality (He's such a nice guy, a lot of fun!) to cloud your professional judgment and responsibilities.

If you accept, or laugh along with the inmate's actions without contradiction and appropriate limit setting, they will assume that their actions and behaviors, no matter how non-compliant, are acceptable. However, when you subsequently violate them for those behaviors, they will turn on you suddenly in betrayed anger.

Inmates in manic states can be very manipulative, while appearing to be friendly and engaging; they are only doing so in an effort to control the relationship. Remember, the inmate may be very provocative trying to set you up for an over-reaction or making you look like a fool. Think of Bugs Bunny and Elmer Fudd, or the Road Runner and the Coyote. You know which role the inmate puts you in.

As stated earlier, they often sexualize interactions; therefore, you must be very cautious that they don't perceive sexual interest on your part based on you letting pass some innuendo or mild flirtatious comment. This applies to same-sex interactions as well as cross-sex.

There is an old expression: "He's a drag," referring to someone who slows the party down. That is not a bad idea with the person in a manic state. As a correctional officer it is not part of your job description to be liked by those inmates you supervise. Remember: Firm, but fair. Therefore:
- Stay centered.
- Don't get swept away or swept up in their energy.
- Focus on slowing things down. Speak slowly, and take things step-by-step.

32.2 Author's Experience: Be Careful—All is Not What It Seems!

WARNING: They may be acting like comedians, but they are not trying to be funny!

This writer recalls a little guy who had lined up over five thousand 'matchbox' cars on every projecting surface of the inside of his house. None were glued, but they were perfectly balanced, even on the molding on the walls! Because he had overdosed, we took him to the hospital. He was given charcoal, and as he sat on a gurney, belching black fluid down his chin into a pan, he was talking non-stop, chirping like a little bird, asking, "Why, if this medicine is so bad, you gave it to a man like me? Why didn't you give me Skittles instead?" And then he yelled, "Chase the rainbow!" as an arc of black vomit spurted out of his mouth. It was both a reasonable question and under the particular circumstances, funny. One of the nurses began to laugh, and he frisbeed the metal basin he was holding right at her head, arches of black vomit spraying all of us, and while we were all ducking, he grabbed her by the throat, screaming, "This isn't funny. Nothing's funny!"

The Medication Struggle: It Is NOT Like Diabetes

As stated earlier, mania is a unique state in which one feels wonderful, healthy, confident, and effective, when one is actually not doing well at all. If the mania is due to abuse of drugs, inmates must stop using if they are to heal. If their mania is a side effect of their medication, then they must see a doctor.

When the problem is a symptom of the inmate's bipolar disorder, medication can usually control the symptoms. However, some inmates with bipolar disorder believe, in some ways correctly, that they will feel worse when they take the medications. Yes, perhaps they will be calm, more organized, sleep better, and not get into trouble. They may avoid crushing periods of depression as well. But life will lose a wonderful glow, and the hours of each day will be more like lead than gold. Unlike almost any other condition, many people with bipolar disorder feel best when they are most ill.

When encouraging an inmate with bipolar disorder to take medications, many people say, "It's a condition like diabetes. You need to take it every day. It's not like medicine for a sore throat that you take until you are cured, and then never have to take again." This is true, but there is a vast difference between diabetes and bipolar disorder. If a diabetic does not take their insulin, they quickly become seriously ill and they feel awful too. <u>On the other hand, the manic person feels far better when they don't take their medications</u>. The only way they will accept medication is if their medicated life is tangibly better to them than the un-medicated carnival of the manic state. Otherwise, it is highly unlikely that the inmate will be compliant with their medication. How this can occur for the inmate in a prison environment is a difficult question indeed.

32.3 Review: Responding To an Inmate in a Manic State

You will recognize the inmate in a manic state because they will display super high energy. They will often be talking very fast and their ideas will 'zigzag' from one to another. They often act like comedians, with a rapid-fire delivery. Their behavior may also be either sexualized or hair-trigger aggressive. In either case, they will very likely be provocative.

- Remain calm and centered.
- Be conscious of their 'brittle' state of mind, in spite of how confidently they behave. Grandiose does not mean healthy or psychologically stable!
- Don't bluntly criticize their actions.
- Don't tease or joke around. If you use any humor, it is for the purpose of slowing them down, not having fun.
- Don't join in what sounds like fun. It is not.
- Over boisterous happiness is actually a precursor to assault or loss of control.
- They may try to provoke you (think of the Road Runner and Coyote, or Bugs Bunny and Elmer Fudd).
- They can be very volatile, exploding into rage with the slightest provocation. Be relaxed but ready for the worst.
- If the inmate is also psychotic, addressing the psychosis (delusions and hallucinations) will probably need to take precedence. In these situations, you basically have a hallucinating or delusional person who also happens to be moving and talking very fast.
- Try to enforce compliance with their doctor's orders, particularly concerning medication.
- Use the 'steam-valve' technique (CHAPTER 31) to get information when the inmate is talking rapidly, zig-zagging from one idea to another, or otherwise so full of energy it is hard to get information from him or her, or effectively direct him or her into desired actions.

CHAPTER 33

Communication with Inmates with Dementia (The Elderly)

The fastest growing population of incarcerated felons is that of the aged.

State prison inmates 55 years of age and older grew from approximately 2.9% of the state prison population in 1979 to near 5% in 2007. In federal prisons, the inmate population 56 years and older grew from 5.1% in 1990 to more than 7% in 2009.[26] This trend has continued in the last decade.

With maximum sentencing guidelines, we are seeing more and more aging inmates, some lapsing into ill health and dementia. They are victimized by younger inmates, require special care, and are a tremendous drain on public resources. One can question if any purpose (rehabilitation, punishment, or public safety) is served by maintaining them in prison, but such questions do not help the situation. They are there and must be managed along with any other inmate.

Effectively dealing with elderly inmates, particularly if they are also mentally disabled, is one of the most challenging situations an officer might face. Officers will almost always outweigh and outmuscle them, but even if the elderly inmate has retained substantial strength (tendon strength, hence grip, is the last to go), they may still be physically fragile.

So, what do you do with an elderly aggressive inmate? If you apply a come-along hold, for example, they easily can get a broken wrist or arm. (This author accidentally did this to a slender wristed woman in a martial arts practice while applying a level of force barely enough, he thought, to get her attention. The result was a broken bone!). If you find it necessary to tackle the elderly inmate or man-handle him or her to the ground, they may end up with a broken pelvis or thigh—injuries like this have killed elderly individuals.

Are there any verbal interventions that might possibly keep the situation under control at a lower level of force with an elderly, demented inmate? Remember, older adults are not a monolithic category. They are people—just like us—simply older. Every character type, every mode of aggression, every mental syndrome, and every de-escalation strategy applies to the elderly as well as those of other age groups. Despite their age, elderly people do assault others. Their rage can emerge from dementia, medical conditions, pain, adverse drug reactions, mental illness, pure meanness or hate, or any number of stressors.

33.1 Concerning Physical Force and the Elderly Inmate

If physical force is required to safely bring an elderly inmate under control, then it is required. However, because of the particular vulnerabilities of elderly people, your defensive tactics instructors should consult with medical specialists, particularly paramedics and emergency medical technicians, regarding the type of physical guidance and restraint that offers the least risk of injury. This should be integrated into your training scenarios.

The elderly inmate, rather than being demented or mentally ill, may be suffering from a complication from drug interactions, or, due to age and confusion, taking the prescribed medications improperly. Medical emergencies due to such medication problems are quite common.

33.2 Human and Tactical Concerns With Elderly, Aggressive Inmates

- Be aware that elderly inmates may be resistant to help or non-compliant with directives:
- When it is not an immediately emergent situation, take a little bit more time. Attempt to 'nibble around the edges,' talking about life, about family. Sometimes the volatile rage that elderly people display comes from a deep depression; they are isolated, confused, and no one seems to care if they live or die. This may be true. Many elderly inmates have lost everyone in their lives, due to a lifelong history of criminality.
- Be prepared to get enormously frustrated at their leaden stubbornness, that "they simply won't do what is good for them." This stubbornness may be fear. Remember that the biggest *change* in their immediate future is death. Any situation suggesting change evokes thoughts of the biggest change—death. **You may think they are defiant; they may simply be scared out of their wits.**
- Don't talk around or about the elderly inmate as if they are not present.
- Don't barrage them with choices, decisions, or too much information.
- Paranoia, (CHAPTER 21) whatever the cause, is one of the frequent triggers of rage in elderly people. As the person becomes suspicious, you can often change the subject, so that the object of their suspicion recedes from their awareness.
- The rage and violence that emerges with elderly people is frequently chaotic. Please refer to CHAPTER 27 on details regarding communication with disorganized people and CHAPTER 49 on de-escalation of people in chaotic states.
- Be aware that the inmate's behavior may very possibly be brought on by improper use of their prescribed medications.

SECTION VII

Suicide

CHAPTER 34

Suicide in Prison

Few correctional officers are certified therapists. Nevertheless, correctional officers should be able to recognize the signs of distress and frustration that often lead to suicide attempts, and should also know what to say or do while trying to get them assistance. The truth is, the correctional officer is not only the 'first responder' in cases of suicidal inmates—they are often the inmate's ongoing, day-to-day contact with the world of the living. Officers are also the 'first noticers' of many suicidal inmates. Sometimes it is just a variation of the inmate's routine or a quiet withdrawal from activities. Only the officers who deal with inmates on a daily basis have the reference points necessary to detect when an inmate may be deteriorating.

The suicidal inmate is not the only individual for whom you should be concerned. Suicide is an act of aggression. The difference between suicide and homicide is often no more than what direction the weapon is pointing. The ability of the correctional officer to recognize and address signs of aggression and suicidal thoughts, which so often go together, is essential to your safety.

Why Would You Suspect That an Inmate Is Suicidal?

Suicide is a problem-solving answer to the seemingly unending pain, trauma, and frustrations of life. However, problem-solving activity that it may be, suicide is also an act of violence that, if successful, results in the death of a human being. Suicide is often expression of anger and always of desperation, and the suicidal inmate often uses a weapon to kill himself/herself. Given these facts, officers should use extreme caution when interacting with a suicidal inmate. Following any verbalizations of suicidal thoughts, especially if the inmate specifically states that they would use a weapon to commit the act, correctional officers should immediately conduct a search of the inmate's cell or living area, once they are safe and secure. You search just as diligently as you would in any case, but with the specific intent of finding a weapon, drugs, poisons, other means of suicide or a letter stating the inmate's intent. Of course, before that search, the inmate must be taken to a safe cell, searched for weapons or pills and given tear resistant clothing. The inmate should then be immediately placed in a higher custody crisis care unit for direct observation by staff pending a threat assessment and mental health evaluation.

Tell the inmate that you are searching them and moving them to a secure cell in order to help them.

34.1 Search the Cell With the Intent of Helping the Inmate
Rather than 'tossing' the cell, keep things ordered. If you trash an inmate's possessions, he or she will not reveal their intentions to staff the next time they are suicidal—and by the way, if they are suicidal, will they be less so if their possessions are messed up, stepped on, or even damaged?

Warning Signs
Many books and training manuals on suicide present lists enumerating the suicide rates among various ethnic groups, age, educational and economic status, traumatic life events, and so forth. Although such general information can suggest some viable warning signs, you need to notice what is significant about the *individual* inmate at hand, not merely to which category he or she conforms. Examples include:

- Inmates who are under the influence of alcohol or drugs are at a higher risk for attempting suicide as they don't have the clarity of thought needed to reason themselves out of it.
- Significant negative changes in the inmate's life, such as divorce, break up of a relationship outside or *within* the prison, the death of a loved one or significant other, or an anniversary of such losses. Then, there are problems within the prison that can include difficulty due to a debt owed, pressure from a gang, sexual assault or other threats to life, limb or integrity, as well as disappointments such as losing visiting privileges, or placement in segregation. Of course, another major stressor is the possibility of a longer term, especially after a recent sentencing.
- Loss of self-image can be profound. We humans are 'social animals,' and any event that radically effects one's social status within inmate hierarchy can be devastating.
- Social isolation, either from ostracism (being cut off from a group of friends or associates) or isolation (confinement that limits human contact).
- Other warning signs may include a radical change in appearance, weight loss, loss of appetite, removing themselves from a work detail, hostility towards peers, workmates, or services staff, alienation from family, social isolation, the giving away of prized possessions, writings or drawings with morbid or despairing themes, a depressed demeanor, and allusions to a lack of a future or to the 'pointlessness of it all,' or paradoxically, reassuring statements when you know nothing has changed for the better, such as: "You don't have to worry about me anymore. I'll be taking care of things. It's not an issue, anymore," etc.
- Sometimes, without knowing why, an officer has a sense of foreboding, or at other times, they think something 'ridiculous,' like, "I don't think that guy will live out his sentence," or "I wonder if this is the last time I will see this inmate." Such thoughts are often an intuitive sense that something is very wrong.

34.2 CAUTION: It's not Just About Inmates—It's About the People with Whom You Serve

Nearly every warning sign regarding suicide with inmates is directly applicable to the officers with whom you work. Correctional Officers are twice as likely to kill themselves as they are to be killed in the line of duty. *The main rule for corrections officers is that everyone goes home at night, and this should include the caveat that our fellow officers are safe after they've left work as well.*

Keep your eyes and ears open for warning signs of psychological pain in your fellow officers, particularly anything that would lead you to believe that they might be thinking of suicide, and be ready to offer a hand. This requires a particular kind of courage—to step up and ask the hard questions to someone, perhaps a friend, who may act as if they do not appreciate your concern. They may resent it intensely, but if they are genuinely suicidal, they are no longer the best judge of what is in their own interests, much less that of their loved ones, who would have to suffer the terrible consequences after they killed themselves. Therefore, pay close attention to the subsequent chapters in this section. Given the terrible stresses that this job can impose, officer safety *must* include the willingness to help protect brother and sister officers from violence to themselves.

NOTE: Some officers have voiced the concern that they will offend a fellow officer if they ask questions about suicide, when that officer is not suicidal. The answer to this concern is: If you are wrong, it is recoverable. You are checking up out of genuine human concern, not only for the officer in question, but also for the rest of your team. Someone who no longer cares if they live or die, is very likely to stop paying attention to danger around them. Just like you would notice if a fellow officer was about to walk into a situation without proper body armor, it is a professional act to check with an officer if they appear to be walking into danger without proper 'emotional armor.'

CHAPTER 35

The Basics of Intervention with an Inmate Who May Be Suicidal

As a correctional officer, you are not qualified nor expected to make a diagnosis of any inmate who has indicated or appears to indicate suicidal ideation. You are expected, however, to immediately seek the intervention of a qualified clinician. In the meantime, the correctional officer should, after notifying staff and supervisor, either place the inmate on a constant and direct observation suicide watch or maintain the inmate in the clinic or infirmary pending clinical evaluation. Do not leave the inmate alone! The correctional officer should also document the occurrence, providing as much detail of his or her observations, intervention efforts and referral to further clinical evaluation.

The officers' documentation will show a continuum of treatment and response to crisis of the particular inmate. It is also important for future case management and/or any agencies with oversight responsibilities such as a case manager.

When attempting to speak with an inmate whom you expect or know is suicidal, you must ask yourself if you are the proper person to ask this inmate any questions at all. Don't believe that because you are 'good with the inmates,' that this particular man or woman will open up to you. Does this particular inmate respect you? Have you acted in ways in the past that would lead them to feel otherwise? Perhaps another officer would do a better job speaking with this individual. We also recommend you document your concerns, complete with the reasons why you believe another officer should speak with the inmate. Don't get your feelings hurt, just get the inmate to the person they might talk with and do not leave them alone if you are convinced the inmate is suicidal.

If time and circumstance require that you are the person to speak with them, at least initially, See the list below for helpful information on what to do when speaking with a possibly suicidal inmate. Some of these strategies may seem contradictory, read one after the next. They are not a checklist—they are a list of possible strategies, one or another which may best suit communication with a specific individual. As you read them, you will probably be able to imagine or recall the type of person you should approach in that specific way).

Location. You need to assure the inmate some privacy, but you don't want a place that is so private that you and the inmate are isolated.

Demeanor. Too much direct eye-contact, or close physical proximity, may shut them down. Speak easily but not overly confidently. If you present yourself as too 'together,' they may experience this as an implicit judgment on them, their misery contrasting so dramatically with your confident demeanor. Sit or stand at an angle (the 'blade' stance – yes, the best tactical stance is also the best way to communicate – see CHAPTER 42), with only occasional direct eye contact with the inmate. Your occasional eye contact will then have significance, rather than being experienced as a constant, intrusive examination. Don't forget your tactical training. Position yourself so that you have an exit strategy, and do not look *away* from the inmate.

Meander. With a wary inmate you may wish to 'wander around,' talking about this and that. As long as they are talking, they are not killing themselves. This gives you time and also helps to build trust.

Ask Direct Questions. When you have a real concern that an inmate is considering or planning suicide, you must be more direct. Don't tiptoe around the subject. Instead of asking an inmate, "Are you thinking of hurting yourself?", ask "Are you thinking of killing yourself?" With some individuals, particularly those who seem to deny the seriousness of their suicidal intention, it is proper to ask "Are you planning to murder yourself?" Such direct questions often come as a relief because it indicates that there is someone who is strong enough to listen to what is really going on inside them. If the inmate is not suicidal, they will let you know. If they are outraged by your questions, explain why you believe they might be suicidal. They should be able to give you a clear explanation why you don't need to be concerned. <u>One final point: asking them if they have thoughts of suicide won't put the idea in their head if it was not already there.</u>

Voice Tone. Speak in a calm matter-of-fact tone of voice. If you sound nervous, you will appear unreliable. If you are joking or off-hand, the inmate will feel that you are not taking them seriously. If you are overly concerned, overly warm, or sensitive, you will sound like a hovering counselor, that soft-voiced, gentle soul who can't be trusted to stand up and fight, but seeks refuge only in being 'nice.' A calm, matter-of-fact tone shows that you are not panicked by their situation, and that you can handle anything they say.

Take Your Time. Act as if you have all the time in the world. If you act like there is little time, the inmate will believe you, and they will rush to a decision or conclusion. *When you take time, you give time,* and the suicidal inmate begins to believe that there is <u>enough</u> time to figure out a better solution than suicide.

Don't Give Advice Too Soon. Until you become more familiar with the situation, don't hand out advice. Even then, keep it to a minimum. For example, if you immediately say, "Think of your family," the individual might think, "Yeah, they'll be sorry. They haven't visited me in seven years. Their tears dropping on my grave are the best payback I can think of!" The assessment process is a means to get them to reveal themselves, so they feel less isolated, and furthermore, so you know the right thing to say.

Never Dare Them to Do It. That kind of stupidity only works in the movies. The ultimate stupid sentence is, "Cutting? If you were serious, you would cut your wrists lengthwise, not cross-wise." The idea here is to 'scare the person straight.' It is obvious the aggressive intervener thinks, that the suicidal person is attention seeking and not serious, and they try to shock them with the reality of what they are doing. In all cases I can recall, such 'interventions' are born out of frustration, irritation, burn-out, or plain dislike of the often repeatedly suicidal person. It is a statement for us, not them. This author met a man who took such advice. His crippled arm looks like corduroy, due to seven elbow-to-wrist razor slashes down to the bone.

Don't Debate. Some inmates use suicidal behavior as a way of attaining some personal power in a world over which they have little control. Debates about the meaning of life, religion, or the immorality of suicide will *break* rapport, particularly if you are 'winning.'

Protect Yourself Emotionally. Quite often the stories that suicidal inmates tell are very painful. However, this can also be a very sophisticated type of manipulation, and inmates who dramatize their problems, only to later minimize them or discount those who tried to help them, can enrage or frustrate us. I am not encouraging cynicism here, but as correctional officers, you can't allow yourselves to become so emotionally involved that you feel betrayed, or simply burned out, if the inmate rejects your efforts to help.

Identify Other Intended Victim(s). Identify the intended victim(s), beyond themselves. Try to ascertain who the suicide is intended to hurt. You will get a better sense if they are also homicidal, intent on taking others along. You can tell if others are intended to suffer by asking "If you do that, who will be at your funeral?" Some people are shocked at the question, so preoccupied with their own pain that they didn't even think that a loved one would have to bury them. Others describe that same scene with happiness, imagining people weeping at the gravesite.

35.1 Dialogue Is the Lifeline.
The most powerful intervention with suicidal individuals is that you are talking. Suicidal inmates feel profoundly alone. They believe that nothing can end their pain, but death. They are often depressed or very bitter and angry. When one is isolated, one does not even feel half-alive, because to be human is to be in relationship with others. When you are able to begin a dialogue with the suicidal inmate, <u>the power, beyond anything you say, is that you are speaking</u>. A sustained, respectful conversation conveys on an almost primal level that they are still worth something—because you, who are worth something, find them worthwhile by speaking to them. By definition, the inmate is no longer alone. Someone is hearing them out. Someone grasps how terrible life is for them. As time passes, the very fact of talking with you can make them feel alive again, and this gives hope, even when their situation has otherwise not changed. As one veteran correctional officer put it: "Other than putting them on a watch until the impulse passes (and even the most carefully planned act of violence against self or others requires the momentary impulse to act on it), the only true suicide prevention is human connection."

CHAPTER 36

Essential Questions

The Basic Questions

The following are the standard questions for assessing suicide risk.[27] There is a progression in which greater specificity indicates greater danger. You are not in the role of a therapist, but even if you were, the basic questions would be the same. You are assessing if the inmate is safe, and determining the need to contact a mental health professional. Don't use the following questions as a mere checklist. Instead, use them in the natural flow of the conversation while understanding that the inmate may wander off on all sorts of tangents before being ready to answer the next question.

> **36.1 Err on the Side of Caution—From a Prison-Based Mental Health Professional**
> Truly, any hint of suicidality should generate a mental health referral. It's a matter of liability. One of the best pieces of advice I was ever given was "All we're really doing is guessing whether or not something is going to happen. So make your decision so that WHEN you guess wrong, people won't look back and say 'What was that officer thinking?'"

The Four Questions

Question One. "Are you planning to kill yourself?" If they answer no, follow up with questions and statements why you believe they might (You received a kite from another inmate who stated that the inmate was going to "end it all," perhaps.). If they can't counter your suspicions satisfactorily, then you need to call emergency response to assure their safety despite their denials.

If the inmate replies something along the lines of, "I don't want to kill myself, but sometimes I pray that I won't get up in the morning," this could be termed passive or soft suicidal ideation. Don't minimize this, as the inmate's pain is very real, although their lack of an immediate plan usually allows you sufficient time to refer these inmates for a mental health evaluation. Should the inmate refuse to answer, but you have reason to believe they may be suicidal, a referral for a more detailed mental health assessment is necessary.

If the inmate answers "yes" that is a clear sign of their thought processes and intent. Follow up this answer with more detailed questioning, or take immediate action to ensure the inmate's safety, perhaps even taking them into higher custody or to a crisis care unit for further evaluation and stabilization. Do not leave the inmate alone.

Question Two. "How would you do it?" Obviously, this question is asked in response to the inmate answering "yes" to question one. If their response is "I don't know," then you should have time to address the issue by negotiating an agreement to accept treatment. If the inmate says that they "could do it all sorts of ways," and offers a long list of possibilities, or simply says, "I'm not telling you that,"—this is manipulation. This doesn't mean they won't try, but their response usually stems more from an "I'll show you I'm serious!" attitude. At this point, you must make it clear to them that such suicidal threats *are* taken seriously and have them evaluated by a mental health professional rather than dancing around, so to speak, trying to coerce from them how serious they really are. If the inmate specifies a particular method (poison, overdose, hanging) or weapon (an edged weapon), the level of risk has just increased exponentially.

Sometimes, the suicidal inmate will offer a plan and a back-up plan, for example, "I want to jump off the tier, but I think I don't have the guts. So, if I can't, I'll just get some drugs on the yard and overdose." This is usually not a manipulative strategy because it denotes careful planning. Among other responses, you will check his cell for stockpiled drugs. (Sometimes inmates 'sort of' tell the truth; in this case, "I'll get some drugs" really meant, "I've got some drugs." Once again, you should immediately conduct a search of the inmate's person, cell, and living areas for possible weapons or other validations of the inmate suicidal intent).

Question Three. Often suicidal inmates may have decided on a method, but it is one that they have not yet acquired or have access to. Be sure to ask follow-up questions to ascertain if they have access to the method they have named. Examples of follow-up questions follow below:
- "Do you have any pills?"
- "What kind?"
- "Where are they?"
- "Do you know what would happen if you took them all?"

Question Four. "When will you do it?" This question helps you gauge immediacy, and to determine if the inmate has established the plan to make others suffer, and if there is anyone else who is 'timed' to suffer, e.g., "On my mom's birthday." The more 'positive' answers you get to these questions, the greater the risk of a lethal outcome.

Follow-up Questions
In most cases, particularly when interviewing an inmate regarding suicidal risk, you will have fully accomplished all that you need to do. You know that the inmate is or is not suicidal, and how close to the act they are. In many cases, however, you may have to keep talking for the following possible reasons:
- They trust you and want to talk more.
- It is a barricade situation, and the inmate is talking on the other side of a door.

As inmates continue to talk, they often pull back from the intent to kill themselves on his or her own, or they will be more amenable to de-escalation because they feel that, at last, someone is willing to listen.

Simple communication brings people away from suicide, even without a solution to the problems that drives them toward it. Below are some follow-up questions that may prove helpful:
- "Have you tried to kill yourself before?"
- "Have you ever tried to kill yourself another way?" Desperate people become very concrete and literal, only thinking of their chosen method. They may have made several attempts before, by other means.
- "Have you ever *felt* like killing yourself before?"
- "What stopped you?" "Who stopped you?" Be sure not to make them feel like they 'failed' when they were not successful in a previous attempt. When they recall someone or something that stopped them, this may help them regain a sense of responsibility for the people who care for them, or some other factor that kept them alive in the past.
- "Has anybody in your family or someone you cared about ever tried to kill themselves?" Such people have 'shown the way,' and this history heightens risk.
- "Have you been drinking? Using any drugs?" *(Don't push this one if you have a sense that the person will be more worried about getting violated for use or possession than finding a solution to the situation.)*
- "What's happened that things are so bad that suicide makes sense?" OR "What happened TODAY that you decided to kill yourself?"
- "What else have you tried to do to get yourself out of this situation?" (Be careful—a defensive person could respond by thinking or saying, "Oh, so you think I'm stupid" or "Now I have to explain myself again—I don't **know** why having a girlfriend waiting for me and getting released in three months isn't enough!!!!!!!"
- Other areas to talk about include if the inmate has suffered any recent losses, is ill, or has little or no social/family support or has been recently diagnosed with severe health concerns

Despite whatever assurances these questions might engender regarding the inmate's real abilities to commit an act of suicide or not, the questions by the correctional officer should be immediately followed by a mental health evaluation by a trained and licensed clinician who will then decide as to whether or not the inmate requires further staff intervention strategies.

The Taxonomy of Suicide

This tool can be used to help gauge the seriousness of the inmate's suicidal intent, and what type of suicide it might be. Given that suicide is a form of murder, let us categorize the act in roughly the same manner as a homicide. See below:

Aggravated First Degree Suicide. This would include killing oneself in a heinous or torturous way, because the person believes he deserves to suffer. Another example would be a suicide calculated so that a loved one will see a mutilated body. A third would be a murder-suicide. The latter is seldom encountered within a prison or prison because the individual seldom has sufficient time or privacy to follow through with the act.

Premeditated First Degree Suicide. This would include any planned suicide. This is the typical pattern for a suicide while incarcerated.

Second Degree Suicide. You usually see this type on a monitor as they are carrying out the act, or come upon their body later. When incarcerated, this form of suicide is usually precipitated by an extreme emotional occurrence, such as a forcible rape of the victim or threats to one's life. It can be exacerbated by intoxication of drugs or alcohol.

Assaultive Self-Harm With Intent to Commit Mayhem (First Degree Self-Assault). The inmate does not mean necessarily to die, but they do something horrible to themselves, often with the intent to show others, "See how much I'm suffering!" or "See how much you make me suffer." The distinction between the previous item and this one is a hard call: you may not even be confidently able to make it. However, the mental health professionals who will deal with such an individual would also find this useful information, if you happened to acquire it.

> **36.2 Example of Intent to Commit Self-Mayhem (No intent to die)**
> An inmate has his cell tossed. His possessions are trashed and he finds his daughter's photograph torn and stepped on. He is so enraged he starts beating his head against the wall, so hard that he is knocked unconscious, with his forehead split open. He says, "I didn't want to die. I didn't even think of that. I just didn't know what to do with what was inside me."

Assaultive Self-Harm. This includes any suicidal gestures, such as cutting oneself and other self-mutilating actions (CHAPTER 37). This gesture is common within prisons by inmates seeking the attention of staff. These gestures seldom result in serious harm or death unless the severity is miscalculated by the inmate perpetrator or by staff.

Self-Sacrifice. Rare though it may be, this would include actions that have the intention of helping others—like throwing oneself in front of a friend so he is not stabbed.

Self-Execution. This includes suicide that is primarily directed by a sense of guilt. Such an individual believes that they deserve to die for some unforgivable transgression. We are confining this category to those who have actually done something terrible, not someone who, due to a sense of pathological guilt brought on by mental illness, decides that they do not deserve to live.

> **36.3 Example: Self-Execution**
>
> One of my consultants described a convicted child molester who hung himself when he discovered his son had been placed to the same prison for child molestation.
>
> Another correctional officer described an inmate who had been arrested for drunk driving and vehicular homicide. He attempted to kill himself when he sobered up and realized what he had done.

Mercy Self-Killing. This category includes so-called 'assisted suicide' or other suicides in which the inmate is seriously ill and wishes to 'die with dignity.'

"I'm Taking My Body Out of Here." This is an attempt at final control over one's own fate. This can range from:
- An 'escape' by those afraid of being killed by other inmates—having the control of doing it oneself is somehow less terrifying than being killed by others
- Most common is the action of someone whose only way of 'defeating' the people who hold him against his will is to kill himself.

Very rarely, suicide can be a protest, a kind of heroic action against intolerable violation or oppression

> **36.4 Example: "It's Your Fault"**
>
> One of my consultants, while Warden of a California State Prison, came upon a suicide by an inmate who, prior to expiring, had written on his body and cell walls his complaints against the prison system, its staff and policies, and how this contributed to his suicide.

CHAPTER 37

Self-Mutilation

One of the most confusing actions that an inmate can take, at least to those outside the situation, is self-mutilation. When it is potentially life-threatening, but somehow has survival 'built in,' it is referred to as 'para-suicidal behavior.' This primarily includes cutting ones wrists or other actions that could, taken to an extreme, have resulted in death. Other actions are not life threatening, and are referred to as 'self-injurious behavior' or 'self-mutilation.' Among self-mutilating behaviors that the author has encountered are:

- Rubbing an eraser on the wrist until all the skin is peeled away and one has a weeping lesion in the flesh.
- Cutting with a sharp object, or deeply gouging the wrists and forearms.
- Repetitively stubbing out a burning cigarette on one's face and genitals.
- Running a needle in and out of the flesh of one's belly.
- Swallowing sharp objects
- Hacking over one's wrists on the corner of a table, and then, after being stitched up, tearing out the stitches with one's teeth and attempting to spray blood on nearby corrections officers.
- Repetitive incidents of slicing open the abdominal wall all the way to the fascia that holds the organs. (A former nurse did this to herself.)

The hallmark of all of these actions is that the inmate does not intend to die. There are a number of reasons why an inmate would commit such acts:

Self-Hatred. The inmate punishes himself or herself through self-torture and/or disfiguration.

Attention Seeking. Attention-seeking cases are usually, *but not always*, typified by less serious wounds. Such inmates, through such acts as superficially cutting their wrists, 'require' others to pay attention to them.

Primitive Medicine. Similar to the historical European and American medical practice of bloodletting to 'cure' a variety of physical and mental health illnesses, these inmates are metaphorically 'draining out' the poisons in their bodies by bleeding themselves.

A Struggle to Feel Something. Some inmates in the throes of deep depression or trauma literally feel numb. Absent any apparent emotions, they use these torturous acts help them feel alive.

Stress Reduction. Physical wounding results in the release of endorphins. These are neuro-chemicals produced by the body that have a pain-relieving effect similar to opiates such as morphine and heroin. A common term for this is the 'runner's high,' that folks experience after a particularly vigorous workout. Inmates can become habituated to this endorphin release, and activities that stimulate it, such as self-mutilation, can become addictive.

> **37.1 Example of Stress Reduction by Self-wounding**
> A young woman told the author that, after years of verbal and emotional abuse by her father, "I felt like I was walking on egg shells all the time. Then, when my mom and I finally left, it was like I couldn't stand any emotions at all. Even when I was happy, I would still feel like I was going to explode." She described one day cutting herself on the forearm with an Exacto knife, and to her shock, felt a sensation of warmth and peace. Several weeks later she tried it again, and it became an addiction.

Rehearsal. Some inmates want to commit suicide, but their underlying fears make them hesitant, resulting in numerous 'failed' attempts at suicide.

Psychosis. Inmates in acute psychotic states, particularly when subject to auditory command hallucinations (CHAPTERS 30 & 31) that dictate the inmate's actions, can inflict horrifying wounds on themselves.

> **37.2 The Line of Self-Mutilation Has Moved**
> We must be aware that the line of self-mutilation has 'moved.' We see individuals with tattoos over the face, multiple piercings, including one's tongue or sexual organs, and others who have voluntarily branded themselves. Many of these people talk about endorphin release. Others claim that they are making their own bodies into works of art. As strange or repulsive as we may find some of these body modifications, this is not an emergency, unless the person puts themselves at medical risk.

The Proper Response to Self-Mutilation by Correctional Officers

You have surely supervised inmates who seem to be in, or seem to create, a constant state of crisis. Everything is an issue, and the most minor problems or setbacks are likely to cause an inappropriate amount of emotional stress and drama. One of the primary outlets for these inmates is repeated suicide attempts, or threats of suicide.

As a correctional officer you should NOT try to manage this type of behavior alone. Instead, you need to consult the other members of the inmate's current treatment team to discuss any concerns for the inmate or their disturbing behaviors. Although the scope of this text does not allow for a discussion of detailed planning for such inmates, let us discuss both the problems they engender and offer an example that gives general principals of case management.

All too often, the focus centers around the person enacting the pathology. Such repetitive para-suicidal actions are, however, acts of violence against the fabric of society, be it prison society or that on the outside. Let us consider the damage they cause:

Compassion Burnout. Quite simply, we get sick of such people. We see them only as manipulative, self-involved pathetic losers. Beyond whatever justification one might find for that point of view concerning a particular inmate, it unfortunately expands. Many officers begin to view all inmates with mental illness, all suicidal people through the distorted lens that burnout creates. This becomes a safety issue. When we begin to view others with contempt, they can easily respond with their own negative emotions. Therefore, interactions between correctional officers and inmates suffering from mental illness become increasingly volatile. Remember, too, that an inmate suffering from mental illness perhaps suicidal as well, might have a negative interaction with one contemptuous officer, and decide to take it out on another, at a later date.

Damage to Operational Effectiveness. Suicidal threats, alone, can take up an enormous amount of man-hours, not only for custody staff, but also for your emergency medical system. When you have such an inmate, a committee needs to be set up to figure out the best way to manage the situation effectively. Such a committee, known as an interdisciplinary treatment team (IDTT), should include representatives from correctional staff, case management, and clinical staff, as well as non-security staff, such as Educators and Program Supervisors (the latter may come up with strategies that become rewards if the inmate doesn't enact para-suicidal behaviors).

Maintain Contact. It is the responsibility of the mental health professionals to maintain contact with the person, and begin to work with them so that they get a sense of reward when NOT using suicidal threats to get attention.

Comprehensive Plan. A comprehensive plan can be set up so that the individual gets more emotional rewards and attention by NOT engaging in para-suicidal gestures. This planning is a function of the particular inmate's IDTT responsibilities.[28]

37.3 Example: Interdisciplinary Treatment Team (IDTT) Intervention With a Para-suicidal Inmate

Inmate Mendez is well known in the correctional and mental health communities for becoming suicidal when he does not get his way, gets confronted, or becomes very stressed or upset. Although Mendez has not actually attempted suicide, he is very willing to escalate behaviors from moderate to extreme in a millisecond, and willing to hurt himself or anyone else to get his way.

He is referred to Acute Care after a suicidal statement and moved to a padded cell and placed in a tear-resistant smock. His welfare checks are increased to every seven minutes.

Acute care may need to see Inmate Mendez several times before he is cleared from the padded cell. All of the correctional staff realize that Mendez benefits from the increased interaction from the staff. Some officers feel manipulated in the process, but they realize this is the plan that moves him through the process and back to his regular housing, so all maintain their professionalism.

Once Mendez is cleared from the padded cell, he is moved to a single man cell and remains in tear-resistant materials—smock and blankets. His welfare checks are lengthened to every 30 minutes, but he still has face-to-face time with officers. His care is then taken over by the in-house Mental Health Case Managers and a medication review is completed with the doctor (if it hasn't been already). Cell door visits are completed with Case Managers and with Officers from the Classification Team. Mendez's physical surroundings transform with his continued cooperation with the Mental Health team. He is eventually given a full uniform and blankets as he works with his Case Managers and with the correctional staff. He earns extras such as books, pencils, and paper until he is eventually moved back into his regular housing.

SECTION VIII

Recognizing Patterns Of Aggression

CHAPTER 38

The Cycle of Aggression

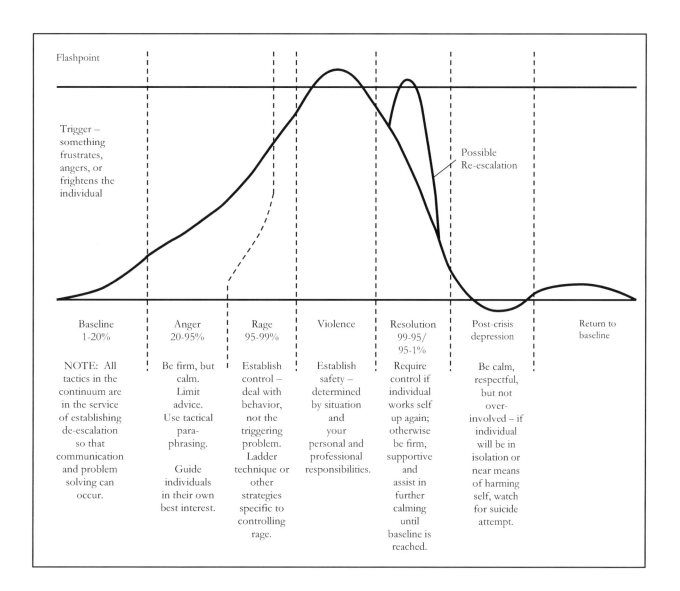

An outburst of aggression occurs in a cycle that starts with relative calm and ends with relative calm. The aggressive cycle often appears to start with an apparent 'triggering event' though, in fact, the crisis may have been burning beneath the surface for some time. The reader may recognize the term trigger, being familiar with it in terms of relapse in regard to substance abuse. The same concept applies with acts of violence. Just as many addicts have certain triggers that elicit the urge to use drugs, aggressive inmates have triggers that *cue* them to become violent.

Baseline: From 0-20

When we are calm, we are at **baseline,** which is represented as '0-20' on the accompanying chart. At baseline, we use the parts of the brain most responsible for our better human characteristics: thinking, creativity, and forming social relationships. The reason that the rating scale goes up to '20' is that I wish to underscore that one can have a little heat and energy, and still be fully rational.

Anger: From 20-95

A triggering event elicits a change in both thinking and feeling. This event can be something that threatens the inmate's sense of safety, frustration at not being able to obtain what they desire, or simply a cue that they are now justified using a skill (aggression) with which they are confident. Once aggression is triggered, the inmate becomes irritable, then angry.

If baseline is presented as being '0-20' on the scale of aggression, with actual violence being '100,' anger represents the numbers 20 through 95. Regardless of the numeric value of their anger, the inmate is trying to communicate with you. Because we perceive their attempts to communicate to be loud, obnoxious, domineering, threatening, or just plain irrational, we often don't construe their actions as communication. The inmate, on the other hand, experiences an increasing sense of frustration, and not infrequently, a sense of helplessness, at their inability to make themselves understood (not that they necessarily are making sense), further fueling their anger.

Think of arguments you have had when, frustrated, you said such things as: "No, that's not what I'm saying! Do I have to explain it again?" or "Let me put it another way!" or "You just don't get it! What do I have to say to make you understand?" We become progressively more intense, often raising our voices (as if that will help the other person understand) because we want the other person to 'get it.' This type of escalation is counter-productive, despite our intentions, because we tend to make less sense when we are angry.

There are several reasons such inmates grow angrier as the perceived or actual conflict continues:
- Many inmates simply can't accept anyone disagreeing with them, especially when they believe they are right.
- When you don't seem to grasp what they are saying, you are perceived as being disinterested, too dumb to understand, or your lack of comprehension implicitly accuses *them* of stupidity or unreasonableness.
- They may believe you think you are "too good to listen to me."
- When you don't agree or comply with them you are frustrating the inmate in achieving something they desire.
- Many inmates have a distorted and hypersensitive sense of 'respect.' The inmate often sees resistance, disagreement, or perceived slights as being disrespectful, causing them to lash out in anger or violence in an effort to regain their 'street cred.'

As inmates become more agitated, the areas of their brain that direct basic emotions take over. At this point, equity, negotiation, or compromise becomes less and less of an option. In their frustration, angry inmates shift, to attempting to dominate you: to *make* you see things their way, or to comply with them.

Anger is accompanied by physical arousal, which functions as a positive feedback loop, driving them forward. As they get more upset, the inmate no longer cares about the truth. They care only about being 'right' and proving others 'wrong.' The disagreement has become a win or lose situation. Therefore, they no longer care about what you have to say—only that you 'get' what they are saying. As long as they are angry, you cannot problem solve with them. Such an inmate interrupts more frequently, cutting others off and picking out the flaws in the other person's argument.

To de-escalate and control an angry inmate, the correctional officer should attempt to *'line up'* with them. This lining-up strategy is exactly the same as what hostage negotiators do to eventually get compliance from the hostage taker. When you line up with the inmate, you prove that you understand (not necessarily approve or agree with – simply understand) what they are saying, thereby proving that their concerns are important. This in itself is powerfully disarming, not only calming them down, but also helping the correctional officer demonstrate that he or she will work to solve the problem.

Rage: From 95-99

As you can see on the chart, rage is represented as 95 to 99 on the aggression scale. How can you tell the difference between anger and rage? When someone is angry, you too, may become angry. You might also become concerned, upset, hurt, confused, and/or frustrated. Usually, however, you are not afraid. Why? Although angry people may *later* become violent if they are further agitated, that is not their aim. Instead, their intention is to communicate with you, albeit dramatically, loudly, or forcefully. At worst, they are trying to dominate or intimidate you into doing what they want. As abhorrent as this may be, it is still communication.

When inmates are enraged, however, they are, in effect, trying to 'switch themselves on' to becoming violent. Many people slowly work themselves into a state of rage as a prelude to violence. Of course, others can lash out violently with seemingly no prior warning, verbal or otherwise. Usually however, even non-communicative inmates will signal their anger or intentions through their body language and other non-verbal forms of communication. Correctional officers should be aware of these warning signs of impending aggression, as manifested on the intuitive level (CHAPTERS 2 & 5) and based on observable behaviors, as discussed throughout this book.

Most of the time, anger does not result in violence. One reason for this is the various self-inhibitors that work to control our behaviors and prevent us from acting out our baser instincts. But within a state of rage, the inmate is *trying to overcome* those inhibiters, so that they can do what they actually desire: act violently. Some of the prime inhibitors are listed below:

Fear of Consequences. The fear of counterattack, legal consequences, time added on, a new charge or sentence, social disapproval, financial costs, and a host of other possible negative outcomes serve to inhibit one's resorting to violence to settle a dispute.

Morality. Most individuals possess a core set of moral or religious principles that prevent them from harming others. Even most criminals have what could be termed 'wolf-pack morality'—if you are a member of the pack, you should be protected (unless you threaten what they perceive as their 'alpha position.')

Self-Image. A man may see himself, for example, as the kind of person who does not hit women, make a public display of aggression, or lose control of himself. Another inmate may have a rule that he never attacks someone, even a correctional officer, from behind. A positive self-image, and fears of tarnishing that image, will often preclude an individual from committing a violent act.

The Relationship. A feeling of responsibility toward the other person, e.g. friendship, trust, respect, love, family relations, etc., will hold an individual from violence.[29]

Learned Helplessness. Some inmates, survivors of abuse for example, have tried to defend themselves in the past and have failed repeatedly. They may believe that fighting back is a futile effort, only leading to further pain and abuse. Their rage, however, is there: inside. There are phrases like, 'a cornered rat,' or 'the worm turns,' which describe a person who has suppressed their rage, sometimes for years, before acting out in violence and rage.

Rage therefore, is a set of behaviors, including both physical actions and verbalizations that serve to do away with one's self-inhibitors, so that nothing holds them back from violence. Inmates in a rage state are no longer trying to communicate; they are working themselves up to an attack.

What is the difference, then between rage and violence? Anger is a rocket ship all fueled up with some fumes coming out, and the countdown initiated. Rage is right before lift-off. The rocket has not yet moved, but there are flames and steam billowing out, making a terrible roar, so loud the ground shakes. It is a moment of explosive, tenuous equilibrium. If you cut off the fuel, you can stop the rocket, even now, but there are only a few moments to act, because the rocket is about to lift off. Lift-off is the equivalent of the initiation of **violence**.

What we *should* experience in the face of rage is fear. This is not a bad thing. <u>Fear is just a wake-up call.</u> Fear tells us that we are in danger and that we must do something—NOW! We will most likely be able to handle the situation, but we had better devote every power we have to survival. Fear switches us on, so that our internal emergency response systems are activated. Fear demands attention, but it should not paralyze us into non-action, mentally or physically, in the face of anger and rage. <u>Remember, a sense of powerlessness is not fear; it is a *conclusion* that some people reach when they are afraid, limiting their ability to control the situation, or to defend themselves.</u>

THE CYCLE OF AGGRESSION

<u>With the enraged inmate, you must establish *control*</u>. De-escalation and control tactics, whether they are verbal or physical, are geared to establish the conditions that make the aggressive inmate no longer dangerous.

> **38.1 From a Veteran Correctional Sergeant: If You Train Yourself Properly, You Are Ready to Function in a State of Fear, and Still Be Ready to Lead**
>
> Early in my supervisory career, a unit of thirty or so violent felons began escalating towards a riot. These inmate were refusing to lockdown, throwing cleaning gear at the windows (mop buckets, etc.) and had broken mop handles to make weapons. They were calling officers names, and were taunting for them to come into the unit. We were at shift change so I had both shifts of officers on the floors.
>
> My first priority was to keep this behavior from spreading to other units, but I didn't have enough radios for every officer. Most of the officers wanted to go into the violent unit first, but since they had done only minimal damage, I knew it was more important to lock all the other inmates down on the floor to prevent the spread of the riot behavior. I started assigning officers in pairs, one with a radio and one without telling them that they had to stay together. I sent them into the calm units to lock the other inmates down.
>
> While this was happening, I was monitoring the violent unit and trying to figure out how many officers I could fit into the elevator, in case the inmates broke through the doors. I was also trying to figure out who to send first and who to send last (besides me—supervisors are the first in and last out.) I was terrified at the thought of losing any of my officers, or of them getting hurt.
>
> Luckily, the situation did not spread. I sent officers into the violent unit in forceful numbers. Using reasonable and effective communication, the violent inmates were locked down with no uses of force and minimal facility damage.
>
> Years later, I confessed to one of the officers involved in the event how scared I was. She said that no-one could tell, and was surprised to hear me say it—she had been scared too. She told me she had kept looking at me, and since I didn't appear to be scared or wound up about the event, she calmed down and figured I had it under control.

38.2 The Difference Between Anger and Rage

Imagine someone hands you a huge plastic container. Through its translucent sides, you can see a dark, hairy shape, a Goliath Bird-Eater, the world's biggest spider. It rustles around the container shifting in your hands like it's filled with mercury. Is it creepy? Sure it is. Is there any reason to be afraid? Not really. As long as the lid is on the container firmly, you are absolutely safe. This is the equivalent of anger. Internally you say, "I'd better keep the lid on this thing."

Now, imagine your 'friend' takes the container back, and to your surprise and horror, takes off the lid. The spider emerges onto the floor right next to your leg. It raises its front legs in threat-display and opens and closes its one-inch fangs. There is something poisonous, hairy, and mean in the room, and it is not enclosed in any container! The spider is out of the box. This, metaphorically, is rage.

However, the fear that now arises within you doesn't mean that you are helpless. You can step on the spider or jump up on a table. If you are ticked off enough, you can grab your 'friend' by the neck and make him sit on it! A belief that you are helplessness near the spider is an interpretation, not a fact. Fear is simply the warning cry—the drums at the brink of battle—that demands that you *must* act right now.

To deal with the enraged person, you must establish *control,* especially if, their behavior presents an immediate threat to you, to themselves, or to others. Control tactics—be they verbal or physical—are geared to establish the conditions that make the aggressive person no longer dangerous. In essence, using our metaphor above, we say, "Put the spider back in the box. Now!"

Violence: 100 on the Scale

Violence does not begin when someone is hit or injured. Violence is perpetrated simply through the fear of imminent danger and attack. Some of the legal terms for this are terroristic threats, harassment or harassment by communication, stalking, and menacing. In short, a violent act occurs whenever there is good reason to believe that you or someone else is about to be hurt. <u>In the face of violence, your guiding principle is to establish safety, and you use most effective means of protecting yourself and those around you.</u> Very often, the best thing to do is to escape and get help. In other times, it means to use overwhelming force.

Although actual physical self-defense tactics are beyond the scope of this book, correctional officers should also avail themselves of any offered defensive tactics training, including the less than lethal weaponry you are provided through your individual agencies. As with any skill, self-defense techniques and tactical responses to crisis situations must be practiced regularly to ensure their viability in the event of an actual confrontation. Many officers do extra training on their own, maintaining themselves in peak combat-ready condition.

38.3 How Combative Skills Contribute To Verbal De-escalation

Studies have shown that SWAT-trained law enforcement officers have the lowest use of force complaints of any unit within police agencies. Why? Because they train, both on the job and off, so that they answer the 'what if' questions. Not only mentally and psychologically, but on a pseudo-instinctive level, they know what they will do if they are assaulted. When you can trust your reflexes, you relax. When you relax (while remaining alert), your confidence and calm causes other people to calm as well.

Officers who have not achieved expertise in physical confrontations (both unarmed and using the weaponry that is a part of one's job) tend to be either naïve ("Nothing's going to happen. I have back-up—I have OC spray—I have a Taser) or nervous. Conflict avoidant officers draw conflict and aggression to them.

A friend of mine functions as a training officer at a state's Basic Academy. He is an expert grappler, and also studies edged-weapon survival. He puts on the padded suit and has the trainees try to fight and survive him for a number of minutes. He physically humbles everyone—not in an unethical or abusive manner, but to test the trainees' fighting spirit. Through this, he underscores that, contrary to one-step sparring drills, real combat is chaos; if one wants to survive, one has to a) be physically fit b) be well trained c) be able to manage fear, panic and anger. He told me that in his last class of thirty-seven soon-to-be officers, only one came up to him later and asked where he could get more training. The other thirty-six, having clearly 'lost the fight,' considered this a once-and-done experience that they could put behind them.

Not only are they ill-prepared to face assaultive inmates, they are ill-prepared to talk with them either, because they will not display the confidence that a trained professional must embody when confronting people who are 'professionals' at violence, aggression and manipulation.

In other words, if you tell an inmate, "Step back," and they step forward and say, "What happens now?"—you better have an answer. Better yet, inmates should already know the answer before they step forward, reading your calm, your confidence and your posture. A well-trained officer has a kind of <u>spaciousness</u> – prepared for the worst, they have the options of offering the best.

CHAPTER 39

Why Would an Inmate Become Aggressive?

Aggression is not an alien or unnatural emotion. Without a capacity for aggression, humanity would never have survived. Yet, much aggression seems far apart from the basic activities of hunting or self-defense. Much of it is irrational, self-destructive, vicious, or cruel. Why would someone be swept by rage when it causes so much harm? Why would they be prepared to throw away a future, even a life, driven by emotions that they might be horrified to have expressed even a few moments later? Why would they choose to attack correctional officers, even in situations that they have little possibility of winning? Correctional officers can better control an aggressive inmate when they understand what has driven the inmate to anger. Below are some of the factors that can drive an inmate to become aggressive:

Feels confused or disorganized. Anger and rage can develop because the inmate is confused or disorganized. They cannot understand what is going on around them, or 'inside' them, due to cognitive distortions or a chaotic situation (too much information for them to figure out). Among those who experience this confusion are those who are mentally ill, autistic, developmentally disabled, intoxicated, elderly inmates (particularly those suffering from dementia), and those in the grip of overwhelming emotions.

Feels enclosed, trapped and/or beset with problems. If you are in prison, this is true, by definition. This is often similar in effect to confusion or disorganization, but it is accompanied by a particular anguish. The inmate usually perceives either a person or entity as the agent of their situation, and they fight desperately to get free from his or her oppression.

Has a fear of attack. The fear of attack elicited by an actual or perceived invasion of personal space is often a precursor to aggression. Each of us has a sense of personal space, a 'bubble' within which an outsider is only permitted if invited (CHAPTER 5). A violation of this personal space can elicit aggressive reactions and behaviors. In stressful or volatile situations, you will be perceived as an attacker if you encroach upon another's personal space, no matter your intentions.

Feels wronged or feels a loss of power. An inmate may resort to aggression if they feel they are being wronged, or feel as if they are losing, or have lost, their sense of autonomy and power. Some inmates suffering from mental illness experience a sense of personal violation when they are being limited in their actions or forced to conform to rules, despite the fact that such restrictions are for their own good. This is especially true of those who are paranoid, who may believe that they are being oppressed by powers beyond their control. Correctional officers are often designated in such an inmate's mind as the representative of the controlling entity.

Is hallucinating or having delusions. Hallucinations and delusions play a significant role in the likelihood of aggression. The inmate may feel compelled to act as the voices demand or in trying to make the hallucinations stop by any means, become violent. On other occasions, the voices, visions, smells, and/or sensations are infuriating: think how you would react if a neighbor played loud music twenty-four hours a day, shined flood-lights on your house, or left the surroundings smelling like a garbage dump.

Drugs, alcohol, and other organic stressors. The use of drugs and alcohol, along with other organic stressors can also make an inmate more likely to become aggressive, *particularly if the inmate also has psychological problems*. By other organic stressors the author is referring to a lack of sleep, a lack of regular exercise, and/or an insufficient or non-nutritious diet. Such deprivations can cause changes in perception, mood, and cognition, which can lead to an increase in irritability and/or hypersensitivity. Drug abuse 'on top of' a psychotic disorder can exponentially increase the risk that an individual will be violent.

Feels shamed or humiliated. One of the most powerful driving forces of aggression is a sense that one has been shamed or humiliated. Shame is not a mild sense of social embarrassment; it is a sense of being exposed and victimized by others with no hope of relief. Shame and humiliation are driving forces for revenge-based aggression, and are also prime motivators for attacks when the inmate remembers, correctly or incorrectly, something the correctional officer did that offended them in the past. They may brood about past grievances, their anger slowly escalating until they explode into rage or violence. A particular problem for correctional officers is where inmates may bear a grudge against a previous correctional officer, and they try to take it out on another.

Is acting out of protective aggression. Inmates may act aggressively out of a sense of protective rage. This type of rage is not confined only to parents, but also as expressed by an inmate who is trying to protect another individual from being victimized. The closer one feels to the victim, the more one's identity is 'merged' with that of the victim and the more aggressive the person will be in their defense.

> ### 39.1 Example of Protective Aggression
> An inmate, a military veteran, feels protective towards another vet, who has brain trauma. He attacks a correctional officer whom he feels treated the injured vet poorly.

Act out of a sense of entitlement or they simply enjoy it. Some inmates may resort to aggression due to a sense of entitlement, or because they enjoy it. In the former case, their attitude is, "If I want it, I deserve it." Others simply take pleasure in intimidating others and acting violently. For them, there is a joy in making others submit and a delight in causing pain.

Anything that elicits profound emotion can cause an inmate to become volatile or aggressive. Emotional stressors include a recent loss through the death of someone close, dysfunctional family dynamics, romantic and other interpersonal relationships, job or housing changes, divorce, infidelity, or feelings of insecurity. Certainly, the criminal justice system elicits strong emotions, and each and every interaction with the correctional officer brings those emotions back, heightening the chances for an aggressive interaction between the officer and inmate. If you go back to SECTION VII on suicide, anything that evokes suicidal ideation can evoke rage or homicidal intent as well. Remember, the only difference between suicide and murder is what direction the weapon is pointing.

Prison gang subculture. Within the inmate gang subculture, violence and acts of violence often play a strong role in defining an inmate's allegiance to the gang, its members and its focus. In addition, many inmates fear the gang more than they fear the consequences of violence they are ordered to do (AKA – "Do the hit or we hit you.").

CHAPTER 40

What Does Escalation Look Like?

As an inmate escalates in their aggressive behavior(s), they are priming their bodies to posture, to intimidate, to fight, and/or to flee. They can display a variety of different behaviors.

Escalation Behaviors

Physical and Emotional Withdrawal. Some inmates will avoid eye contact, stop speaking, or respond only with short phrases or monosyllabic answers. Of course, some inmates are more naturally withdrawn and reserved; this does not mean that they are readying themselves for an aggressive outburst. Instead, here we are discussing a heretofore friendly and engaging inmate who lapses into sullen hostility or refuses to engage in conversation.

> **40.1 Physical and Emotional Withdrawal**
>
> If you notice an inmate behaving in this manner you should approach them and engage them in order to elicit a response. For example, you may ask "Inmate Cane, every day, when I see you in the morning, you said hello, and ask me how my day is going. But today, you turned your back on me. Something's bothering you today." Note that you did not ask, "What's going on?" Direct questions will merely give the inmate an opportunity to ignore you or reply with simple answers such as "Nothing" or "I don't know." By treating their behavior as a given, you are more likely to get a truthful response, such as "I just heard my uncle died, and I don't want to talk to anyone now." or "You know what's going on! You know what you did!" Such a response is the quickest way of ascertaining if the withdrawn inmate is a threat to you or anyone else.

Nervous, Anxious, or Frightened Demeanor. Such inmates usually lash out in defense. They are not looking for a fight; they are trying to protect themselves.

Overwhelmed or Disorganized Behavior. Inmates who speak in repetitive loops, muttering incoherently to themselves or pacing, are displaying symptoms of either a chaotic mental state or intoxication. Inmates in this state can be unpredictable, and they may react to a correctional officer's attempts to communicate with sudden, unexpected aggression.

Hostility. Any inmate displaying open expressions of dislike or hatred should obviously put the correctional officer on guard.

Seduction. Seduction is not reserved for just sexual expressions or desires. In communication from inmate to correctional officer, the inmate tries to get the correctional officer to collude with them, perhaps in an attempt to convince them to not file a violation report, or perhaps in an attempt to place the correctional officer in a compromising position. The perfect phrase of such an inmate is, "C'mon, officer, you know me . . . ." Seduction is masked aggression, and when it fails, the inmate, who perceives himself or herself to be smarter than you, frequently explodes in rage. You not getting conned is interpreted as 'disrespect.'

Mood Swings (CHAPTER 18). These involve rapid shifts in mood and emotional affect, from boisterous to morose, then shifting to belligerence. Such inmates present a particular risk due to their unpredictability and their inability to control their own emotions.

Hypersensitivity. Hypersensitivity is most common with inmates experiencing paranoia (CHAPTER 21), but others can also be hypersensitive. Hypersensitive inmates may complain of being stared at, watched, or controlled, and feel perpetually under threat of attack. Ironically, when they have no apparent enemy, they will create one. They feel most stable when targeting someone. The hypersensitive inmate can react aggressively to even the most inoffensive and harmless attempts at communication.

Authority Complex. Many inmates have difficulty with accepting authority. When a correctional officer tries to set limits or say 'no,' these inmates become outraged, refusing to comply with rules. Their attitude is simply an expression of their hatred for authority.

Electric Tension. This is the feeling you get before a thunderstorm hits: it could be called 'intuitive correctional awareness.' We can't underscore highly enough that you must ALWAYS trust this feeling, this intuitive sense that you are approaching a dangerous situation (CHAPTERS 4 & 5).

Changes in Cognition

Cognitive Distortions. Cognitive distortions are thinking patterns where the inmate makes broad, negative assumptions. For example, an inmate makes an angry comment to a teacher in a classroom and assumes he will be written up. Therefore, when he sees a correctional officer coming towards his cell, he is already convinced of the injustice he believes will be perpetrated upon him.

Interpersonal Cognitive Distortions. This occurs when the inmate mishears, based on their own negative expectations what the correctional officer is saying. For example, "Kennedy, you have to start complying fully with the committee rules, or I will have no choice but to issue you a rules violation report." And her response is, "YOU ARE WRITING ME UP???!!!!!"

Becoming Less Amenable to Reconciliation or Negotiation. The inmate focuses on dominating the situation, on winning the argument, or on taking out their frustrations on the object of their anger, rather than trying to find a peaceful resolution. The inmate focuses on being 'right,' and not on the facts. Because only their own ideas and desires have any importance to them, they refuse to consider other perspectives, something typical of almost all angry people.

Deterioration of Concentration and Memory. This causes difficulty in the inmate's ability to communicate, to solve problems, or to recall problem-solving skills. As their information processing skills deteriorate, their **judgment consequently becomes worse and worse**. They can't evaluate what is really in their own self-interest.

> ### 40.2 Example: Deterioration in Judgment
> An inmate is being moved to protective custody for a violation. He blames his cell-mate for this, and without thinking of the consequences, blurts out that his "cellie' is running an illegal business in the prison. Not only is it not true in this case, he is now marked as a snitch.

Changes in Patterns of Verbal Interactions

Silence. Potentially aggressive inmates may lapse into a morose, sullen silence, often accompanied by hunched shoulders, knitted brows, and glaring at the floor or at other people.

Sarcasm. Sarcasm can be considered to be hostility shaded in humor or passive-aggressive phrases. Inmates may jeer at you, or sneer scornfully, demeaning your position. Many inmates don't view correctional officers as true members of the law enforcement establishment. Sarcasm should also be interpreted as thinly veiled threats, and these must be taken seriously, lest the inmate believes that he or she can continue to treat a correctional officer with disrespect without fear of consequence.

> ### 40.3. Example of Sarcasm as Veiled Threats
> One of my consultants described speaking to an inmate during a routine tour of the facility. The inmate went on to relate his contempt for law enforcement in general and stated that once released (his parole date was within thirty days), he would be in a position to "educate some of you guys, because being here is worth my own degree in criminal justice, and 'street justice,' too, if you know what I'm saying." This inmate was immediately placed in segregation, received a rules violation report for making terrorist threats and received additional sixty days of incarceration as well as a referral to his parole officer for possible high control placement.

Deliberate Provocation. Inmates may deliberately do or say things to upset or irritate a correctional officer. Provocation is a challenge, an attempt to elicit a response from the correctional officer that will justify the inmate in becoming increasingly hostile, or violent.

Playing Word Games. Inmates may deliberately twist or misinterpret what correctional officer says, trying to confuse them or make you question your own memories of previous encounters. Inmates sometimes misremember or 'forget' directives, and then try to blame the correctional officer for their position. This is why proper note taking and documentation is vital.

Abusive or Obscene Language. The use of abusive or obscene language should put the correctional officer on guard immediately, especially if the language is threatening or portends a violent act. In these cases, the inmate uses language to shock or stun the recipient, causing the correctional officer to focus on what the inmate is saying, and not on what they are doing (such as moving closer, or surreptitiously reaching for a weapon).

Repeated Demands or Complaints. Some inmates will make repeated complaints towards or about the correctional officer for the inmate's derelictions in following established rules and policies, such as arriving to work on time, mail delivery, meal quality and quantity, medical care, or perceived lack of, etc. By making constant demands of their correctional officer, the inmate is looking for a pretext to legitimize their sense of grievance, creating an issue they consider to be worth fighting over, or at least disturbing the correctional officer's composure.

Low-Grade Aggression to Wear You Down and Make You Unaware. Inmates can use constant complaints and other obnoxious behavior to cause an officer to mentally shut down when in proximity to that particular inmate. The officer automatically thinks, "Here he is again," and mentally shuts off. They are then blind to the inmate actually 'stepping up' on this occasion to carry out an assault.

Clipped or Pressured Speech. Some inmates try to hide their aggression by appearing to be overly polite. They often use very formal or stilted language, presenting themselves as being in control when they are actually seething with aggression or a sense of injustice. A typical phrase would be, "What do you mean, officer. I-am-not-angry." This is often the hallmark speech of someone with paranoid traits (CHAPTER 21).

Implicit Threats. As with threatening sarcastic remarks, any implied threats made by an inmate must never go unanswered or ignored. An inmate who boasts of past acts of violence, or who warns a correctional officer that they might not be able to stop themselves from reacting the same way in the future, must be dealt with quickly and directly. If the situation is threatening enough to warrant the inmate's removal from the general population for a period of time, it should be documented and the inmate placed into temporary segregation pending a review of the circumstances and the potential threat persecuted by the inmate.

Changes in Physical Organization and Disorganization

Facial Expressions. Facial expressions can vary a lot, depending on the mode of aggression. The following list is not hard-and-fast, but there is real likelihood when the following facial expressions are displayed, the person means:
- **Clenched Teeth.** An attempt to contain or control intense emotions.
- **Bared Teeth.** A threat display. You may have noticed certain people smiling who are really baring their teeth. In this case, the smile doesn't 'touch the eyes.'
- **Frowning.** Is often associated with anger.
- **Staring Eyes.** Particularly if there is tension all-around the eyes. Can be an attempt at intimidation or manipulation; targeting the other as prey.
- **Biting or Compressing the Lips.** Is associated with barely controllable intense emotions.
- **Quivering Lips.** Is associated with fear or unhappiness.
- **Tightening the Lips.** Is associated with an attempt to control or contain intense emotion.
- **Pulsating Veins in the Neck**. Is associated with building anger and rage.
- **Dilated Pupils.** Is associated with drug intoxication.
- **Avoiding All Eye Contact**. When coupled with other expressions of aggression, this can be associated with planning an attack, hiding intentions of an attack, or, paradoxically, an attempt to disengage so that they won't be forced to fight. Remember that this kind of avoidance may simply be that, particularly in the case of individual suffering from mental illness or those with rigid personalities—it should be considered one component in a larger picture.

Voiding. When angered, some people have an urge to void themselves, clearing their bodies for the fight. Nausea and vomiting can occur with reduced blood flow to the gut. Other people feel a need to urinate or have an onset of diarrhea. These behaviors occur when an individual is in a state of intense fear or otherwise full of adrenaline.

Breathing. Different breathing patterns are indicative of different modes of aggression
- Inmates who are gearing themselves up for an attack often take deep breaths, which can be slow or fast, depending on how quickly their anger is building.
- Those going into defensive aggression, fearing they will be harmed, usually breathe in a shallow, rapid, and irregular pattern, almost like panting or gasping. Some hyperventilate, breathing so fast that they go into a panic state. They may become violent out of a terror-induced panic.
- Inmates who *want* the confrontation (the belligerent), and are looking forward to it often breathe very deeply, from the abdomen through the chest.
- Predatory inmates and others who are 'professionals' at violence often maintain a smooth easy breathing pattern throughout.

Changes in Actions

As an inmate becomes increasingly tense and agitated they may try to discharge the tension by pacing, often typified by rapid jerky movements. However, more predatory inmates tend to relax when they are preparing for an attack (leopards are relaxed when taking prey).

Deliberate Rejection in Word and Deed. Some inmates simply pay no heed to any directives by the correctional officer to enforce compliance. Their behavior makes their intentions abundantly clear, and nothing a correctional officer does will change their non-compliant behavior and/or criminal activity.

Posturing. As an inmate becomes angry, they will begin to posture, inflating their chests and spreading their arms to make themselves look bigger, invading their victim's personal space, pacing, smacking their fist in their hand, breathing faster, etc. They may move in quick jerky starts and stops, moving toward their victim and then back again repeatedly, as if working themselves up to attack. These actions are an effort to intimidate, prior to adopting a fighting pose.

Positioning. Inmates looking for a fight or confrontation square off directly in front of their target, *in your face,* while those looking for a victim tend to move to the *corner* of the person, trying to obtain an angle on them so that they can attack more easily.

Fighting Pose. A combative stance, as opposed to posturing, is often a crouch, with the chin tucked in and the hands raised. In some instances, the inmate may brandish a fist or a weapon. Be aware, however, that those most skilled at violence can often attack from a position of complete relaxation. One subset of aggressors, the predatory (CHAPTER 52), tends to **relax** when they are preparing for an attack. They are at home with violence, like a tiger or a snake. Predators sometimes smile while making eye contact with you.

40.4. Experience: You Don't Have to Look Tough to Be Dangerous

Those best at being dangerous often don't act dangerous. This author was acquainted with a man with a reputation in some circles as the best street fighter in a section of Tokyo. He was middle-aged, short, pudgy, and out of shape. He couldn't box or wrestle. However, every morning, for one half hour, he would stand in front of a mirror, and practice smiling, relaxing or gazing with a puppy-dog-like apology—perfecting utter harmlessness. Right beside the mirror was a small leather bag at head height. That was how he practiced his nearly perfect sucker punch, where he'd step on a foot, followed by a palm-heel uppercut, followed immediately by a head stomping, as his victim hit the ground.

Trespassing and Power Testing. An aggressive inmate will intrude on their victim's personal space, 'accidentally' bumping into them, spitting on the floor, faking a punch with just a hitch of a shoulder, or waving their hands close to the other person.

Visual Sexual Assault. Male inmates, in particular, will use their eyes to trespass on female correctional officers, running their gaze over their bodies in what can only be considered a 'visual rape.' (NOTE: This form of visual assault also occurs male-on- male, female-on-female and female-on-male). This is one reason why all staff in prisons should have the inmate lead the way to the interview room or office. Female officers, especially, should never allow a male inmate to follow them back to their office. A good correctional rule of thumb is to never escort an inmate or enter an office with an inmate without at least one additional staff member for back-up purposes and to notify central control as well as your supervisor as to your intentions.

Displacement Activities. Aggressors may hit, kick, or throw objects in an effort (that always fails) to discharge tension, as a threat display, or as a 'warm up' to an attack.

Making a Dramatic Scene. The inmate 'acts crazy,' either to get closer to you than you would let someone who was purposefully targeting you, or to get you so preoccupied with calming them down, you lose sight of larger tactical concerns.

Diversion. The inmate purposely engages the officer's attention through acting out or other gesture to divert the officer from a pre-planned activity by inmates in another or adjacent location. The activity might be an assault or drug/contraband transaction, escape, etc. Beyond this, a deliberate assault can be enacted by one or more inmates distracting an officer while another carries out the assault.

The Edge of Attack

Skin Tone. An angry inmate has a flushed face—the pale skinned turn red, and the dark-skinned turn even darker. In essence, blood at the surface of the skin is a threat display, as if to say, "See how angry I am!" Note, however, that flushing occurs for other reasons: some drugs, meth among them, are associated with flushed skin. Do not, therefore, over-value flushed skin as an indicator that the inmate is 'only angry.'

If they blanch—light skinned people turn bone-white, and dark-skinned people get a grayish tone—this indicates RAGE. The threat is not potential—it is NOW.

Pacing. Increased pacing, while muttering to oneself, is arousing, bringing oneself closer and closer to the edge or attack. Some inmates engage in more and more displacement activity: hitting, kicking, and throwing things.

Internalize All Signs. Other inmates will **internalize** all signs of incipient assault, and thus, when the assault does occur, it seems to appear instantaneously. Right before an attack, however, the inmate often stops breathing for a moment. This is often accompanied by stillness, the 'calm before the storm,' as if you aren't there. In the latter case, the inmate will sometimes have a 'thousand-yard stare,' where he or she seems to look beyond or through you. Some inmates, particularly, those with psychosis, get eerie smiles on their faces, that hold no mirth. As the attack is incipient, these inmates can 'lose it'—shaking, yelling, and acting berserk.

Explosion and the Aftermath

The crisis will be some form of assault, either verbal or physical. As discussed throughout this text you must do whatever you must do to ensure your own safety and that of those around you, up to and including the use of force to control the inmate and the situation.

After the explosive episode, the aggressive inmate moves to the *resolution* phase in which they gradually, sometimes *very* gradually, return to baseline. Their body relaxes, cognitions improve, and their actions are less stilted and threatening. After resolution, there is often a *post-crisis depression*, which is due partly to the physical depletion one experiences after the rush of adrenaline that accompanies any threatening situation, and which is partly psychological. The inmate may be remorseful, apologetic, resentful, or merely withdrawn. In some cases, they are happy, as if blowing out tension from their body, and demonstrating to themselves, at least, that they are not a hundred percent controlled by the prison and it's staff.

SECTION IX

The De-Escalation Of Angry Inmates

CHAPTER 41

Preemptive De-escalation

In many instances the correctional officer can use the tactic of preemptive de-escalation to calm an inmate who seems to be brooding or obsessed with anything from a legitimate grievance to a delusion. An early intervention can enable the correctional officer to avert a crisis before it happens. This technique may be more useful with an inmate with whom the correctional officer is familiar as he or she will be familiar with characteristic changes in the inmate's demeanor, although, of course, the correctional officer should certainly be able to recognize any inmate's escalating irritability and frustration.

Perhaps an inmate is a little heated, but still rational. Nonetheless, they are upset. Simply ask what they want or need. If you have a solution to the problem, explain it clearly to them. Always try to explain the process. <u>Give them an idea how long it will take and what they should do in the interim</u>. Many inmates in this state will brood and then flame up if they don't know how long they have to wait or what to expect. With the proper information they de-escalate on their own. This is particularly valid with service-level complaints. This may even work when the answer is not the one they want as long as you explain why and what their options are.

If you notice that the inmate is truly irritated, however, you should not necessarily attempt to address their irritation immediately. In many circumstances, try and draw them into a conversation about a benign subject such as the weather, or another area of interest to the inmate. Such seemingly harmless topics can be used as an assessment tool. If they resist your trying to help them refocus, this tells you immediately that the situation is becoming serious, and your primary goal becomes one of preventing an escalation of the inmate's anger and frustration.

Begin by stating impartially that you believe something is upsetting them, and that they don't appear to be themselves today. Don't pose your concern as a question, such as "What's wrong with you today?" or "Why do you seem so upset? Is there some sort of a problem?" Remember, when you ask a question, you give the inmate an opportunity to simply 'close the door' and deny that there is a problem. Instead, use phrases like, "You are really down today. Something is going on." or "You looked really pissed off after your talk with your case manager." These phrases give the inmate an opening to present their problem to you without feeling they are being interrogated.

If the inmate does reveal what's upsetting them, and is willing to discuss the issue, you can use open ended questions regarding possible solutions that require them to respond, such as "I see why you are so upset, but how do you think you can take care of it?" or "What do you think can be done to resolve this?" Open-ended questions are intended to bring the inmate into the conversation by making them consider their options and offer their own solutions. This also gives the correctional officer an opening to suggest other potential solutions to their problem, or to discuss the possible ramifications of the inmate's suggestions.

> **41.1 Example: Open-ended Questions as a Threat Assessment Tool**
> **CORRECTIONAL OFFICER.** "So how do you think you can take care of the problem?"
>
> **Inmate.** "I'm gonna cut his throat. I told them not to cell me with no sex offender."

Please note however, that even open-ended questions should only be addressed to an inmate who is mildly upset or agitated, not to one who is extremely angry, much less enraged. Questions are used to 'slow down' the inmate to make them think. Enraged inmates are beyond thinking. Likewise, stop asking questions if you notice that the questions are *making* the inmate angrier. Questions demand an answer, and an angry or enraged inmate will view your continued questioning as an interrogation or a failure to understand their problem.

Correctional officers can sometimes assist inmates in developing positive outcomes by reminding them of any negative consequences that may have resulted from previous crises or problems when the inmate resorted to anger or violence. Encourage them to use the strategies they have learned to deal with difficult situations: everything from walking away, exercising, writing a kite, etc.—whatever has worked for them in the past.

Sometimes the situation can be resolved simply by allowing the inmate to tell their story in order to get 'it' off their chest. There is no need to problem solve and no need to interrupt. In such cases, listening with attention and respect is all that is needed.

> **41.2 Caution: Getting Something Off Their Chest Versus Venting**
> Correctional officers must differentiate between an inmate 'getting something off their chest' and venting. Venting can be viewed as a form of verbal aggression, albeit toward someone who is not present. The danger is that venting in and of itself becomes arousing to the inmate. Then, because he or she has allowed it, the correctional officer will have to step in and de-escalate the inmate, perhaps directing the conversation on to another topic, before the inmate has worked themselves into a state of rage. In that process, they may turn on you.
>
> In addition, venting is used by some inmates to elicit a sympathetic response by other inmates in the area, which can lead to a dangerous, possibly riotous situation (CHAPTER 54).

CHAPTER 42

Physical Organization in the Face of Aggression

In CHAPTER 5, I discussed the study of body spacing as a means of honing intuitive skills. In this segment, I will discuss the subject of body language, body spacing, and positioning on a tactical level.

Tactical concerns such as whether to sit or stand when interacting with an inmate(s), the time and location of the interview, the issues being discussed, and the history of the individual inmate all have a direct impact on a correctional officer's ability to defend himself or herself. How you stand, how you breathe, your eye contact, and your gestures are all essential factors in calming aggressive inmates. You can say all the right things, but if you look like you are afraid, irritated, or angry, your verbal interventions and commands will have little to no effect, and the situation will only get worse. An unshakeable calm, a knowledge that you can handle any violence the inmate might offer, gives you the power—and therefore, credibility—to <u>negotiate</u> a safe resolution.

How to Organize your Body

Breathe With Your Entire Torso, Not High In The Chest. When you breathe rapidly with your chest, you tend to hyperventilate, which 'tells' the brain that you're in trouble because you need more oxygen now! Deep, powerful chest breathing, where you pump the air in-and-out, on the other hand, excites the more primal areas of the brain: not flight, but fight. I strongly recommend that you master 'circular breathing' (CHAPTER 9). However, for those who aren't able to effectively use circular breathing, or when one has to teach people in a short time, the simpler method to tactical breathing, referred to here as 'numbered breathing.' is to inhale on a (your optimum) count, pause your breath on your optimum count, and exhale on your optimum count. (It's traditionally taught as 4-4-4, but many people do not breathe in that particular pattern). At any rate, people tend to calm around people who are powerfully calm themselves. Proper breathing is the quickest avenue towards that end.

42.1 Concerning Tactical Breathing Verses Crisis-fueled Breathing

Think of correctional officers who walk into volatile situations and everyone simply calms down. Think, also, of officers who escalate the situation the moment they arrive. Were you to track their respective breathing patterns, you would probably be able to predict what was going to happen after observing two or three breaths.

Standing or Sitting. You always have to judge if you should be standing up or sitting down as you converse. In the office setting, you will most likely be seated, and your office furniture should be arranged to facilitate your safety. However, remaining seated when someone is menacing you is unwise. You will be standing in the yard or the tiers, and of course, in any tactical situation. At these times you should be aware of potential avenues of escape, and not allow yourself to be maneuvered into a position where your exit route is blocked.

Move Slowly and Smoothly. Agitated inmates, particularly those who are suffering from mentally illness, startle easily, and any sudden movements or gestures on your part may be interpreted as an attack, or simply surprise the inmate into a physical reaction. [NOTE: Explaining what you are doing can often calm down the confused or fearful inmate, because they fear – and attack – what they don't understand.] By breathing slowly and moving smoothly, you are trying to get the inmate to mirror your actions and attitude. Not surprisingly, overt frustration, anger, or hostility toward the inmate will cause them to become more fearful and/or aggressive, increasing the likelihood of a physical altercation. Don't make any sudden moves, unless the fight has started. (In that case, of course, you need to be moving faster and more powerfully than your attacker).

Establish Eye Contact. In most cases, try and establish some type of eye contact. As with the other aspects of body language discussed above, you must be both non-threatening and non-threatened. Glaring at the inmate with hostility or darting your gaze around nervously will just serve to make the inmate more ill at ease, and may actually cause them to attack preemptively.

- Some inmates in psychotic states find eye contact to be very invasive. When they are calm, or only slightly agitated, angle your body ('blade stance') in such a way so that they don't feel confronted, and limit eye-contact (while still being aware of their hands and feet). Even with these inmates, however, you must make eye contact to establish control if they escalate into real aggression.
- Some inmates may be so intimidating that you feel apprehensive about making eye contact with them. Others are so chaotic, manipulative, or disorganized that you find yourself unable to focus on what to do or say when your eyes meet. In situations like these, look between their eyes, at the bridge of the nose or the center of the forehead. You will find yourself far calmer, and the inmate, *if aggressive*, will not be able to tell the difference. You will just appear very strong.
- There is a disinterested 'no-eye-contact' (CHAPTER 51) that can be used with *aggressive-manipulative* people: in essence, you look past one ear, while still being aware, of course, of their hands and feet.

Regardless of the exact nature of the situation or the inmate's mental state, never look away from the aggressive inmate. If you turn your attention away from the inmate for even an instant you have given them an opportunity to attack undetected. An attack takes but a split second, especially in close quarters, despite your body positioning and spacing. The inmate must be aware that *you* are aware.

Stand at an Angle. This is sometimes called a 'blade stance,' because you stand with one foot in front of the other, the back foot at a forty-five-degree angle with some space between, thus angling your body. Don't line your feet up, heel to heel ('T-Stance'). There should be at least a fist or two spaces between where your heels fall on the "east-west" axis. Interestingly, this combatively effective stance is calming, as the inmate can tolerate your proximity better than if you were standing squarely in front of them, a more confrontational posture.

You should also sit with a 'seated blade stance.' Sit on the edge of your chair, which is slightly angled, with your lead foot flat on the floor, and the other placed on the ball of the foot. Your lead foot is directly at the inmate, with the trailing foot a little to the side. You look interested and attentive, but in fact, you can easily get up without the use of your hands, or need to lean forward to get back on your feet.

Space Between You and the Inmate. Don't stand too close to the inmate, particularly one who is emotionally or psychologically distressed. Correctional officers can't lose sight of the fact that inmates also have a sense of personal space, and some inmates, especially those suffering from mental illness, may have an *extreme* view of personal spacing issues. Some of these inmates will see any intrusion into their zone as an attack, and may respond with violence. Correctional officers have to carefully consider how close they get to an aggressive or disorganized inmate. <u>You should be able to define, tactically, why you are close to the inmate. If there is not a good tactical reason, give them more space, so that the inmate doesn't feel pressured or intimidated.</u> Finally, do not get so absorbed in communicating with them that you are not aware of their agitation at your proximity.

Don't Allow the Inmate to Stand Too Close to You. Just as correctional officers must be aware of proper spacing between themselves and the inmate, they must also warn the inmate when he or she approaches too closely. If an inmate keeps trespassing into personal space, tell them calmly something like, "Inmate Rigaki, I know this is important to you, but you are standing too close. Step back three steps and you can tell me the rest of the situation." You should not display any signs of fear or unease. By responding calmly and firmly, you are letting the inmate know that you are alert and aware of danger, as well as able to take care of yourself. Of course, if they do not immediately comply, then you must shift to commands and prepare to defend yourself.

Keep Your Hand Quiet. When communicating with an aggressive inmate, correctional officers should minimize hand gestures and other movements that could be misinterpreted as an attack. When adopting a comfortable stance, clasp one wrist with the other hand. Don't clasp one hand in the other because you may begin wringing them unconsciously if you get nervous, making you look scared and perhaps evoking the aggression you are trying to avoid. The same thing can occur if you keep your hands 'open.' The adrenalin may make your hands tremble or you simply won't know what to do with them.

By clasping your wrist, you broaden yourself slightly. You will feel solid rather than nervous. Furthermore, you can easily bring your hands upwards to fend off or block a strike if you have to, without looking like you are ready to do so. There is no apparent fight in your stance, just strength.

Use Your Hands as a Calming Fence. Fences lend a feeling of security.[30] When you place both of your hands, in front of you, palms out, you establish a boundary between you and the inmate. The arms should angle from the body at about thirty degrees, and the hands should be relaxed and curved slightly. Your hands should be relaxed, and not clenched in a rigid, fighting posture. Your hands and arms should express that you are closed off to physical contact, but open to listening. Of course, were an inmate to come close enough their body or hands touch yours, physical contact must be interpreted as assault. You can use your upraised hands to push away or fend off the inmate if necessary.

Another option is to hold your hands at about chest height, palms up, with the back of one hand in the palm of the other. In this case, you can 'talk' a little with your hands, moving them in unison. You are moving naturally, but at the same time minimizing your gestures. The advantage of this posture, however, is that your hands are higher, even more ready to ward off an attack. If the inmate amps up, you can turn your hands outwards in a 'fence,' and as they come back down, turn the palms back inwards.

PHYSICAL ORGANIZATION IN THE FACE OF AGGRESSION

Interview stance

Ready stance

> ### 42.2 One Hand versus Two
> Paradoxically, holding up *one* hand, although weaker from an unarmed combative perspective, is more likely to provoke the inmate. Rather than a fence, a single hand becomes the leading point of a triangle, your shoulders being the other two points. Inmates may experience this as if your hand is up to shut their mouth. Of course, if you need to keep your other hand on your weapon, that supersedes such considerations.

Don't Touch the Irritated Person Hoping to Calm Them Down. Of course, the only times you will touch any inmate should be to handcuff them, physically control them, or protect yourself.

Try to Get the Inmate to Sit Down. Pacing and stomping around is stimulating, and when you are standing, you are readier to fight. On the other hand, we associate sitting with peaceful communication. Have the inmate sit down, or a chair or bunk is not immediately available, have the inmate escorted to an area, i.e., watch commander's office, counselor's office, etc. where the inmate can sit and be contained away from the inmate general population. Should the inmate repeatedly rise out of their chair, the situation is obviously escalating. In any meeting when you both are seated, if the inmate stands, you should stand as well, because otherwise you are at an immediate disadvantage.

If Inmate Attempts to Disengage. In situations where you do not need to place the inmate in custody or restraint, and they try to disengage to cool down—let them. Assaults frequently occur when the inmate tries to disengage, but the correctional officer insists on working things out *right now*. Of course, if they must be detained for institutional or safety reasons, if the inmate is too enraged, or has overtly threatened to commit an act of violence *after* they leave, then safety becomes the correctional officer's more immediate concern, and the inmate must be detained until the issue is resolved satisfactorily.

42.3 One Officer's Experience: Inmates Waving their Hands or Standing When They Should Be Seated

Honesty is usually the best way to go with inmates that are not out of control but are agitated. There have been many situations in which I have told an inmate that I can't concentrate on what they are say if they wave their arms around while they are speaking. If they ask if I am scared (about them waving their arms around) I tell them I'm not scared but I am careful! But mostly I want to hear what they have to say and for me to be able to concentrate I need to not have their arms waving around my face.

I use the same logic to get inmates to sit down while they talk to me. This gives me (a five-foot two-inch female) at least a second of get away time from a larger, agitated, potential adversary. When they ask if I'm scared, I tell them: "I'm only five foot two and I prefer to look people in the eye while I listen rather than get a crick in my neck—everyone is taller than me." If they won't sit down or quit waving their hands—these are signs that I need to leave or get back up.

CHAPTER 43

Tone and Quality of Your Voice

Use a firm, low pitch. When facing an aggressor, try to pitch your voice a little lower than is usual for you; it should also be firm and strong. An angry person will focus on your tone rather than the content of your words. Don't betray any negative or angry emotions. A bored tone with either impatience or condescension is guaranteed to evoke more anger, not less. A calm, low-pitched voice communicates to the inmate that you are in control of yourself and the situation.

When you pitch your voice lower, you feel a little vibration in your chest. Under stress, our voices tend to go up in pitch. When you feel the vibration of your voice in your chest, you get immediate feedback that you have taken control back of your own body, restoring your sense of power.

Also, throughout the animal kingdom, a low vibration in the chest is a signal of dominance.

Slow down. Generally, you should speak a little slower than the inmate you are de-escalating. By slowing down, you are trying to get them to resonate with your slower energy, and also to keep yourself from being swept up in their aggression. However, don't speak with an exaggerated slow-motion quality, or they will think you are trying to hypnotize them.

Don't be condescending. When communicating with an angry inmate, don't use a condescending or patronizing tone. Talking to inmates, even those with a mental illness as if they were children, will cause them to become even more angry and agitated.

When necessary, give loud firm commands. For inmates who are very disorganized or angry, the use of a low-pitched voice may not be effective, because it won't penetrate through the fog of their hysteria or agitation. Whenever necessary, correctional officers should give the inmate clear, firm, and loud commands to cease and desist. You let the inmate know that you are in command, while at the same time offering them an opportunity to negotiate a safe resolution to the crisis.

Use of a dramatic voice Sometimes the best tactic is to use a dramatic voice, loud and somewhat enthusiastic, using charisma to grab attention. This is particularly true with some inmates who have a childish demeanor, perhaps suffering from dementia or those who are developmentally disabled. I will sometimes accompany this voice with broad physical gestures, making a bit of a drama out of the whole thing.

> **43.1 Example of the Use of a Dramatic Voice**
>
> A developmentally disabled inmate is upset because she thinks people in the dining area are laughing at her. You say, "Dobson, I SEE you are upset! Now COME ON over here and tell me about it!" Indicate with your body where you want her to go, moving as if you are absolutely certain she will comply. "C'mon. I want you to tell me EXACTLY what happened! EVERY word! Let's go over here where no one can bother us!"
>
> Show her that not only are you giving her your complete attention, but the drama means that she is important, the center of the action. By moving her somewhere else to talk, you remove her from the scene that is upsetting her.

When to use the 'battle cry.' When the inmate is moving toward you to attack, or is otherwise presenting immediate danger to another you should roar like a lion to startle and freeze the inmate's motion momentarily with commands like "STAY BACK" or "STEP AWAY," so you can evade, counter, or escape. The way you do this is as follows:

- Open your eyes WIDE!
- "Slam" your stomach BACKWARD to try and connect your navel and your spinal column.
- Tighten your throat. (This will be a little painful to some people, leaving a raw throat for the next day, but it's worth it if it saves you or someone else from harm.)
- **ROAR** a command.

> **43.2 Choice of Words for a Battle Cry**
>
> When an inmate, already close to you, is moving toward you with hostile intent, don't command that they "Stop" Or "Freeze" They may <u>comply</u> and still be too close. Instead, command that they **"Step Back"** or **"Move Back"** or **"Back Off."**
>
> The commands **"Stop"** or **"Freeze"** should be used to arrest an action that will, in itself, result in harm; for example, if an inmate is about to assault another person, throw something, or to shock them into momentary immobility, so that you can effectively deploy a mass of officers or a weapon to stop their threat.
>
> **"Get down on the ground!"** or **"On the floor, now!"** are combative orders, with immediate negative consequences for non-compliance.

CHAPTER 44

Across the Spectrum of Anger

All of the de-escalation techniques outlined in this section are for an inmate between 20-95 on the aggression scale. They are contraindicated with an enraged inmate who is between 95-99. (CHAPTER 38)

> **44.1 Strategies for Angry Inmates Versus Enraged Inmates**
> Strategies used to de-escalate angry people don't work with <u>enraged</u> inmates. In fact, they will very likely further escalate the situation. Imagine trying to 'validate' a berserk drug intoxicated individual in a psychotic state: "I see you want to rip my brains out of my skull and smear them on the walls. You've been having a rough day today."
>
> Conversely, using strategies that are suitable for enraged people (control tactics) with angry ones will flame them upwards *into* rage. Imagine coming home and your spouse tells you that he or she is not happy at all that you forgot the groceries in the trunk of the car, and you say, "Step back. Give me five feet right now!" It's all about using the right tactics.

The correctional officer must always center themselves before stepping into the conflict and establishing control of the situation and the inmate. (If you have properly trained in the procedures in SECTION III, centering is an almost instantaneous act.)

If you don't establish safety for yourself and others, you can be of no assistance to the inmate, or anyone else. This does not mean that you should cease talking with, reassuring, or negotiating with the inmate. What the author means is that everything you do must have a tactical basis. In the sections that follow, the reader will be introduced to a variety of de-escalation techniques, some of which may appear to be polar opposites of each other. Some are applicable over a wide range of circumstances, whereas others may only be useful in very specific situations. You use them like a jazz musician uses notes and phrases: to improvise as best fits the scene.

Here are some guidelines for handling the angry inmates, many of which may also prove useful for those who suffer from mentally illness. Do remember that inmates suffering from mental illness may present a somewhat different problem regarding de-escalation as opposed to 'regular' inmates, because their fears, concerns, and outbursts may be due to their illness, and not necessarily their desire for something specific:

De-escalate, and then solve the problem. Your focus should be on what the inmate is doing, not the cause of their anger. <u>You can't solve a problem with an angry person. Solving a problem with an angry person is like trying to feed a baby that is too hungry to eat</u>. First eliminate the anger, and then engage in problem-solving.

Officer presence. The correctional officers' presence can sometimes be enough to calm an inmate down. 'Presence,' however, does not merely mean that you are 'there.' It means that you have established, through your stance and demeanor, an authority that can't be ignored. This, absolutely, does not always mean 'looming' over the inmate, or presenting the intention of an immediate use of force if your directives are not complied with. Rather, 'presence' is assuming the right stance and attitude to most likely achieve compliance on the part of the inmate.

Watchful waiting. A crisis always requires a moment-by-moment decision on the best course of action. Sometimes, all that is necessary is that you remain centered and ready, as the inmate calms himself or herself without any assistance from anyone else. This does NOT mean that you ignore them, but sometimes the best control tactic is letting them control themselves.

Trust your hunches. As the author has noted several times throughout this book, correctional officers should pay attention to their 'gut feelings.' If you have a vague sense that something is wrong with the inmate, you are probably right. Assess the inmate's behaviors, both verbal and non-verbal. What do you see? Have you seen this pattern before? How is the inmate interacting with other people? Have they been having any problems recently? What is different now from the way they act normally?

One point of contact. When *de-escalating* an inmate, only one person should be communicating with them. This becomes more relevant the angrier they become. Trying to talk to two or more people at once, particularly if *they* are not in complete agreement, will cause the angry inmate to become more and more confused, as well as making him or her feel surrounded and overwhelmed. <u>This does not imply that only one person should be present with the inmate—of course you have back-up. Just make sure that one officer, only, should be talking.</u>

Be what you want *them* to be. Speak calmly, control your breathing, and maintain an upright and non-threatening posture, all the while remaining ready to respond to any attack. Your intention is that the inmate will *template* to your behavior and demeanor. This is not an unattainable goal. In a crisis situation people tend to mirror the behavior of the most powerful individual with whom they are interacting. If correctional officers are out of control, the inmate will feel even more threatened, and become even more aggressive. If you are calm, however, you can imbue the situation with that calm.

Tell me—don't show me. As elementary a suggestion as this might sound, the following illustrates the power of this intervention. An inmate, very upset, begins swearing at a correctional officer. She replies, "Inmate Clifford, it is absolutely clear that you are upset. Furious! And I am <u>able</u> to help you with this. But I won't do that when you swear at me. You can tell me why you are upset; you don't need to show me."

Demonstrate empathy. Empathy is not the same as sympathy, that feeling of sorrow for the person's plight. Empathy simply means that you understand, approximately, what other people are feeling based on their physical organization, what they say and how they say it. Use phrases such as, "I understand you are…." or "What you are saying really makes sense." Or "I imagine I'd feel the same way…." We thereby demonstrate that we grasp what the inmate is experiencing without necessarily agreeing with it.

44.2 Caution: DO NOT Overuse Empathic Techniques
Don't overuse this, or you will sound like a parody of a therapist. You will either be viewed with contempt or accused of trying to manipulate the inmate. (For many inmates, being understood is being 'tracked,' and being tracked is being controlled.) Like everything else I have discussed, it is tactical communication, to be used sparingly at just the right time.

Be professional. Some officers act in far too friendly and informal a manner. Professional distance gives the subject of your attention a clear understanding of the true nature of your relationship with them. Correctional officers should not allow inmates to call them buddy, pal, dude, babe, or any other form of casual address that implies a friendship or intimate relationship. Furthermore, you are not CO's, much less 'guards' or 'screws.' Conversely, the officers should address inmates with human respect. Use their name, not just "Hey you."

Stealth team up. Incorporate them into your 'team' by talking to them with 'stealth agreements.' When they accept something you say, even unconsciously, they begin to feel that they are working with you, not against you. In short, 'you and me become we.' Such statements as listed below are helpful in teaming:
- "Let's you and me go over here."
- "Yes, we do have a problem. Let's see what we can do to figure this out."

Give praise for their good ideas and/or positive acts. Don't be over-effusive, but highlight any positive moves the inmate makes. <u>Seriously: many of your inmates have had so little positive feedback in their lives that they can perceive a little praise as a major thing. This will encourage them to offer more productive solutions</u>. However, praise is not a 'put up,' to make them feel good, as if a few mere compliments will solve everything. 'Ride' the praise into a problem-solving solution. Note the examples listed below:
- "I like that idea! I think we can make it work. You have a few phone calls to make."
- "I'm impressed how you decided to ignore that guy. You are making some good decisions lately. If you can bring that attitude home with you, you could conceivably get out of here on time. Honestly, if you can handle the kind of b.s. that guy was trying to give you—you can handle the last few months here."

Humor. This is the ability to see a situation from another perspective, can sometimes work like magic. However, you must be careful—it only is helpful when the inmate is at low levels of escalation—irritation—rather than strong anger. If they are too upset or agitated, their response to a joke or humorous comment is likely to be, "You are making fun of me," or "This is serious. You think this is a joke?"

> **44.3 Author's Experience (Not in a Correctional Environment)**
> Many years ago, this author was in a social gathering, a mixed-race group, when one of the men, an ex-con with a history of assaults, started singing a little song, "I got a bullet for every white man here, because everyone should die." I smiled at him and said, "That won't work on me. I can only be killed by a silver bullet, followed by garlic and a stake through the heart." I looked at him blandly, and he gave me a momentary hard stare. Then we both broke into laughter, and the atmosphere in the room lightened considerably.

Distract. Particularly with cognitively impaired inmates, it is often best to simply distract them. Their anger is driven by feelings and sensations, rather than by what they are thinking. If you can change the focus of their attention, their anger often dissipates.

Honesty is golden. In any interaction with any inmate, correctional officers must be honest and forthright, never making promises (or threats) that can't be kept. This is especially true when de-escalating an angry and potentially aggressive inmate. Don't try to fool the inmate or agree to their demands in the heat of the moment. If you do suggest a solution, be clear as to what the limitations are, and exactly what your legal responsibilities are as a correctional officer. The last thing you should do is leave the inmate feeling betrayed after the incident has been resolved. In fact, should the inmate receive an adverse action, the correctional officer has a responsibility to advise them of the violation process (after the crisis has been resolved safely), and of any recommendations you will make for evaluations, treatment options, or transfer to an appropriate facility.

You will never get 'X,' but 'Y' is a possibility. If you think of de-escalation as negotiation, then you have the opportunity to achieve a compromise solution to the problem. Because the inmate is very unlikely to realize their original goal, whatever it is, you can offer them a secondary goal or solution. However, since many inmates take negotiation as concession, believing they will get everything they demand, you must be absolutely clear with them, "You want X, but X simply can't happen. I'm going to offer you Y."

Keep in mind that with de-escalation of *angry* inmates, you are not trying to intimidate them into giving up, but rather to have the inmate *choose* a second or third option because they eventually realize that they are not going to accomplish their original intentions. (The tactics and intent are different with an enraged or violent inmate.)

Preserving the inmate's self-respect: A safety tactic when in negotiation mode. Regardless of the inmate's motivations, correctional officers should allow the inmate to save face. Try to resolve the situation so that the inmate can separate with pride intact. Even if they have not achieved their original goal, the inmate should at least have a certain amount of respect for the professional way that the correctional officer handled the situation.

Another point I would like to make here is that word of your behavior as a correctional officer travels quickly through the prison. Indeed, one of my consultants, a veteran correctional sergeant, can recall a number of occasions when, on meeting a new inmate for the first time, They said something like, "Yeah, I heard about you. You are stand-up." On the other hand, if you treat an inmate in a disrespectful manner, lie to them, or go back on your word, your reputation will precede you when dealing with other inmates, leading to confrontational relationships where you go.

A private space. As a general rule, de-escalation is best accomplished without an audience, although this is often unavoidable. Correctional officers also need to judge when to intervene with an inmate who is either violating a rule or policy or is clearly not following staff instructions. As an example, an inmate who takes an extra helping of dessert in a crowded dining hall should be dealt with later when he exits the dining hall rather than being confronted over a relatively minor infraction in front of scores of his peers where he may feel compelled to act out, thus escalating a minor incident into a major occurrence. Crowds always make things worse:
- Disorganized inmates may be frightened by onlookers.
- Enraged or more predatory inmates may become excited by the crowd or begin to attack others who are present.
- 'Bluffers' may be afraid they will lose face. Therefore, in front of others they feel they have to remain aggressive or obstinate.
- Manipulative inmates will use the crowd to their own advantage, by acting out to an even greater degree in an attempt to turn the onlookers against you.

CHAPTER 45

Diamonds in the Rough: Essential Strategies for De-escalation of Anger

Codes for Living: Following the Access Route

Inmates, perhaps even more so than others, have a set of codes by which they live. Some of those codes are based on the culture into which they are born, and others are based on the culture or lifestyle they adopt. Some of these codes are passed down within a family, or inmates may create a code in reaction or resistance to the social codes they were handed. Then there are the codes of whatever prison gang they may affiliate with, while other inmates develop their own credo, unique to themselves. Inmates with mental illness may develop an eccentric set of rules congruent only with their mental illness or character disorder.

The heart of their code is often a phrase or two words that sum up their deepest values. When people talk about themselves, their codes of living are often woven throughout their speech. This is especially true with an angry person, whose reason(s) for their outrage is often their belief that their code is being threatened or compromised:
- They perceive that others are demanding they violate their code.
- They believe they are facing a choice that, if wrongly decided, forces them to violate their code.
- They take offense when others don't conform to their code.
- They think another's actions require them to respond, lest they violate their code.

Angry inmates will very often proclaim their values and code for living in their explanation or tirade, and correctional officers should be able to identify that core value in 1 or 2 words or phrases.

45.1 Examples of Personal Codes

Inmate 1. "I'm a man. He can't talk about me that way."
Inmate 2. "Think of how I feel. If someone did that to you, wouldn't you be upset?"
Inmate 3. "Are you saying I'm not going to get transferred? I did the job and you owe me. Whether you like it or not isn't the issue, you owe me!"
Inmate 4. "I was standing there all alone. Everyone was looking at me. Talking about me!"

What is most important to each of these inmates in the above examples?
- Inmate 1's is pride.
- Inmate 2's is empathy (AKA, "You don't get what I feel and you should.")

- Inmate 3's is mutual obligation.
- Inmate 4's is fear of being shamed.

The code is an access route to the inmate. **Use the code to reach the inmate.** When you incorporate their code in your response, you are recognizing (<u>not approving</u>!) the inmate's values, however misguided or anti-social they may be. This is what the inmate often means by 'respect.' This connection, however tenuous, allows you to work with the inmate toward a resolution. Take note of the following:

- If you perceive that personal integrity is a core issue of concern to a male inmate, frame your responses with the same theme. "I wouldn't want people talking about you as a man who can't control himself."
- To the young inmate who believes someone treated him with disrespect (an enormous source of conflict and violence within any prison): you can say "Man, I can see how angry you are. I'd be angry too if someone said that to me, but if you try to hurt him, you'll end up losing. You'll lose your program, your 'good time,' your job and your visiting privileges. Yeah, I know you think he *disrespected* you, but if you assault him, you would be letting him *own* you. He says three words, and your response means you lose your chance at getting back to your family in less than three months! Is that what you want?"
- Sometimes a code is situational, something as simple as the weather. "Look, Frank, it's a hot day, I'm tired, and I guess you are too. I don't care who's right here, really. I just want to finish this paperwork so you can get that appointment with your psychiatrist. The computers are down and so is the air conditioning, so we have to figure out some other way to get through to them. These days are nasty. Here we are, all stressed out just because we're both hot and tired."
- An inmate with a psychological disorder can get so focused on an issue that they get 'tunnel vision,' and it is all they can think about. In effect, the problem defines their existence at the moment. A correctional officer replies, "You are absolutely right, those meds are disgusting. They must taste terrible, but if they didn't work so well, your doctor wouldn't ask you to take such foul-tasting things. But they do work, don't they?"

Break the Pattern

Correctional officers often find themselves in the same argument(s) over and over again, and often with different inmates! In order to detect any patterns or behaviors that may have negatively affected your communication with an inmate, you can easily perform an After-Action Review of your *own* actions and responses in past disputes, noting 'hot buttons' (CHAPTER 8). Honest self-reflection will quickly reveal any patterns of behavior, personal style, even *your* personal codes, that may have had a detrimental effect on your relationship with a particular inmate, or group of similar inmates. As with any occupation, correctional officers can get 'caught in a rut' that only deepens with prolonged interaction with inmates, especially those who suffer from mental illness.

At times however, you may be forced to more dramatically break the pattern of interaction between you and an inmate, by doing or saying something that makes continuing the dispute absolutely impossible.

In many cases, you will use a dramatic voice or display somewhat uncharacteristic or unexpected behaviors. This technique is not recommended for 'routine' episodes of de-escalation, and most definitely not as an opening in any encounter. However, breaking the pattern can be effective because many inmates expect their victims, including correctional officers, to react in a somewhat predictable manner to their displays of threat, anger or violence. By reacting in an unanticipated manner, you can throw the inmate off balance. This tactic can work with very angry individuals. It sometimes takes the fight out of the interchange like suddenly letting out the air from a tire.

Breaking the pattern may seem like magic, but instead, this is a highly intuitive skill that is developed with time and experience. Because future behavior is unpredictable, correctional officers can't prepare an array of specialized catch-phrases or tactics, ready to disarm an aggressive or disturbed inmate. This technique is pure improvisation, grounded in the same strong and powerful calm that we have written about throughout this manual. If you *consciously* try to be creative, or if you are excited about what a hilarious thing you are about to say, you may indeed say something funny, but it will be at the wrong time, to the wrong inmate. When you are in control of yourself, with the mainline skills of de-escalation at hand, such improvisation will simply emerge. Below are a few examples of breaking the pattern:

45.2 Breaking the Pattern #1 "I Know Where You Live"

One correctional officer, new at a prison, was walking across the yard and was spotted by an inmate who went to the same high school. In front of other inmates, he yelled out, "Hey, I know where you live!" Without even turning, she said over her shoulder, "Everybody knows where I live," and kept walking.

The other inmates began laughing at the first one, and she did not have trouble from him subsequently (of course, she upped her precautions, just in case.

45.3 Breaking the Pattern #2 with a Mentally Disturbed Inmate

One severely disturbed inmate had a compulsion to shred his sheets and mattress. When he ran out of that, he began smearing feces on the walls.

One officer gave him a large paper bag, with very strict instructions. He was told to carefully tear the bottom of the bag off, leaving a three-inch rim all the way around. He was then told to shred the paper in pieces no more than two millimeters in size, and fill up the bottom of the bag. When he finished, he would receive another paper bag.

In this case, it worked. The inmate was not destroying things out of a sense of malevolence. It was a compulsion, part of his illness, and he was absolutely happy to work on the paper bags, thereby eliminating both property destruction and the feces smearing.

45.4 Breaking the Pattern #3 in a Forensic Unit

An officer in a forensic unit for the criminally insane has, over the years, frequently been threatened with assault. In every case, he responds with something like "What? I don't have a Ford 150. I like Dodges, but they aren't so good this year."

Inmate "I'm not talking about trucks. I'm talking about pounding your face in!"

Officer "Sorry I don't have time for that now. All I can think about is trucks. Do you think, maybe, I should get a Toyota? I hear they are good, but I don't know about buying a foreign truck. But I hear they use a lot of American parts."

Inmate "I'm not talking about trucks. I'm gonna kick your ass!"

Officer "No, seriously. You think maybe a Ford is OK?"

The officer told me that, invariably, about this point, the inmate stomps off, muttering something about him being crazy or an idiot. He has never been assaulted in the time he has worked there.

45.5 Important Caution on Breaking the Pattern

Sometimes a 'breaking the pattern' strategy makes a funny story later. For example, I recall one law enforcement officer accused of a repulsive sexual act by individual resisting arrest, and the officer yelled out, pretending to be frustrated and embarrassed, "Goddam it. You make one mistake fifteen years ago and they never let you forget."

The arrestee put up his hands, and comforting said, "Whoa brother. It's OK. I made a few bad one's myself. You get over it after a while," and then turned around, bent over the officer's car and allowed himself to be hand-cuffed.

[Parenthetically, is that not the epitome of 'officer presence?' One phrase and a resisting individual not only complies with the arrest, but offers the officer emotional support in the process!]

I chose that story to illustrate the sometimes funny, sometimes absurd situations that can occur. The truth is, however, that if you try to 'make a legend,' say something funny, look at your team and say, "Watch this . . ." The strategy will backfire. The inmate will be insulted, feel degraded or enraged. Why? Because in this instance, you are doing it at the inmate's expense.

When this strategy works, you aren't smiling or amped up, thinking how well this will play later. Rather, you are absolutely calm, and something, as deep as the marrow of your bones, says, "This is what needs to be said to take control and calm things down." <u>If you are not calm, centered, AND ready for things to go sideways anyway, then don't use a 'break the pattern' strategy.</u>

Some Guidelines for Limit Setting

As soon as you draw a line, it will become the main focus of your interchange. Don't ever set a limit that you cannot enforce or one that is not reasonable and simple to understand.

Beleaguered by mental illness, struggling with substance abuse, beaten down by poverty or unemployment, inmates often experience their lives fragmenting into pieces. When the rules shift, they can become profoundly anxious. When dealing with such people, **limit setting** is a kindness rather than oppression.

The following will help in setting a "full stop" limit:

Your tone of voice should be matter-of-fact, rather than critical. Simply <u>remind</u> them of the rule or <u>set</u> a proper limit (a new rule, so to speak).

Give clear directives with no wiggle room. For example, you say in a confident, commanding voice, "Inmate Taylor, lower your voice."

Give praise if he complies. Give him a brief mark of 'approval' and continue with the verbal control.

If he does not comply with the directive, depersonalize the reiteration. "Inmate Taylor, you are required to lower your voice." Don't say, "I expect you to…." The individual should experience what you are saying as the 'law,' an institutional command or policy, rather than a personal issue between the inmate and you.

Don't get them caught up in manipulative word games. Don't respond to professed ignorance, excuses, or confusion. You are using this tactic because there is no ambiguity regarding the transgression and no ambiguity as to what the consequence will be.

Silence

Sometimes, the most powerful thing you can do is to be silent. Be sure that you are not being passive-aggressive, fuming in silent anger, or appearing to ignore or dismiss the inmate. Instead, you should wait, quietly and powerfully. Keep your facial expressions calm, your posture centered, and carefully listen. Nod your head calmly as you listen, doing so slowly and intermittently. In many cultures, including the United States, nodding your head too rapidly indicates that you want the other person to hurry up and finish, or worse, just shut up.

Silence, however, is not that easy, particularly for the person who is suffering the brunt of another's anger. There are three ways to listen silently, and two of them will make people angrier.

Contemptuous silence. You are tired of the dispute, and tired of the inmate. You fidget, you sigh, and most significantly, you roll your eyes upwards to one side, and twist one corner of your mouth. In almost every culture, this facial expression and behavior express an attitude of contempt, and is guaranteed to provoke anger or rage. (Think of how mad you get when your teenager does this.)

Stonewall silence. When you stonewall, your demeanor shows that you have no interest in what they have to say or why they are saying it. You can to do this inadvertently by entering notes into a file while the inmate is talking, or by taking a phone call during an interview. Other times, it is calculated and deliberate. Such dismissive behavior can evoke anxiety or anger in the inmate who wants to get through to you, only to find that there's a 'wall' in the way. As a result, the inmate will do anything to 'get through to you,' including trying to tear down that wall.

In addition to upsetting the inmate, such indifferent behaviors on your part will also increase risk, and decrease your ability to defend yourself from attack because your attention is improperly focused on your computer screen or your telephone conversation, instead of where it should be—on the inmate.

Interested silence. This is the right way to listen silently. When you have been listening quietly, the inmate often interrupts to ask, "Aren't you going to say something?" or "Don't you have any ideas?" If they don't stop, and continue to talk and talk, *you* may have to interrupt them. Do this by advancing a hand slightly at waist level or a little higher, fingers curved, palms down. (You don't want the inmate to interpret your hand movement as a 'shut up' gesture.) You should also lean toward the inmate slightly, indicating that it's your turn to speak. If they don't notice your hand gesture, put both hands up in front of you in a 'fence,' and tell them to stop a moment, in a voice that is loud and holds a little humor. "Inmate Schultz, wait a minute. You 'gotta' give me a chance to say something! Listen to me a second!"

After interrupting the inmate, the first thing you should do is to sum up your understanding of what he or she just said. This proves that you were indeed listening to them, and are interested in solving their problem. Once you have summed it up, you can either go into problem-solving mode, or, if they are still heated, shift into "tactical paraphrasing" (CHAPTER 46).

CHAPTER 46

Tactical Paraphrasing: The Gold Standard with Angry and Agitated Inmates Suffering from Mental Illness

What Is Paraphrasing?

Paraphrasing is perhaps the most important technique for calming **angry** individuals. You sum up in a phrase or sentence what the angry inmate has just said in a paragraph. If you paraphrase accurately, you have established that you have 'gotten' it that far, so they don't have to repeat it, or try to say it in other words.

If you <u>don't</u> show that you 'get' it, the inmate will feel compelled to repeat and/or elaborate that layer of the problem with more and more intensity. As they get more intense, they usually get more irrational, and their ability to communicate breaks down even further. <u>The best thing about paraphrasing is that you don't have to be 'smart' and interpret anything. You simply have to listen carefully</u>.

It is like peeling off a single layer of an onion so that you can be shown the next one. As you peel off each layer, the inmate gets to the next layer that is driving them. They might start out complaining about a correctional officer who sanctioned them for an infraction, and that paraphrased, they tell you that their wife lost her job and if they don't get out in time for Christmas, the family will be in financial trouble, and that paraphrased, tells you that their wife is threatening to move back east to live with her parents, and that paraphrased, start talking about suicide.

Paraphrasing establishes that you are truly listening and have understood what they have said. There is another component where we also take a slightly activist approach. We <u>select</u> what we will sum up from the complex, sometimes almost incoherent, communication that the inmate has just given us, choosing the *most rational* aspect of what they have just said.

This method is 'self-correcting,' whereas passive summation, called 'mirroring,' can make things worse. If you sum up an angry inmate's worst impulses, they will find themselves in agreement with you. Inadvertently, you have lined up with what desires destruction. If you sum up an aspect of what they have said that is in the direction of conflict resolution, you will draw out of them that which *does* wish to resolve the conflict. On the other hand, if they are, in fact, bent on mayhem, they will correct you by escalating what they are saying, believing that you are not getting the message. Remember, they are trying to communicate. All you have to do is paraphrase up <u>what you understand</u> from what they said. When you get it right, they go to the next layer.

> **46.1 Example of Correct and Incorrect Paraphrasing**
>
> **Angry Inmate.** "I am so mad at my daughter that I could just choke her when I get out of here!"
>
> 1. Incorrect paraphrase: "You want to murder your daughter."
>
> 2. Correct paraphrase: "You are *really* furious with her!"
>
> If you have, in two accurately paraphrased the meaning of the angry father's intention, you will naturally go on to the next layer of his complaint.
>
> **Angry Inmate.** "You won't believe what she did. My wife comes home and found her on the couch lip-locking that punk from down the street. You know, one of those scumbags who epoxies his hair in corkscrew spikes?"
>
> If, however, the second example is *inaccurate*, and he really *means* number one, the angry father will correct you with more vehemence.
>
> **Angry Inmate.** "No, *(not really furious)* I honestly intend to loop a belt around her neck and slowly strangle her. Seriously! I'm getting out in a month. She better not be home when I get back there."

<u>Why not simply ask the person what's going on? If they want to tell me, why don't they just answer the questions?</u> Asking questions is usually not a good idea with really angry inmates. They already believe you <u>have to</u> 'get' what they are saying, and a question shows that you have not done so. Still angry and now frustrated at their failure, this makes them try harder, albeit with less coherence than before. They experience failure over and over—they can't get through to you! When anger is combined with this sense of powerlessness, the inmate feels like he is 'losing' to a more powerful other. In essence, they experience a question, a demand for an answer, as putting you in a dominant position in regard to them.

> **46.2 Example: An Illustration Showing How Irritating Questions Can Be**
>
> Imagine coming home after a bad day. You are hot, tired, and frustrated. You walk into your house, drop your gear on the floor, sigh loudly, and walk toward the shower. Your spouse says, "Did you have a bad day?" Isn't this irritating? Isn't it *obvious* you've had a bad day? After all these years together, and he or she doesn't know when a bad day just walked into the house! On the other hand, imagine your spouse observing you and saying, "Bad day, huh?" You continue walking towards the shower, and say, "I don't want to talk now. I just want a shower. I'll talk to you later." You are not 'forced' to explain yourself.

How to Use Paraphrasing Successfully

It is very important that your voice is strong. You speak to the inmate as someone who has the power within to take care of himself or herself and their problem, not as someone who is fragile or volatile (even if they are). You contact the strong aspect of the inmate, the future looking side, that which is striving for strength, looking for integrity. Sometimes, you can use a dramatic summation: "You are really furious about this!" Here, you sum up the inmate's mood with your voice and posture, in addition to what is being said. If you contact the weak, or the insecure, you may foster regression to a less mature level of action. Childish action is often impulsive or violent.

46.3 Example: A Successful Use of Paraphrasing With an Inmate Suffering from Mental Illness

Inmate. "I never get enough sleep."

CORRECTIONAL OFFICER. "You look really tired."

Inmate. "I don't know how I look, but I feel exhausted!"

When you are inaccurate in your summation, the other usually corrects you. He is not arguing with you, just tuning up the signal.

CORRECTIONAL OFFICER. "You've been up late the last couple days and waking early too, and now you are really tired, aren't you?"

You can include extra information that sums up the experience the other is having. This is for the purpose of steering the inmate toward problem-solving while not giving advice. It also allows you to assess how responsive he is to you. In other words, if you add a little something, is he even able to hear it?

Inmate. "I am not tired at night."

CORRECTIONAL OFFICER. "You can't fall asleep when you hit your rack, huh?"

Notice the tag lines like, "huh?" or "aren't you?" These are not really questions. They follow statements and give the other an <u>invitation</u> to correct you or give you more information.

Inmate. "I don't even bother trying to sleep. I just lie there looking at the ceiling."

CORRECTIONAL OFFICER. "It seems like a waste of time, and then you wake up early anyway. It'd be fine if you weren't tired."

The second sentence by the officer, is an attempt to sum up what he believes are the inmate's feelings about his sleep cycle. It is also another assessment; he offers him something to agree with or correct.

Inmate. "Yeah, I'd be fine if I wasn't tired. I'd just be sleepless and do more. But I'm too tired for that. I wonder if I need to talk to Dr. Montour. I think I need something to help me sleep. When I don't sleep, I go crazy"

Imagine that this inmate has bipolar disorder, is very resistant to talking about his medications, but usually gets in lots of trouble when he doesn't take them. If the officer had responded to his initial statement about being tired by suggesting he go to the doctor immediately ('problem-solving'), the inmate might have angrily stopped talking or argued with him. By listening and showing step-by-step that he understood him, the correctional officer got him to find the 'buried layer' of his concern by himself.

46.4 Example of Successful Use Paraphrasing With an Inmate Who Often Becomes Suicidal when Frustrated

Female Inmate. "I can't believe it. She is so stupid!"

CORRECTIONAL OFFICER. "You are really upset!"

Inmate. "No! I'm really furious!"

Note: When you sum up imprecisely, the other usually corrects you. This is as if she were tuning up the signal rather than arguing with you. Notice, too, that the officer did not go directly to: 'Who is she?'

CORRECTIONAL OFFICER. "Inmate Scott, I haven't seen you this mad in a long time."

Note: You can include extra information ("in a long time," for example). This is for the purpose of slightly steering the person in a positive direction. It also helps to assess how responsive she is to you. In other words, if you add a little something, is she even able to hear it? In this case, you are validating that she has shown that she is able to maintain control of herself for awhile

Inmate. "I know. But nobody's ever done anything like this to me!"

CORRECTIONAL OFFICER. "This is something new, huh?"

Inmate. "Yeah, I asked her to hook up after our NA meeting, and she said "yes," and then, in front of everybody, she said she was just joking."

CORRECTIONAL OFFICER. "That must have been embarrassing!"

Inmate. "I was ashamed. It was just like when my mom left. I felt like I wasn't good enough for anybody."

You just got the story without a single question. She even trusts you enough to tell you something real about her past. Now you are in a position to do a threat assessment, to determine if she is either suicidal or has aggressive intentions towards the woman who shamed her.

Using Paraphrasing to Communicate With Individuals Who Are Severely Mentally Ill

Paraphrasing can be remarkably effective for communication with severely inmates suffering from mental illness. Given the internal chaos that people experience when psychotic, manic, or disorganized, it is essential that we don't add to their sense of confusion by barraging them with questions or attempting to solve their problems by taking over and telling them what they should feel or do.

46.5 Example of Tactical Paraphrasing With an Individual in a Severely Psychotic State
After inmates complained about Murray's 'strange behavior,' correctional officers interviewed him, and found him in what appeared to be a decompensated state.

Murray tells the officer that he was electric and that the other inmates knew he was electric and just didn't understand him. He complains of hearing voices that sometimes told him to do acts that scared him.

CORRECTIONAL OFFICER. "Pretty confusing, huh?"

Inmate. "You are darn right it's confusing. How'd you like to be in my head?"

CORRECTIONAL OFFICER. "I wouldn't want to be in a confused head. It must be hard to think."

Inmate. "Hard to think and scary. The voices say scary things. They tell me to hurt me."

CORRECTIONAL OFFICER. "You are telling me about it now. I think you want some help."

Inmate. *(nodding)* "Yeah, I don't want to bleed."

CORRECTIONAL OFFICER. "Somebody would make you bleed."

Murray. "Yeah, them, in my head. Make me bleed and other people too."

CORRECTIONAL OFFICER. "You are not bleeding now."

Murray. "Yeah, not yet. They want me to take the blade under my mattress and cut."

Notice the officer's last sentence. Notice that the officer didn't ask one question, and he or she got that the inmate is being driven to cut himself and others, and found out where the shank is. Questions could have thrown Murray off track, making his communication more confusing and harder to assess for risk. By making a matter-of-fact statement, the officer takes a lot of psychological pressure off the inmate, and it is easier for him to re-organize enough to be able to communicate.

Remember, though, that paraphrasing is self-correcting. Murray might have replied, in response to the last statement: "There's no blood out here. I'm holding it in." It's at that point you see that he's been clamping his wrist with the other hand. He lets it go and the blood from the cut veins starts pouring out.

Core

We know we have reached the core level when there is no more 'progress.' The inmate **spins his wheels**. They may use different words, but they say essentially the same thing over and over again. Some inmates express relief at being finally understood. Others exhibit an intensification of emotion, because you have reached that which is most upsetting to them. When you reach core, and it is clear that you are on the same wavelength, you can begin problem-solving. This can be:

- Further paraphrasing, where you show greater and greater understanding about what they are upset about.
- A summation of the core problem. For example, "You trusted him, and he stole your cigarettes. I can understand why you'd be so mad at him. You are due out of here in two months. You know he did this to mess up your release date, but you tell me if you don't do something, you will not survive two months. Yet you want to go home. We have to figure out a way that you can really win without getting into trouble."
- By paraphrasing them every step of the way, you establish that you are a person of trust. In some cases, you can now be quite directive, because most people are willing to accept advice or even instruction from people they trust.
- With others, we are ready to engage in a collaborative process of problem-solving, trying to figure out a way to solve the situation that is in the best interest of everyone involved.

Don't Waste It

Paraphrasing is almost a cliché, so much so that I can imagine some of you rolling your eyes when you read the title of this chapter. This technique is too important to abandon, and at the same time, it must be used carefully, i.e., *rarely*. If inmates get too used to you using paraphrasing, they will cut you off, because you will appear to them to be giving nothing back, except mirroring. It is 'cold fare' compared to a dialogue. If the individual is not angry and *requiring* you to use de-escalation tactics, don't use paraphrasing. Simply talk with them.

If there is a crisis, however, and *if* the inmate does not believe they are understood, now paraphrasing comes into its own. Paraphrasing can have an almost electrifying effect with an angry individual. Imagine the feeling when you try to pull a splinter from under your fingernail, and after ten long minutes of aggravating struggle, you get a hold of it finally and pull it out of your nail bed. That is the sense you get when, angry and desperate to be heard, you realize that the other person 'got it.'

46.6 How to master paraphrasing

If you view paraphrasing as a 'specialized,' pseudo-counseling technique, you probably won't want to do it—and you won't be good at it anyway. When you are hit by adrenaline, you will stumble over your words if you try to remember to say things like:
- "So, what you are sharing with me is . . ."
- "What I hear you saying is . . ."

Don't do this! many inmates will find you irritating, and you will be in your head at a time where you must be aware of what's going on in front of you.

You are, in fact, a master of paraphrasing. You do it all the time simply keeping a conversation going, saying things like:
- "Your kid flunked out, huh?"
- "You're not getting a raise."
- "You hate that guy."
- "She's the one."

In short, the natural statements you intersperse in any conversation are perfect paraphrasing. However, because you do this unconsciously, it's hard to tap into as an *emergency technique.*

It's easy to perfect, however. Consider this—how many conversations do you have a day? Twenty? Thirty?

In each and every conversation, at an arbitrary moment of your choosing, paraphrase the next thing they say. Just once. They won't even notice. But because you made a conscious decision to do this, your brain notices. That means you have practiced that skill twenty to forty times a day. Consider how good your tourniquet skills or firearms ability would be if you do twenty repetitions a day—it will be automatic! Similarly, if you do this every day, you will be able to step into crisis-oriented paraphrasing without hesitation. It will be so natural to you that you do not even have to think about it.

CHAPTER 47

Big Mistakes That Seemed Like Such Good Ideas at the Time

De-escalation requires on-the-scene improvisation, in a very fluid and dynamic setting, often with volatile and unpredictable inmates. In such a highly charged atmosphere, where clear communication is necessary to prevent any misunderstandings that may worsen the situation, correctional officers must think quickly, but calmly, before speaking.

By maintaining a professional emotional distance, and not reacting personally to anything the inmate may say, you will be less likely to escalate an already heated situation. Nobody is perfect; however, many mistakes are very obvious, and the moment something leaves your mouth, you think, "Uh-oh. I shouldn't have said that!" Fortunately, this can often be prevented by taking a moment to gather thoughts before responding to what the inmate has said. Sometimes holding up your hands to give them pause, will also give you time to gather your own resources, and then reply.

Some mistakes are subtler. On certain days, you may be tired, not feeling well, or be distracted by family matters perhaps, and de-escalating an angry inmate is the last thing you wish to do. Not surprisingly, risk increases when you are at less than your optimum ability and awareness, and you are more likely to make a mistake in your communications at these times. You actually need to be more alert when you are not at your best.

The following topics are areas the author believes correctional officers should take special note, so as not to make innocent mistakes that may lead suddenly to escalating encounters with angry inmates:

Ingratiation. Don't try to ingratiate yourself ('suck up') with the inmate; don't pretend that a potentially aggressive situation or encounter has not developed; and, don't ignore the aggressive behavior or language while calmly going about your business in the hopes that the inmate will eventually tire himself or herself out.

<u>We usually see this with people who really shouldn't be correctional officers</u>. They are too nice, too naïve, or too intimidated. That said, everybody has leverage points, and any one of us can slip up.

One of the paradoxes of ingratiation is that correctional officers who allow the inmate to control their interactions often present themselves as having a 'special rapport' with an inmate who, in fact, intimidates them. Oddly enough, these same officers, who try to avoid conflict, or 'make nice,' are often suppressing a lot of anger at being controlled. They displace this on those who call them on what they are doing. Thus, one of the first signs that the correctional officer is ingratiating himself or herself is an attitude of self-righteousness, a defense mechanism that enables them to avoid questioning the violations of their own integrity. The following factors are also signs of ingratiation toward the inmate:

- You worry about 'how things are going' between yourself and the inmate, and react accordingly.
- You are sometimes ashamed of your actions, or believe that you act in a cowardly fashion in the way you interact with the inmate.
- You believe you are caring and nice, so you react with shocked outrage when an inmate is blaming or aggressive toward you, as if you and the inmate have made some sort of transaction that they have now betrayed.
- You allow the other inmate to speak to you in overly familiar or rude terms.
- You are 'grateful' that an intimidating inmate seems to like you or approve of you.

The mistake of trying to find common ground. Sometimes, correctional officers will try to connect with an inmate by telling them how they must feel, by confessing to having the same issues, or claiming to have gone through a similar situation. Statements like, "I know how you feel," "I know you love your son," or "When I was in the hood . . . " are statements that the angry inmate may not agree with at all. They then decide to prove you wrong by demonstrating that they are NOT what you just said they are. Most inmates will perceive an officer talking this way as 'sucking up' to them, or if paranoid, trying to soften them up by pretending to be alike.

The mistake of allowing venting. Pure venting is an expression of energy, such as going for a run after a difficult day, or chopping wood until fatigued, so that you can 'let go' of an unpleasant incident, or just a bad day at work. However, generalized aggression expressed verbally in front of others (tantrums), or aggression expressed about one person to another is also designated by the same term.

I previously referred to letting an inmate 'get something off their chest' (CHAPTER 41). This is not the same as venting. The purpose of the former action is to get finished with something by talking about it; the purpose of the latter is to stoke oneself up into higher levels of aggression.

Many people have a false idea about aggression, and imagine it to be some kind of psychological fluid that builds up pressure inside of us. When we vent (hence the word), these people believe that we get rid of the anger and then become peaceful, similar to a valve releasing pressure from a water line. Aggression, however, is not a fluid; it is state of arousal. Just like any other state of arousal—sexuality, happiness, excited interest—additional stimuli elicit more arousal. When you shout, yell, complain, kick things, or the like, you are stimulating yourself to greater and greater aggression. Therefore, if you allow an inmate to vent, the angrier they will become.

Don't attempt to make any distinctions between venting directed at other people, and either anger or rage directed towards you. Simply consider it for what it is—aggression. When you let an inmate vent about other people, they perceive that you are giving implicit approval to their verbal complaints and abuse. If you listen to their venting silently, without de-escalating or controlling their verbal escalation, they believe you are on their side. However, when they get so angry that they start to become dangerous and *then* you object, they will turn on you. Thus, whenever an inmate begins to vent, de-escalate and control them.

Obvious mistakes we shouldn't make but do anyway. Although some of the items included in the following list have been discussed elsewhere in this book, they are repeated here as a reminder to the reader of the seemingly minor, yet crucial, details of de-escalation. Correctional officers should NOT:

- Make threats or promise consequences they can't keep. False promises or implied threats, which the inmate may know the correctional officer is incapable of keeping, will lessen your credibility. The failure to follow through on promises made or consequences threatened will also serve to undermine your authority with the inmate after the incident has been resolved.
- Bombard the inmate with choices, questions, and solutions, as this will only overwhelm the inmate, especially if they are suffering from mental illness.
- Ask an upset inmate, 'Why?' Asking a 'why' question demands an answer or an explanation from the inmate, something they may be quite unwilling, or unable, to do. "Why" questions should only be used when you have used paraphrasing to reach the core problem successfully (CHAPTER 46).
- Talk down to the inmate as if they were stupid or ignorant. Don't roll your eyes or sigh heavily while the inmate is trying to communicate with you. Don't interrupt as they speak, particularly to correct what they are saying. On the other hand, interruption of aggressive verbalizations or pointless monologues on the part of the inmate, *is* the right thing to do.
- Analyze their behavior while de-escalating. Problem-solving and evaluations can be completed after safe de-escalation.
- Share the inmate's private information in front of others.
- Take things personally when the inmate attacks your character or professionalism. The measure of the true professional is NOT taking things personally (CHAPTER 8).
- Allow the inmate to trespass on your personal boundaries, or violate theirs. The safety issues inherent in personal spacing issues are quite obvious. Safety is enhanced when one enforces a strong, professional hierarchical relationship with the inmate.
- Adopt an authoritarian or demeaning attitude, particularly in front of their peers or other onlookers, including fellow officers. Authoritarian attitudes and behaviors are some of the most common precipitants of assault by inmates.
- Tell an angry or enraged inmate to 'calm down.' It never works.

47.2 CAUTION: The Worst, Stupid, and Unethical Mistake: 'Lighting the inmate up'

Let's be honest here. Not every correctional officers is a paragon of humanity. Even most of you, the good guys, are not perfect. None of us are at our best in periods of high stress, and even less so when we are in danger, when we are demeaned, and when our best intentions are sometimes spit on or worse. When you have an inmate who is, for example, smearing feces on himself, even devouring it, and nothing you can do can stop the foul odor and behavior, it's easy to soon view the person as less than human. (This is quite apart from the fact that something is going terribly wrong that an inmate is acting in such a debased way.)

Without effective leadership and a strong sense of both solidarity and personal integrity, a group culture can arise in which correctional officers devolve into 'guards.' Group culture can lead people to egg each other on, and mild incidents of teasing can escalate into taunting and provocation.

To be quite blunt about it, it can start to get funny to 'light an inmate up.' By this, I mean saying or doing things to inflame the inmate suffering from mental illness, because the burned-out toxic group culture gets off on 'f**king with him.' Clear enough?

It happens and it's wrong. Not only is it unethical, as what is right about provoking an individual who, due to their illness, is helpless to stop their reactions and sometimes painfully ridiculous responses? Beyond that, it is unprofessional. If you rightly state that beyond all else, officers must focus on safety, how is this served when officers act in a way that justifiably would cause anyone to view them as enemies. Remember, too, that it will not only be the officer who provokes the inmate who is so regarded. Anyone wearing the uniform will be seen the same way. Not only are other officers at risk in your facility, so too, will other officers in the facility the inmate is transferred to be at risk, or police officers out on the street, and they do not even know they've been set up in this manner. Furthermore, so, too, will the officer out with his or her family in the community who is recognized by the <u>now-released, once-again-unmedicated-100%-hating-correctional-officers</u> former inmate who, as far as he or she is concerned, was psychologically tortured during their last incarceration.

It is, therefore, not only a mark of a professional to keep your own dignity and integrity. It is equally the mark of a professional to assist the inmates, even the most mentally disturbed, keep theirs as well.

SECTION X

Managing Rage and Violence

CHAPTER 48

Preface to Rage and Violence

Rage and anger are not merely different in degree; they are different modes of being, just as water, once past the boiling point, becomes steam. Frustrated inmates posture or otherwise act angrily to establish dominance, or to force agreement or compliance from others. If nothing else, their goal is to communicate their feelings, although, due to their lack of interpersonal skills, their mental illness, or the effects of drugs and/or alcohol, they often resort to anger in an attempt to make themselves heard.

The reader will recall that anger is denoted as falling between 20-95 on the aggressiveness scale (SECTION IX). This represents a very broad range of arousal, ranging from mildly irritated to truly irate. Rage however, occupies a much smaller fraction of the scale, from 95- 99. When in a state of rage, the inmate desires to commit mayhem. Enraged inmates are in a 'threshold' state, their anger and rage escalating until they have overcome any moral or personal constraints that might otherwise prohibit them from committing the ultimate expression of rage—violence.

<u>Therefore, all of the strategies described in the previous chapters dealing with the angry inmate are more or less useless with one who is truly enraged</u>. Sometimes the only viable option for the correctional officer is to remove himself or herself from the situation until reinforcements can be summoned. In others, you are suddenly in combat.

There are various types of rage, and correctional officers need to recognize what type of rage the inmate is expressing, because there are different verbal control strategies to deal with each type. Fortunately, an enraged person's behavior is quite obvious, and after reading this section of the book, you will be able to identify what type of rage the inmate is exhibiting rather easily, allowing you to employ the appropriate strategies to control them.[31]

48.1 IMPORTANT CAUTION

Here, and in several other areas of this book, I have used animal symbols to aid in the understanding of various types of rage or other behavior. For example, I use the image of a leopard or a shark in describing predatory rage.

These are thought devices, to help you 'catch' patterns of dangerous behavior in a single glance. They are not intended to be used in either paperwork or communication to describe inmates. They are descriptors of *styles* of behavior, not people.

In our hypersensitive times, such a reference to a specific inmate may be misconstrued as stigmatizing that individual as 'being an animal.' This is absolutely not intended—the images are to assist in understanding modes of behavior, not character. Nonetheless, such images should remain aids of understanding, not terms of reference.

CHAPTER 49

Chaotic Rage: A Consideration of Rage Emerging from Various Disorganized States

Chaotic rage is typified by profound disorganization of cognitive and perceptual processes, and can be engendered by severe psychosis that has 'crossed over' into a delirium state, whether engendered from mania, intoxication, drug withdrawal, severe developmental disability, senile dementia, overwhelming emotions, or as a result of brain injury or trauma. Enraged disorganized inmates are often very impulsive and unpredictable, striking out in all directions. They may not be coordinated in their actions, but they are fully committed, meaning that they have no fear of injury or consequences to hold them back. They are also often indifferent to, or unaware of, pain or injury to themselves. However, not every person in a chaotic rage state is uncoordinated: with trained fighters, combative reflexes are almost instinctive, and thus, even though they are cognitively shattered, they can still fight, throwing punches and kicks with accuracy.

I am hearing more and more reports of 'synthetic cannabinoid,' know as SPICE, being smuggled into prisons. A single dose of this class of drugs can plunge an inmate into a berserk, chaotic state—and some are using it regularly.

My symbol for this state is TAZ, the fanged, whirling tornado of arms and legs, in the Warner Brother's cartoons.

Unlike a classic psychosis, the most salient characteristic of chaotic rage is the near impossibility of establishing *any* lines of communication. Inmates in this state often can't logically string words together, communicating in ways that are comprehensible only to themselves. They may utter cascades of words making no sense whatsoever, or grunts, moans, and mumbling. Others make sentences based on rhymes, puns, or cross-meanings, their brains capriciously linking words together based on sounds, not meanings. Delirious inmates may laugh or babble, completely at variance to the seriousness of the situation. They may speak in repetitive loops, fixating on one subject, which could be real, hallucinatory, or such a manifestation of their disorganization that you don't even know what they are talking about.

Delirious inmates can easily become quite frightened or irritable, especially if they are overwhelmed with stimuli, such as a large number of onlookers or the presence of several correctional officers. They may begin yelling, screaming, lashing out physically, or engaging in self-injurious acts such as scratching and gouging their own flesh, gouging their eyes, striking themselves repeatedly, or banging their head against the wall or ground. Such behaviors should be considered medical emergencies, and proper medical attention must be summoned as soon as possible. Ideally, medical staff should stage nearby while the correctional officers are establishing the safe control and resolution of the crisis. **Even a few minutes delay in medical attention, once the inmate is secured, can be fatal. Chaotic rage can be a sign of a life-threatening emergency, and inmates manifesting it must receive adequate medical assessment and intervention as soon as possible.**

Verbal Control of Chaotic Rage

Disorganized or delirious inmates are among the most difficult to verbally control, because comprehension and coherent cognitive processes are among the first faculties they lose. Because of their impulsiveness and unpredictability, correctional officers must be on guard against a sudden attack. Therefore, knowledge of any triggers that might have set them off in the past is very useful.

One person, usually the supervising correctional officer, needs to take command and control of the situation and direct other officers as to what they should do, i.e., clearing the room of others, providing site security to prevent others from entering the area, phoning for emergency medical assistance, etc.

Use calm movements, and a firm but reassuring voice. Chaotic inmates often experience poor motor control, vertigo, disorientation, etc. Slow movements and a strong, quiet tone of voice can help orient them physically and emotionally.

Repetition is the best strategy. Use simple, concrete commands with no more than a single 'subject' in each sentence—short sentences, little words. Use only one thought at a time, as complex sentences will be confusing, and thus threatening or irritating. For example, say slowly, "Sit down, Williams. Sit down. Sit down. Williams, sit down." **I mean MUCH slower than you think you should speaking. Your voice should be heavy, almost 'hypnotic' – do not change the pitch, the speech or the tempo of your repetitive command.**

Deflection. Disorganized inmates in chaotic rage states are sometimes susceptible to being deflected to another topic, although this is unlikely when they have entered fully into chaotic rage. You can sometimes fabricate a theme that catches their attention and seems to engage higher thought processes, delaying their outburst of rage until help can arrive. Think of this as a momentary "Island of Sanity." The island of sanity I described above (CHAPTER 31) can be thought of as relatively permanent. This is more like a life raft. It may not be helpful during the next incident, but it helps keep the chaotic inmate focused on one thing—**NOW**.

CHAOTIC RAGE: A CONSIDERATION OF RAGE EMERGING FROM VARIOUS DISORGANIZED STATES

> **49.1 Example of Deflection: Dealing With an Inmate in a Chaotic Rage State**
> A correctional officer approached a delirious inmate and said, "Jimmy Jones, what are you doing here, I haven't seen you since high school." As he kept rattling off fictitious memories to the man, the delirious inmate gazed into his eyes in confusion, rocking back and forth in rhythm with the officer's words. The officer was successful in capturing the inmate's attention, until more officers could arrive. To illustrate how dangerous this situation was for that single officer, the moment the other officers tried to physically control him, the man exploded into a violent attack, requiring a number of officers to subdue him.

Paraphrasing. Use tactical paraphrasing to validate and acknowledge their confusion and/or fear. For example, use phrases such as, "Really scary, huh?" Or "You are really worried, aren't you?"

Use their name. One of the last things we 'retain' is our name, so use their name, repetitively, interspersing it frequently in your commands in order to get their attention before initiating attempts to redirect them to another activity. *This is a situation where their first name, rather than "Inmate Jones" is probably preferable, because the first name is more fundamental.*

Physical contact for one reason only. Be very cautious about body contact with chaotic inmates, as this may be experienced as invasive, or even as an attack. Correctional officers should make physical contact only as a means of physical control, of self-defense, to take the inmate into custody, or to prevent the inmate from harming themselves or any other people present.

No distractions. Minimize such distracting behaviors on your part as extraneous body movements. Your movements should be calming and also only be those useful in helping the person understand what is going on.

Non-verbal communication is paramount. Because of their difficulty in attending to what you say, non-verbal communication is a paramount concern. A calm reassuring presence, manifesting both strength and assurance is your best hope of helping to stabilize an inmate in chaotic rage.

Only one person should be talking to the inmate No matter how wonderful each of the phrases two or more officers are saying, all that results is chaotic word salad. Signal the other officers by saying, "James, you are only talking to me. These officers are here to help, but you are only talking to me." Signal with a hand to the other officers to stop talking. Another way to head this problem of is in preparation for contact (a cell extraction, an attempt to physically control the inmate elsewhere), one officer states, "I've got lead. I'll be talking to him."

Be ready for the worst. Be ready at any time to use physical intervention tactics. Inmates manifesting chaotic rage are profoundly dangerous.

49.2 WARNING: Disorganized Inmates Can Be Unpredictable and Explosive—But They Are Not The Only People Who Shift To Chaotic Rage

Disorganized inmates (male and female) are among the most difficult to de-escalate verbally because words and coherent cognitive processes are the first thing that they lose. You must, therefore, be prepared to evade a sudden attack, and further, be prepared, throughout, to use physical control tactics to ensure your safety as well as that of others.

However, not only disorganized people go into chaotic rage states. Individuals with a history of head injury and those with epilepsy (both in pre-ictal and post-ictal states – that's before and after the seizure) can be explosively assaultive. Some individuals with head injuries can maintain their combative skills, but some (and almost always an individual with epilepsy in a pre-ictal/post-ictal state) will manifest aggression in sudden chaotic rage. Perhaps the only way to prepare for this is to be aware, if possible, if the inmate has a history of head injury or epilepsy, then there is a distinct possibility that, when stressed or confronted, they may shift almost instantaneously into a chaotic rage state. (Consider many of our young veterans coming home from the Middle East, victims of IEDs; consider those who were in auto accidents; or victims of severe physical abuse).

How would correctional officers know this history? Often, you will not. However, if this history becomes available—particularly if an inmate, who usually is quite 'normal' in behavior—then, if possible, they should be flagged as someone who can explode into chaotic rage. Part of safety planning, thereafter, should be trying to figure out what sets this particular inmate off. For example: a lot of random noise, flashing lights (associated with seizures), particular types of confrontations, etc.

Catatonia: Special Considerations

Catatonia is a very rare, very bizarre condition in which an inmate stays in a fixed posture, not congruent with injury or seizure. Catatonia is caused either by mental illness (schizophrenia) or an organic condition, for example, drug use. The catatonic inmate's posture may be quite awkward or twisted, seeming to require great flexibility. A classic symptom of true catatonia is 'waxy immobility,' whereby if someone else moves their body or limbs, he or she maintains the posture into which they were moved. Such inmates will often be totally unresponsive to speech, touch, even pain, and there seems to be no way to establish any communication with them. Others are rigid in posture, locked into place. Sometimes profoundly depressed, withdrawn people, are also referred to as catatonic, but in this case, the inmate usually slumps down or lies, unmoving in his or her cot.

Considerable caution is needed in dealing with immobile inmates, for several reasons. First, they may be injured or having a seizure and may need medical attention. A second consideration is malingering, faking infirmity to draw officers in to a vulnerable position. The third, specific to this section, is genuine catatonia. <u>One way to regard catatonia is to view the individual as exerting one hundred percent of their will to *not* interact with the outside world</u>. Trying to help, you may be tempted to make physical contact, yell forcefully, or clap your hands in front of their face, in an effort to get them to respond when they are unsecured. This can be a disastrous mistake. Imagine the incredible exertion of will required to maintain immobility for hours, even days, without movement, without response, without even blinking in some cases. Now imagine disturbing this equilibrium. The result is what is clinically called 'catatonic rage.' The catatonic inmate shifts from one hundred percent stillness to one hundred percent explosive motion. The author can recall an incident where a law enforcement officer's career was ended by such an individual who, all of one-hundred-ten pounds, suddenly grabbed hold of his arm and yanking as if he was cracking a whip, ripping through all the ligaments of his shoulder and shoulder blade.

Although you may think the inmate is unaware, they *can* hear you. Therefore, speak calmly and respectfully; don't joke around. Inmates can have very long memories of being shamed, and if you speak about or treat the catatonic inmate as an object rather than as a person, you may evoke a terrible sense of humiliation. In their frozen state, they may not be able to respond immediately, but months or years later, someone or something may trigger an episode of postponed rage. Beyond that, everyone, even a person in a coma, deserves to be treated with respect. Even if it seems that the person can't hear a word that you are saying, act as if they are listening to every word.

Whenever an inmate is immobile and unresponsive, correctional officers should summon medical attention. If you have any suspicion that the inmate may be catatonic, have them placed in restraints and transported to the medical clinic or a hospital where they can be evaluated safely. <u>As you move them, treat them like a bomb about to go off: firm hands, *lots* of hands, and one person talking. Stay smooth, in control and powerful. Do not grab at their limbs, digging your fingers into their flesh.</u>

Make sure that medical staff are aware that they are dealing with someone who is catatonic in behavior, and that they should not disturb them any more than is necessary when they are, as yet, unsecured. Testing reactivity to pain, light, or noise (shouting in their ear, for example), should not occur until the individual is safely in restraints. When you move them to a gurney, make sure you have sufficient numbers to safely manage them, just in case they were to explode suddenly while being moved.

Excited Delirium Syndrome (See Detailed Protocol in Appendix B)

Excited delirium is a rare condition at the extreme end of the hyper-aroused wing of the delirium spectrum. Etiology can be varied, but it is most commonly associated with long-term use of stimulants; particularly cocaine and methamphetamine. Single doses of such drugs as PCP, Ketamine, binges on cathinones such as methylenedioxypyrovalerone (so called "bath salts") and SPICE, and very rarely, psychedelic drugs such as 'magic mushrooms,'" can cause chaotic rage states. It is also associated with ex-

treme manic or psychotic excitement, and can be precipitated by a variety of purely medical conditions. It is typified by some, if not all of the following:
- A sudden onset of extreme agitation;
- Pervasive terror, often without object;
- Chaotic, sudden shifts in emotions;
- Disorientation;
- Screaming, pressured incoherent speech, grunting, or irrational statements;
- Aggression to inanimate objects, particularly shiny objects like glass and mirrors;
- Hyper-arousal with <u>unbelievable strength and endurance</u>;
- <u>Insensitivity to pain</u>;
- Hyperthermia (high body temperature) accompanied by stripping off clothes;
- Most notably, violent resistance to others, before, during, and after arrest or restraint.

Accompanying their almost unbelievable level of physical arousal and resistance to both physical and mechanical restraints is possible respiratory and cardiac arrest. **These people die!** The usual pattern is that they struggle with incredible power and then, suddenly, they stop moving. Or sometime after the fight is over, they become quiet, either in a stupor or in seeming normality, and then they die, usually from cardiac arrest. This can look remarkably similar to a seizure, also a very dangerous syndrome.

These days, most excited delirium is associated with long term amphetamine or cocaine abuse. As mentioned above, single doses of other substances can cause excited delirium. It also arises with combative individual suffering from severe mental illness, those who are epileptic or head injured, as well as some who are developmentally disabled.

<u>If they haven't been already called, get an emergency medical team on the scene immediately! Correct protocol demands that emergency medical staff should already be staged, and ready to intervene medically the *instant* the subject is physically subdued.</u>

Such individuals can be appallingly dangerous both to others and to themselves. **We can't emphasize strongly enough that this is a medical emergency manifesting as physical danger, and usually requiring both correctional officer and emergency medical intervention to physically secure the inmate so that they can be treated.**

You will, almost surely, be unable to verbally de-escalate the inmate in excited delirium, but if they are not presenting an immediate assault risk, make the attempt using the principles delineated above. Why?
- In some rare cases, you may be able to de-escalate them. How? Some people in delirium states, 'flicker' in and out of delirium—in the moments they clear, you can sometimes direct them: away from the edge of a tier, or sitting down so that you can secure them in restraints.
- You may be able to gain partial compliance that makes it easier to take them into physical custody.

- If nothing else you will 'buy time,' allowing sufficient emergency personnel to muster, making the restraint that will be necessary to get them help more feasible. By getting the subject focused on you, they stop moving. This will make it substantially easier to deploy less-lethal means than if they are running amok.

49.3 The Longer the Struggle, the More Likely the Death

Individuals in Excited Delirium states die from a number of causes: heart failure, acute acidosis, rhabdomyolysis (the breakdown of muscle fibers into the bloodstream, causing kidney failure), to name only a few. One basic principle that must be remember: <u>the longer the struggle and the more intense the exertion, the more likely the person will die.</u> Therefore, medical intervention that may include, among other things, physical restraint, intubation, IV of chilled saline solution and immediate sedation must occur as quickly as possible. Verbal intervention techniques are for the purpose of minimizing the struggle, buying time to assemble sufficient officers to effectively and immediately put the person under total physical control, or in some cases, to get the inmate focused on one officer so that their movement is stabilized long enough to put them effectively under physical control.

In many cases, however, there is no time for verbal interventions. Their use is dictated solely by safety concerns—what is the most effective way to get the inmate under total physical control while minimizing the duration and intensity of the struggle.

Please refer to Appendix B for a detailed protocol on response to Excited Delirium.

49.4 Excited Delirium Or Chaotic Rage—What's In A Name?

Most individuals who go into chaotic rage aren't in an excited delirium, but it is possible, even in a prison setting. Furthermore, I strongly urge all individuals involved in crisis response be familiarized on how to deal with such individuals. A joint training of all who may be involved in the restraint and treatment of such individuals is imperative. You need to have an established protocol to ensure other inmate safety, law enforcement safety, and the safety, as best as you can accomplish it, of the delirious subject. **Please refer to Appendix B for a detailed protocol on response to Excited Delirium that can be implemented (and adapted as needed) in your facility.**

Greater knowledge about this syndrome has led to several new problems:
- The protocol for Excited Delirium is to subdue the individual as quickly as possible to get them the medical attention they need, as well as protecting everyone from the appalling violence they may enact. As most individuals suffering from mental illness, even including severely disorganized people, are NOT in excited delirium states, this protocol can seem to directly contradict the model of verbal de-escalation that I have offered in this book. <u>In brief: with most individuals with mental illness, take extra time to talk them into compliance; but with individuals manifesting excited delirium, subdue them as quickly as possible</u>. However, a careful reading of this text reveals a fine-tuned set of interventions, including how to approach a disorganized individual, even one manifesting Chaotic Rage. As I have emphasized throughout the text that assessment is behaviorally based, any dangerous behavior on the part of the person of concern should elicit a well-practiced physical response.
- Because Excited Delirium has finally begun to be recognized by the medical community as a genuine medical syndrome, this could conceivably complicate things for officers. Psychosis, unlike schizophrenia, is a general term. However, if an officer uses the term Excited Delirium, he or she might be accused of diagnosing the person. Therefore, I recommend the use of the general term, Chaotic Rage, in establishing your protocols, because it is fully descriptive, encompassing both the disorganization AND the agitation that such individuals display. Furthermore, the officer isn't required to make a distinction between a person with genuine excited delirium, from a pruno intoxicated elderly inmate who also has mild Alzheimer's Disorder or a distraught grief-stricken inmate in a chaotic state. All parties can use this descriptive term, which will activate a specific protocol, without running the risk of being either over-specific or being accused of engaging in amateur diagnosis. Medical staff will sort out the genuine excited delirium cases, from others, and render appropriate aid in each case. The correctional officers' protocol is the same, whenever someone presents with a chaotic rage set of behaviors.

CHAPTER 50

Terrified Rage

> **50.1 Terrified Rage Versus Chaotic Rage**
> Be aware that the line between terrified rage and chaotic rage can be very fine. The terrified inmate, overwhelmed, can shift into chaotic rage. When facing an inmate in a state of either pure terror or terrified rage, be prepared, therefore, to shift to protocols suitable to assisting individuals in chaotic states (CHAPTER 49).

What Terrified Rage Looks Like

Terrified inmates believe that they will be violated or abused. They appear apprehensive and furtive, looking halfway ready to run, halfway ready to strike. Their voice can be pleading, whiny, or fearful, and their eyes are often wide-open or darting from place to place.

The mouths of some terrified inmates gape open slightly, as they breathe in panicky, short gasps, while others press their lips together in a quivering pucker. Their skin tone is often ashen (if dark skinned) or pale—blanched or grey (if light skinned). Some make threatening gestures with a flailing overhand blow, while others primarily use a fending off gesture, as if trying to ward off attack. Their body posture can be described as concave; they pull away from you or hold themselves tightly in fear. Terrified inmates also exhibit heightened levels of physical arousal, accompanied by panting, sweating, and/or trembling. They may back themselves into a wall or corner. They also may yell, seeming to be threatening and pleading simultaneously, using such phrases as, "Stay back! You get away from me! I will hit you!! I will! You stay back!" There is a hollow quality to the voice as if there is not 'foundation.' This is due to the tightening of the abdomen and diaphragm, so that not only breathing, but also speech is high in their chest.

Causes for Terrified Rage

Severely frightened inmates often suffer from paranoid delusions, fear of the unknown or terrifying hallucinations. At other times, they are afraid of a loss of control or of being laughed at or humiliated. Some are afraid that they are in terrible trouble with someone based on psychotic delusions. Finally, for any one of a number of reasons, they are simply terrified of you. **Imagine a snarling wolf cornered, backed up against a cliff face.** It is a frightened animal with fangs—do you think that what it really needs right now is a hug?

De-Escalation of Terrified Rage

Your goal here is to reduce the inmate's sense of danger. Maintain a safe, distance, and relax your posture. Make sure your movements are unhurried, and that your voice is firm, confident, and reassuring. If direct eye contact is reassuring for the inmate, do so; if intimidating, don't. How will you know? Notice if their body relaxes or tenses in response to your eye contact or its lack. Of course, you should never take your eyes *off* of them. Do not look penetratingly into their eyes if they are terrified by the eye contact.

Reassuring phrases that are also commands. Initiate a litany of reassuring phrases, speaking <u>slowly</u>, with frequent pauses: "I know you are scared, that's okay. Put down the chair, you don't need that. *I keep it safe here.* You can put it down now. I'm way over here. Go ahead. Sit down. *I keep it safe here."* <u>Don't say, "I'll protect you" or "I won't hurt you." Many inmates who go into terrified rage have been hurt by people who said those kinds of phrases.</u> However, when you say "I keep **it** safe here," you are telling them, "This is my territory and no one, including you, will be hurt on my territory. I am taking responsibility, and because of me, you will be safe."

By saying something similar to what they expect to hear, *yet somehow different*, you cause a '*glitch*' in their thought process. "What did he say?" He didn't say, 'I'll keep you safe.' That's what my dad used to say before he hurt me. What's different in what he said?" You thereby cause him to 're-engage' the parts of his brain that actually thinks things through as opposed that which just reacts.

Within all this, tell them to, for example, "Drop the blade. Drop the blade. You don't need that. I keep it safe." Don't shout. The command should be firm, but level voiced. Otherwise, they will key off your shout and amp upwards.

And if they begin to step forward with the weapon, CALMLY say, "Step back. Andrew. Step back. I will Tase you if you step forward. Step back. . . . That's good. You stay there and we are way over here."

Also, "You are just talking to me, Andrew. These officers are with me. They help me keep it safe, but you are just talking to me."

The inmate's body language will also indicate that they are calming down. Their breathing will get a little shuddery or be expressed in short high-pitched gasps. They may slump onto their bunk or onto the floor as if physically exhausted, even beginning to weep. Maintain your reassuring litany.

Breathe with me. Shift to the command, "Breath with me." Begin audibly breathing a little slower than the panicky inmate. As they stare at you, trying to match your breath, slow yours down a little more. Pace them down until they are breathing slowly.

Half-step approach. Ideally, you would command them to come to you, and following your commands, place themselves in a position where they can be safely restrained. If they do not step forward when so ordered, you and your team may have to advance. Slowly approach them. If they show signs of becoming frightened again, pause, move back slightly, and continue to speak to them reassuringly. As you approach the inmate, move in 'half steps.' For example, move the right foot a full step, then bring the left foot *up* to the right foot—pause. Move either right or left foot forward, and then bring the other foot forward *up* to the lead foot—pause. The advantage of moving this way is that you stay balanced, in case the inmate suddenly attacks. Additionally, if the inmate becomes somewhat agitated, you can smoothly ease backward, creating more space between you, and continue your verbal control.

Finally, I have found that when I move in half-steps, the terrified person simply does not get as frightened as when I move one foot in front of the other.

50.2 Maintain Correctional Awareness

Of all styles of verbal control that you use, this one sounds and appears to be most 'benign'—even kind. Nonetheless, the terrified person can be extremely dangerous. That is why I chose an image of a 'cornered wolf.' It wants to get away from you, but if you've got it cornered, you have a desperate being that can take your head off.

Officer presence includes the ability to speak kindly and softly while being prepared for combat, if that is necessary.

CHAPTER 51

Hot Rage

> **51.1 Some Good Advice From A Veteran Officer**
> "Hot rage explodes when officers can't calm the inmate down for a variety of reasons, didn't take the time to calm them down, or the officers themselves were so pissed off that *they* got the inmate into that stage. One out of three is not our fault. Three out of three become our responsibility."

When you think of an inmate who is on the edge of violence, hot rage usually comes to mind. Think of an individual who is yelling and screaming, brandishing their fists or another weapon, and threatening to do harm; they throw things, tip over chairs, and engage in other forms of violent behavior.

Such behaviors are often thought to be instinctual, a product of our primitive 'flight or fight' response to danger. However, instinctual aggression is usually uncoordinated and flailing, and falls under the category of terrorized or chaotic aggression.

Hot rage, however, is coordinated: a learned behavior, trained through repetition, learned through modeling, and reinforced through success. This doesn't mean that hot rage is the equivalent of the actions of a professional fighter, who coolly and calmly prepares his line of attack and focuses his aggression on his opponent. Instead, hot rage is a deeply ingrained combination of primitive drives and trained actions. Such pseudo-instinctual behaviors are actions that have either been repeated so often, or are so ingrained in powerful early experiences that they function almost like reflexes. For example, some inmates with long histories of abuse lash out in rage whenever frightened, frustrated or threatened, with no ability to evaluate whether or not they are currently in real danger. At the same time, they target where best to hit, and frequently, choose a time and a place where they believe they have the best chance of success.

On a more functional level, a good fighter who loses his temper does not necessarily lose his coordination. He does his best to knock his opponent senseless, but he automatically takes a stance with chin tucked in—shoulders rolled forward, and punches with his entire body lined up so that the power of the blow is amplified by his body weight and the torque of his hips.

General Information About Hot Rage

The more often someone goes into a state of hot rage, the more comfortable he/she is with their rage, and the easier it becomes to be violent. Hot rage is often a behavior that has led to short-term success in the past, such as scaring and beating a selected victim either for criminal gain or just for the fun of it. In a state of hot rage, such an inmate has no concern about longer-term consequences, much less guilt. For some, there is a sense of liberation, even a paradoxical kind of joy when they peak into rage. All one's fears and insecurities disappear, and one is left with only the ecstasy of the pure act. For this reason, some inmates desire rage, because that ecstatic state is, to them, the best thing they ever feel.

Displacement on Objects. This is a common factor of hot rage, meaning the inmate's anger is displaced, at least temporarily, toward an inanimate object instead of you or another individual. This also includes picking things up and slamming them down, throwing things, punching or kicking walls, furniture, or other nearby objects. More predatory inmates use displacement as a tactic to make the target of their aggression more fearful, while warming themselves up for an attack.

Peer Group Influence. Hot rage is also associated with peer group influence and masculine display, a primitive attempt to dominate a group or eliminate perceived competition. This can be especially problematic if the inmate begins acting out ('fronting') in front of a group of onlookers, and then, to save face, he or she must attack anyone representing authority.

Frustration. Frustration does not usually elicit rage in healthy people. When frustrated desires are coupled with something personal, the inmate may use rage and even violence as a way of either trying to force what they want, or to destroy what they perceive as keeping them from it. Hot rage can be a 'transference' in which the correctional officer is a representative or stand-in for someone else who frustrated or controlled them. In their mind, you are the emblem of everyone who ever controlled them or put them down, an agent of all law enforcement or societies rules, or simply an easy target to express hatred and violence.

There are various types of hot rage, each typified by almost unendurably intense feelings. I distinguish three subtypes: Fury, Bluffing, and Aggressive-Manipulation. These three subtypes will be discussed later in this chapter.

51.2 Example: Hot Rage Escalates Into Violence

An inmate sees a hardened con select out a young new inmate for sexual assault. He is setting him up, by giving him cigarettes, a debt he will not be able to pay. To the first inmate, this kid looks just like his own son, and he intervenes, saying, "That's just a kid. Let him be." The angry rapist shoves him and says, "Mind your own business, or I'll do you, too."

The man later described hearing a high-pitched noise, and his vision turning black-and-white. He comes to finding himself atop the man, pounding his face into the concrete.

General De-Escalation of Hot Rage: the Ladder
The primary method of verbal control for hot rage is called <u>The Ladder</u>. This is an ideal technique for someone who is beginning to get threatening. It is used only for rage, that gray zone between anger (even extreme anger) and violence. The inmate is no longer trying to communicate with you, and they are right on the edge of assault—in a sense, doing a war dance to work out inhibitions to committing violence.

The technique itself is simple. Identify the most dangerous behavior and repetitively demand that it cease. Use short sentences and easily understood commands. Once they stop that particular dangerous behavior, identify the next problematic behavior and use the same technique; continue until the inmate is de-escalated. **This technique is only effective right before, during, and after the peak of the crisis** because it is a control tactic rather than the 'Lining Up' *de-escalation* tactic used for anger. Control tactics will provoke rage in a merely angry inmate, someone we might have over-estimated, due to his loud tone, or dramatic behaviors. **As described earlier, facing an enraged inmate causes us to experience fear in a way that anger does not.** The danger is NOW, not merely a possibility should the situation continue to deteriorate.

Establishing a Hierarchy of Danger
The general hierarchy of dangerous behaviors, from most to least, is as follows:
- Brandishing an object or a weapon in a menacing way (NOTE: If they are too close, or are trying to use the weapon, this is violence, not rage);
- Approaching or standing too close to you with menacing intent (NOTE: if they are *too* close, or approaching too fast, this, too, is violence);
- Kicking objects, punching walls, or throwing things around (displacement activity);
- Pacing, stomping, and inflating the body in an aggressive manner (posturing);
- Shouting or, conversely, talking in low, menacing tones;
- Using language that is intended to violate, demean, or degrade.

The Ladder is not merely a verbal intervention. Like any other control tactic with an aggressive inmate, you must move as needed to maintain the optimum space to both defend yourself, and exert maximum influence upon the aggressor. If they are very close or threatening, not only should your hands be up, prepared to ward off any attack, but also as a gesture that is both calming and dominant. On other occasions, you should, as previously described, clasp the wrist of one hand with the other hand.

Give the inmate a straightforward command to stop their most dangerous behavior. By keeping things so simple, you can use your mind to look for escape routes, where weapons might be, or how to get help. By holding to a demand that the most dangerous behavior stops, you are displaying clarity and strength to the aggressor, as well as helping him or her focus *their mind* on the most problematic thing he or she is doing. You should not scream or shout—that won't get through, and will increase their aggressive energy. Rather, your voice should be strong, low, and commanding (CHAPTER 43).

After a couple of repetitions, always add, "We'll talk about it when you . . . ." followed by the same command. Once that behavior is stopped, pick the next most problematic behavior (the next 'rung' of the Ladder), and command/require that it stop. If the aggressor does calm down and stops **all** the aggressive behaviors, including assaultive language, THEN set a firm and direct limit.

This is not the time to try and think of something brilliant or life changing to say. By keeping things simple, you can continue to look for escape routes, identify potential weapons, and attempt to get help. You should intersperse your sentences frequently with their name, using this to pace and break the rhythm of your commands, as well as 'calling them back' to a more personal interaction. In addition, by holding to a demand that a specific behavior stops, you are helping them focus *their mind* on their most problematic behavior, then the next, and on down the rungs of the Ladder. Continue working your way down the rungs until the inmate is no longer in a state of rage. If the inmate re-escalates to a higher and more dangerous activity, simply return to that rung of the Ladder and begin again. Remember to stand and use your voice as described in the previous sections.

The last 'rung' is probably swearing or other obscene language. Remember, some inmates swear as punctuation, without any hostile intent. They may be crude, but they are not trying to be verbally violent. If that kind of language offends you, it is something you will deal with at another time, during moments of calm. However, if the swearing is an attempt to violate you, it **must** be dealt with in proper order. However, don't focus on the language, no matter how vile, if the person is *doing* something dangerous. Remember that predatory inmates will use language to shock, distract, immobilize, or terrorize. Their behavior is far more dangerous than anything they are saying.

51.3 CAUTION: The Ladder Is for Rage, Not Anger
Remember, the Ladder should only be used with an enraged inmate. Using this technique with an angry individual will cause them to escalate into rage. In most cases, de-escalation tactics suitable to dealing with angry inmates are sufficient.

51.4 Example of the Ladder
Your voice is firm, low pitched and commanding, as you "descend" down the rungs. In the following scenario, each statement is, of course, in response to something the aggressor has done or said. Don't talk too fast. Command presence, not hysteria!

"Step back, Step back, Jameson, we'll talk about it when you step back." Continuing, "Jameson, Step back, Step back, Jameson, we will talk about it when you step back."

"Stop kicking things, Jameson, Stop kicking things, We'll talk about it when you stop kicking things."

"Jameson, I can't follow you when you pace around, sit down and we can talk, Sit down, Jameson."

Notice the paradoxical message, that you can't 'follow' him. Of course, you could, if you wanted to. This is another example of what I call a 'brain glitch,' the same as we do with the individual in Terrified Rage (**CHAPTER 50**), *when we say, "I keep it safe here." You are trying to catch their attention as they try to make sense of what you said. We want them thinking again, trying to figure out what you said and why you said it. We want the part of the brain that thinks things through taking over from the part that is driving them towards violence.*

Imagine they have stepped forward again. Go right back to a 'higher rung' on the ladder.

"Step back! Jameson! Step back and we'll talk. We will TALK about it when you step back, Jameson. Step - - - - -back."

Don't get frustrated and add, "I said, 'Step back!'" That extra phrase makes you appear weak, as if you think he didn't hear you the first time. By simply, strongly, powerfully repeating yourself, you are saying that there is no other option but to step back—and if the inmate doesn't, then they will be put under physical control.

"Sit down Jameson. We will talk about it when you sit down. We can't talk when you are walking around. We will talk about it when you sit down."

"Lower your voice. I can't hear you when you yell that loud. Lower you voice and we will talk."

Here is a second paradoxical communication. Of course, you can hear an aggressor who is shouting loudly. Once again, you are trying to create a 'glitch' where he tries to figure out what you mean when you say you can't hear him when he is yelling.

"Talk to me with the same respect that I talk to you. We will talk about it when you stop swearing. Stop swearing. Jameson. We will talk when you talk to me with respect, the same way I talk to you."

Remember, some people swear as punctuation. They have no hostile intent whatsoever. If the individual is swearing in this manner, it is not a problem. For example, "Officer, I'm sorry, I was just mad at my f**king case manager, and s**t, you happened to arrive at just the wrong damn moment."

However, if the swearing is an attempt to violate you, it must be dealt with in proper order. However, don't focus on the language, no matter how vile, if the aggressor is doing something dangerous. Remember that predatory individuals will use language to shock, distract, immobilize or terrorize. What they are doing is far more dangerous than anything they are saying.

51.5 The ONE STEP LADDER—A Strategy Specific to Corrections

Very often, circumstances do not allow the step-by-step tactic of The Ladder. Maybe there are other surrounding inmates also getting amped up, or perhaps, based on previous knowledge, this particular inmate would regard The Ladder as giving them time and freedom to continue to escalate. In this case, many institutions have a simple phrase, 'Cell Up!" or "Lock Down" being two examples. This is a one-step command—one that may be repeated a number of times in a dispassionate but powerful way. If the inmate complies, that will be the end of things for now (although there may be other consequences later). If they do not comply, they have 'crossed an un-crossable line,' and physical means will be used to gain control.

Hot Rage Subtype #1: Fury

What does fury look like? Furious inmates are very tense, looking as if they are about to explode. **For a mental image, if they are of big stature, think of a grizzly bear; if they are smaller, think of a wolverine.** In either case, the image suggests an animal that will tear you to pieces if it perceives danger, if it is provoked, or if it believes itself to be cornered. Many inmates, both with a mental health diagnoses and without, display fury, and it is particularly common among those who have suffered head injuries. Furious inmates may show some of the following physical manifestations of their rage:

- Their voice, whether loud, or low and quiet, has a menacing and belligerent tone.
- Their skin tone is flushed as they become angered, turning red or purplish in color. As they become even more enraged, however, their skin blanches, and they turn pale or ashen (depending on their skin tone, light or dark), as the blood pools in the internal organs.
- They often pace, inflate their upper body, hit or kick objects, or strike their hands together ominously, punching one fist into the other hand. Some punch themselves.
- They tend to stare into your eyes directly, or glower from under their brows, with a furious and hostile look on their face.
- Their eyes will appear red or inflamed; usually their eyes are wide open, with tension around the eye sockets and facial muscles.
- Physical arousal, blood pressure, and muscular tension all increase. You may notice veins popping out of the skin, particularly around the neck.
- They may display a smile that shows no humor or joy. Others snarl, or compress their lips with a twist, as if they have a foul taste in their mouth. Still others bare their teeth, or clench their jaws so tightly that the muscles stand out in bunches.
- They are very impulsive, and unconcerned with possible consequences.
- Their breathing is often loud and strained.

- They may claim to be disrespected, humiliated, or shamed. Others will allege that they are not getting their questions answered and their problem solved, or that no one listened or cared. They may rant about 'the system' and claim that they are out of alternatives or solutions. This is not 'communication.' They are doing this to 'jack themselves up,' to justify the violence they desire to enact.
- At their most dangerous point, they may become calm, break off eye-contact, or adopt a thousand-yard stare.

Stance. When confronting a furious inmate your posture and tone should be confident, commanding, even imposing. Maintain direct eye contact, and frequently use their name. Stand directly in front of the inmate, using a blade stance, but out of range of an immediate blow. This best prepares you to escape along tangents to his attack, to ward off blows, and if necessary, to fight back. With the blade stance, you are already 'chambered' to do this. As described earlier, your hands are either up in a fence, or the wrist of one arm is clasped in the hand of the other in front of you at waist level, or in the most extreme situations, you already have your hands on your weaponry or in a combative pose.

Spacing. Stand too close and you will appear to be challenging them, too far and you will be seen as fearful—a potential victim. You may have to move forward or backward to maintain this spacing. In either event, move smoothly, without flinching on the one hand or any sudden or threatening gestures on the other. When you move with a relaxed body, you are readier to protect yourself, yet you don't appear as if you are trying to initiate a physical altercation.

Vocal tone. Your voice is strong and forceful. Don't, however, shout. Instead, keep your voice low-pitched and calm, dropping it into your chest where it resonates, as enraged people, in particular, react violently to threatening or angry vocal tones. The only time you would shout is a 'battle cry' that you use only when you are trying to psychologically dominate them, or stop an actual attack.

You will use the Ladder in its most orthodox form—with your voice pitched low and powerful. You should feel it vibrate in your chest. The inmate will exhibit one of only three actions:
- They keep on coming—you will do what you have to do ensure safety.
- They get close and when you tell them to step back, they say, "Make me"—you will do what you have to do to ensure safety.
- They comply—when individuals in hot rage comply with the command to step back, they usually do so yelling and screaming— "You can't tell me what to do." You will continue down the Ladder, step by step.

Don't let down your guard after 'victory.' Once you have them de-escalated, you must maintain control. This can mean anything from taking them into custody to simply 'reading them the riot act' and putting them on notice that they came dangerously close to being hurt. Only <u>after</u> setting very strong limits would you shift into problem-solving, even with an individual suffering from mental illness. Otherwise, they will assume that the best way to get a reward—your attention or help—is to abuse you.

Hot Rage Subtype #2: Bluff Aggression

The aggressively bluffing inmate is like a gorilla beating his chest, a display of aggression designed to keep you at a distance. There is a sense of bluster, however rather than the pent-up, explosive pressure of the enraged inmate. However, their manifest behavior appears much the same as the individual displaying fury, hence the image of the enraged gorilla. At fifty yards, could you tell the difference between a charging gorilla and a charging grizzly bear? Both are huge, hairy beasts that apparently mean you harm. In all likelihood, the gorilla would prefer to be left alone, rather than engaging in combat, but he postures as if he wants nothing more than tear you to pieces, and if he perceives no other alternative to violence, that's what he will do.

How can you tell the difference between a furious inmate and a bluffer, if their behaviors are so similar? When facing a furious inmate, fear/adrenaline is your natural and likely response. You instinctual mind, that part of you that places survival above all else, demands your immediate attention, and it uses fear to accomplish this. An aggressive bluffer, in a state of hot rage, may also elicit fear, but this fear will be accompanied by another emotion. You will find yourself a bit irritated, thinking how stupid (yet potentially dangerous) this incident has become, and that if the bluffer was not in front of other inmates, or in another case, if someone had not chosen to taunt him as being less than a man, this dangerous situation would never have developed.

The enraged bluffer *often* displays aggression for the benefit of friends or other onlookers. On many occasions these people have provoked him or her to 'prove' they are tough. Maybe they have been set up by a prison gang, and they are trying to 'honorably' be put in segregation to get away from them—the only way they can accomplish that is combat with officers.

In reality, they are actually *frightened that they will be found out as being frightened, intimidated, or succumbing to authority.* These inmates can become quite violent if they feel a strong sense of peer pressure to resist your commands and efforts to de-escalate them. Because they are performing in front of an audience, they will often attack to protect their image. Sometimes bluffers are alone, but they still have an audience, an image inside their own head to which they believe they must conform. You will often hear this in their self-talk as they amp themselves up. "You don't know who you are talking to. Do you have any idea who I am?"

Many bullies, having a long record of violence, actually function day-to-day in 'bluff mode.' They are in a perpetual quest to prove to others, and even more so, themselves, that they are not frightened or insecure. As a result, they repeatedly solicit situations where they must either intimidate others or resort to violence. Correctional officers must short-circuit this behavior.

One thing which lone correctional officers simply shouldn't do is to try and 'out tough' the inmate by refusing to back down or leave the scene. This is merely bluffing behavior *on your part*, and the inmate's audience will only amplify their calls for the inmate to be even more resistant. As the author has stated many times throughout this book, don't personalize any of your encounters with your inmates, and if professional prudence dictates that you should enact a tactical retreat, then do so!

Correctional officers need to recognize that the aggressive bluffer is not really in confrontation with you; they are *pretending* that they are, and are dangerous because they may believe they need to prove themselves by refusing to back-down. Another aspect of bluffing is that when frightened, the bluffing inmate will move towards you, so that no one will see how frightened they truly are.

Matter of fact tone. When you have sufficient force, or there is no retreat possible, control using the Ladder, much as you would with an individual in fury, but with a much more matter-of-fact tone.

'Conversational eye contact. Your eye-contact, too, is matter-of-fact, as if you are having a conversation rather than a confrontation.

No need for a fight. Rather than having your hands in front of you (either clasped or in a fence position), open your hands, slightly to the sides, palm up. You can still protect yourself just as easily, but your posture appears non-threatening, more open and relaxed. Your body language expresses, "There is no *need* for a fight here."

Help them 'save face,' but don't let them win. Remember, these inmates will attack out of the fear of being 'found out' by their peers. Your task becomes one of *helping them to save face*, rather than issuing forceful commands and instructions. In doing so, you will greatly reduce the risk of violence. However, correctional officers can't allow the inmate to *win the encounter* with concessions or agreements, and there must be some form of consequence subsequent to the resolution of the crisis. The imposition of punishment or consequences can come later, especially if the inmate is *not* taken into immediate custody.

When exerting verbal control on the enraged bluffer:
- Don't point out their fears in front of others. They will feel the need to defend their honor.
- Don't try to be more forceful than they are, or appear overly domineering or condescending, as their self-image may require them to strike out. If they are not responsive to a more low-key approach and continue to escalate, you may have a furious inmate (see above) who happens to be in front of other people or a bluffer who has shifted into fury. In this case, you **'turn up the dial.'**

<u>Adopt a more powerful tone and stance, and shift into the more forceful version of the Ladder technique for the furious individual.</u>
- Remember, the inmate's audience is what makes them dangerous. If possible, removing them from their audience will often result in the inmate calming down on their own.

51:6 The Bluffer's Strut
When you tell such an inmate to step back and do it well, aggressive bluffers often strut back with a smirk, sometimes glancing around and making eye-contact with onlookers. This is for the benefit of the audience, and their own self-image. They are trying to show that they are not afraid, and in control of the situation.

51.7 The Bluffer Debriefed and Properly Managed After the Confrontation
Speaking to a person who was in Bluff-Rage AFTER you have them under complete control:

"Morrison, I'm glad this worked out with no one getting hurt. Had you not chosen to sit down and talk, you very likely would have ended up being face down on the floor. No. Listen to me for a minute. I'm not disrespecting you—that's why you and I are over here talking instead of in front of them *(indicating the onlookers)*. I'm telling you, it was a very near thing. Again, I'm glad this has worked out that you and I are standing here talking."

"Next time, though, don't do this in front of <u>them</u>" *(referring to the other inmates for whom he was on display, and actually put a little contempt in your voice when you say the word 'them' as if to indicate that Morrison is better/cooler/stronger than those people he is trying to impress.)*

"Come to me and talk to me one man to another" OR "one woman to another" ("one adult to another" in male-female conversations). "You shouldn't put your personal business in front of them." You will observe him "puff up," feeling himself to be flattered. You then continue, "Okay. Are we clear for next time?" "Good. Now as for this time...." Then set the same types of limits as you did with the individual in a state of FURY, which will often include the phrase, "You are going Seg. You can walk or you can be dragged. I'd prefer that those guys don't have to see you getting dragged. But that's up to you."

They are more likely to accept the disciplinary action when their ego is built up enough to take the hit.

Hot Rage Subtype #3: Controlling Aggressive Manipulation

Aggressive manipulation is a *strategy*, not a symptom of illness. Such inmates are calculating, trying to monitor the effects of their actions. They are not constrained by feelings of honor, integrity, or pride; their goal is win any way they can. Sometimes, you can tell when you are being manipulated ('played') because you are confused about why the inmate is upset, or the purpose of his argument. The aggressive manipulator changes either his mood or the subject of the complaint frequently, displaying some or all of the behaviors of manipulative and sociopathic Individuals (SECTION V).

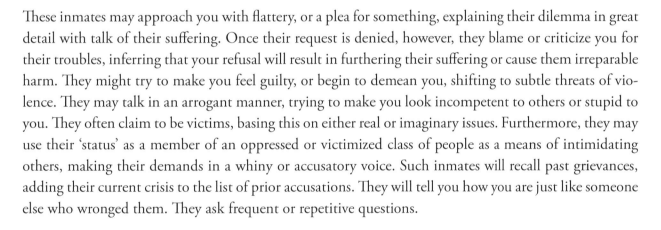

Aggressive-manipulative inmates may have a long history of losing control, particularly when their desires are frustrated, or when they believe they are not given what they feel they are entitled. They frequently have a history of various character disorders (habitual behavioral styles that make others miserable).

These inmates may approach you with flattery, or a plea for something, explaining their dilemma in great detail with talk of their suffering. Once their request is denied, however, they blame or criticize you for their troubles, inferring that your refusal will result in furthering their suffering or cause them irreparable harm. They might try to make you feel guilty, or begin to demean you, shifting to subtle threats of violence. They may talk in an arrogant manner, trying to make you look incompetent to others or stupid to you. They often claim to be victims, basing this on either real or imaginary issues. Furthermore, they may use their 'status' as a member of an oppressed or victimized class of people as a means of intimidating others, making their demands in a whiny or accusatory voice. Such inmates will recall past grievances, adding their current crisis to the list of prior accusations. They will tell you how you are just like someone else who wronged them. They ask frequent or repetitive questions.

Manipulation isn't fake. It is what it is. Manipulation does not mean false threat, and manipulative inmates will often harm others. The difference between an aggressive-manipulator and those in a state of pure fury is that the furious inmate's inhibitions are swept aside by their rage. You will often hear terms like, "He just lost it" to explain such behavior. The aggressive-manipulator, on the other hand, is mostly under control. He or she attempts to monitor your responses and the situation as a whole to assess if his or her actions and behaviors are successful.

The manipulative individual doesn't stay in control. Although the inmate's behavior may be calculating, that does not mean he or she will stay in control. Remember, the manipulative individual believes he or she is smarter than you. When you aren't played, and they try tactic after tactic, and you continue to resist or deflect the manipulation, they get more and more frustrated. And, they get insulted—you not being 'played,' means you think you are smarter than they are, and other people know it. You are, in their mind, disrespecting them. As the inmate becomes more and more intense and frustrated, his or her judgment deteriorates, and he or she may concoct a rationalization for violence that makes sense to him in the moment.

Basic control strategy—cut it off before it gets started. Inmates who use this strategy attempt to twist your feelings and emotions, making you doubt yourself, making you ashamed or scared, for example, to get what they want. Don't buy into it. If you recognize this strategy early on in your interaction with the inmate, the best strategy is to cut it off at the onset. **The symbolic image for these inmates is a large rat—NOT because it is meant to be demeaning, but because rats are survivors.** They are all about winning, not honor, not image, winning by whatever means they can. Dealing with the aggressive-manipulator is like being placed in a maze. Your task is to walk right through the 'walls.'

Looking past without looking away. Making eye contact enables another person to truly see you as you are, and in return, see them as well. Aggressive-manipulative inmates don't care about you, and they use apparent feelings of contact and intimacy to 'read' you and control others. They are interested in gaining information that they can use to their benefit. Similarly, they will use their own eyes to create a false sense of trust or intimacy, as it suits them to confuse you, misdirect your attention, or dominate you. Rather than making eye contact, look past one ear.

> **51.8 Don't Look Away**
> Don't look away. While looking past an ear, you can still see what they are doing. If you look away, you will be assaulted and not even know it is coming. This disengaged look, done properly, indicates that you won't participate in the degradation that manipulation creates.

Using the 'Detached Ladder' with Aggressive Manipulators. If your attempts at control and de-escalation of their manipulative strategies are unsuccessful, the inmate may escalate into a rage state. What distinguishes this from pure fury is that, even now, they continue to read and monitor you for advantage. Internally, they are asking: have they succeeded in intimidating you; have they succeeded in distracting or throwing you off balance so that you are open to an attack; have they got you trying to 'bargain' your way to safety? At the same time, they begin to 'lose it,' as it becomes more apparent that their strategic application of intimidation is unsuccessful. Furthermore, they get increasingly frustrated because they believe their manipulation *should* be working, primarily because it has worked so well for them in the past.

Once the opportunistic-manipulative inmate begins to escalate his or her strategies, you may have to use the Ladder as a means of control and de-escalation. In this case, however, your tone of voice should be matter-of fact and slightly detached. Your tone should express—"I'm not buying in. You are trying to play me, and I'm not playing the game."

In essence, aggressive-manipulative rage is a merger of hot rage and predatory rage (see other sections in this chapter as well as CHAPTER 52). When dealing with such inmates, correctional officers should:
- Stand relaxed and ready to evade a blow and counter the attack.
- Start with disinterested eyes, looking past their ear, but taking in their entire posture and movements.
- If they continue to amp up, loop your eyes from looking past their ear to direct firm eye contact.

51.9 Locking Eyes (THE LOOP)

If the inmate escalates into *fury*, or if they continue to be otherwise non-compliant, turn from looking past the ear to looking right in their eyes, accompanied by a firm command to stop what they are doing. When you turn your head to look directly in their eyes, roll it slightly up and then down as if sighting a weapon. Speak powerfully and directly, just as you do with the inmate who is in a state of fury. If you have ever raised a teenager, you have almost surely done this. In essence, once you make eye-contact with the aggressive-manipulative inmate, treat them as you would the furious type.

- Express flat disinterest in their demands, accusations, and complaints.
- Use the repetitive commands of the Ladder technique. Your vocal tone should be flat. Don't negotiate. Don't discuss other matters as long as the manipulative behavior continues.

Several things can happen with the aggressive-manipulative inmate when you attempt to control their rage:
- Your flat disinterest indicates that they can't 'get to you.' After trying several different avenues, they give up, or shift to another strategy.
- In more heated situations, they will flare into a fury (or pseudo-fury).
- When you 'lock in' eye-contact, they may 'bounce' off into another tactic—sudden tears for example.
- If the behavior does not stop immediately upon being 'hit' with your eyes, this means that an attack is imminent. You will shift into the verbal control techniques used for controlling FURY, or take appropriate action to ensure your safety in the event of violence.

CHAPTER 52

Predatory or Cool Rage

Inmates expressing this type of rage are intimidators who threaten with either vague innuendoes or explicit threats. Their aggressive behavior is calculated, but unlike the manipulator, violence is often their first choice rather than one of many options. The predatory inmate may deliver threats in cool, dangerous tones, often *after* a clear and strongly stated demand. Then they offer you a chance to avoid injury if you comply. A variant tactic is to *pretend* being out of control. This is in contrast to a genuine attack, an action that they are also eminently capable of and willing to carry out. **My symbol for them is either a leopard or a shark, depending on if they present as 'warm-blooded' or 'stone cold.'**

While these inmates seethe with hostility and contempt for others, they have developed these emotions as a deliberate weapon of terror, perhaps even enjoyment. The 'shark' subtype is out-there, all the time; the 'leopard' subtype can cover their emotions up at will.

Paradoxically, their physical arousal is often low. Their heart rate can actually go down and they can be charming and engaging, even as they prepare to commit an act of violence. This disconnect between appearances and intentions can cause some correctional officers to lower their guard because they may have a hard time believing that such a seemingly nice guy is ready and willing to terrorize others psychologically, or hurt them physically. (One of the reasons I chose a leopard as a symbol of the 'warm blooded predator' is that there is no more attractive, yet untamable animal on the planet. They are strong enough to carry an animal twice their weight up in a tree; they will step aside from an elephant, yet stand down a tiger. They can hide in tall grass, on rocks or leaves, yet they are strikingly attractive.)

These inmates actually have no inhibitions regarding their aggression other than tactical calculation or self-interest. They have no capacity for sympathy or guilt, and many experience low levels of anxiety in situations that would frighten ordinary people. Every time they intimidate someone successfully, their behavior is reinforced, and they view non-action on your part, either during the confrontation or afterward, as either weakness or tacit approval, thereby increasing the likelihood of similar behavior in the future.

The best response is a combination of overwhelming force and professionalism.[32] The former is obvious. Never be in a situation where you are vulnerable with such an individual. 'Professionalism' means, simply, that you make your control 'institutional,' not 'personal.' When you are dealing with them, they should not have a problem with you, personally—their problem is between themselves and correctional facility, whose rules they are breaking. As a correctional officer, you are merely the agent of that institution.

What to Do When You Don't Have Overwhelming Force

Your basic task is to demonstrate that you are not prey, and that the inmate's attempts at intimidation will simply not work.

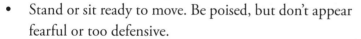

Most predatory inmates don't wish to interact with someone whom they *can't* intimidate or otherwise control through emotional abuse or physical posturing. Instead, they seek weaker, more subservient victims, where their chances of success are great. When engaging a predatory inmate correctional officers should remember the following:

- Stand or sit ready to move. Be poised, but don't appear fearful or too defensive.
- Avoid gesturing or expressive movements. Fear often causes your movements to be awkward, and the inmate will see this as confirmation of their control over you.
- Be open and strategic in everything you do: the way you position your body, your voice, and your posture. The predator is skilled in reading body language and assessing weakness. Don't hide it: protect yourself openly, and don't change your actions based on what they say, whether they come on hard or soft: i.e., either intimidation, or their efforts to put you at ease or promises of compliance.
- Another tactic the predator may use in these circumstances is to use anything you do against you, either making fun of you or accusing you that *you* are out of control, paranoid, or acting strangely. For example, they may say, "Do you really think you can get to that Taser before I can get to you?" Ignore all that, and openly act to keep yourself safe.
- Don't make explicit or unrealistic threats, such as "If any of your people come near my family, I will kill you!" To the predator, that tells him what you *won't* do. In his mind, if you really meant it, you would do it now. An explicit threat is an empty threat.
- Don't over-react to vague threats, or he or she will interpret your reaction as a victory. If, however, the inmate makes an explicit threat to harm you then they should be put into custody immediately or shortly after the encounter (after you have removed yourself from the situation safely and returned with sufficient force). Correctional officers can't allow *any* inmate to threaten them with physical violence without the swift and sure response of punishment.
- Don't comply with any of the inmate's orders or demands that you *should not* carry out your professional duties and responsibilities.

Cryptic Consequences

Cryptic consequences is the strategic response to the predator when you don't have overwhelming force and need to extricate yourself from the situation. Keep your voice matter-of-fact, and give clear and direct statements of *potential* consequences. If you can, smile. **These consequences are of a special type, clear, but cryptic,** e.g., "You know what would happen if you did that." In this case, don't tell them what would happen. <u>Let their imagination take over</u>. These vague consequences are a mirror of their own method of intimidation, and they may react to you as "not prey, not edible, not worth the trouble."

- If they say, "What are you talking about?" you should reply, "You know exactly what I am talking about." When the predator responds to your cryptic consequence with questions or with confusing statements that would make your statement illogical, simply say, "You know what is going on here. You know what is happening."
- You may have to intersperse your vague consequences with Ladder commands if they escalate their behavior.
- Try not to get 'trapped' in eye contact. But if you look away, you will clearly have lost. So look between their eyes, or look with an empty stare. Imagine turning your eyes to buttons. They will look like a cut-out or silhouette. Your eyes are flat, with no attempt to 'penetrate' or make contact. (You should make sustained eye-contact only if in a fight for your life. Then, you must shift focus, trying to penetrate his or her eyes as if you were a laser beam).
- Don't over-react to threats, or they will interpret your reaction as a victory.
- Your entire goal is to convince them that it isn't worth it to hurt you. Once you have succeeded and are free, you need to get help.

To reiterate, you don't have to prove that you're bigger, tougher, or more dangerous. You're establishing that you're merely on to their game and aren't, by nature, someone to victimize. Like a leopard who chooses *not* to chase an antelope because it is moving too smoothly, showing that it is healthy and strong, the predator is likely to disengage, if you don't give him anything to attack or discount (an attempt to intimidate them with a direct threat) or if you try to negotiate (something they have no interest in).

52.1 Example: Interaction With Predatory Inmate When the Officer is Without Back-up and Cannot Escape

Predator. "This is very simple, Officer. I think you and I can agree that you misinterpreted what I said about payback. Look, I understand. You must have been having a bad day, and you over-reacted. This can be fixed very easily. Just call the captain and tell them that you didn't quote me accurately, that you've been overworked lately and misjudged the situation. See, I bet you love your family as much as I do. You've got your child in a good school over at Echo Lake. Actually, it's amazing, that's one of the last schools in this area that still lets the kids out for recess. And gives them freedom to play! Only one teacher watching!

Oh, sorry, I'm a little off track. What I'm saying is that I bet you would be devastated if anything happened to your family. I'm the same. I am really worried that a misunderstanding could cause me to lose my 'good time,' and my child will be deprived of his father that much longer. The problem is that what is happening to my family is you! And this is a problem you could fix, unless you are really sitting there telling me that you want to destroy my life and that of my child. IS THAT WHAT YOU ARE SAYING??!!!!"

CORRECTIONAL OFFICER. *(With a little smile and a strong, confident voice)* "I am really glad we are having this conversation, because it's good that we both understand each other."

Predator. "So, you'll make the call."

CORRECTIONAL OFFICER. "You know what's going to happen."

Predator. "Suppose you tell me."

CORRECTIONAL OFFICER. "There's no need to do that. You know exactly what's going on."

Predator. "Are you threatening me?"

CORRECTIONAL OFFICER. "I don't know where you got that idea. In fact, we both know the situation here."

Predator. *(Walking away)* "You think this is over. You better watch your back."

To reiterate, you don't have to prove that you are bigger, tougher, or more dangerous. Merely establish that you are on to his game, you are not someone who will be victimized, and that there will certainly be consequences for their actions. Predatory inmates are likely to disengage if you don't react to their threats as they wish. And be aware of this: Such an interaction could go on for much longer before you get to safety when a) the inmate withdraws as above b) other officers check on you, because you have been 'over the horizon line' too long.

Final thought: You are isolated, without back-up or at least, without sufficient back-up. All the time you are using cryptic consequences, you are also doing circular/tactical breathing, staying calm and balanced—and prepared to fight for your life without hesitation if the predatory inmate chooses to attack, or if their actions ('lighting up' other inmates puts you increasingly in danger).

52.2 CAUTION: Cryptic Consequences Are Only for the Rarest of Inmates in the Rarest of Situations

You ONLY use this strategy with the openly predatory, ONLY when they are escalating into predatory rage, **and only when you don't have sufficient force or backup to place them immediately under full control.** In other words, it should never happen, but you need to know what to do if it does.

CHAPTER 53

De-escalation of Inmates with Developmental Disabilities

Inmates with developmental disabilities present a special situation. The preferred de-escalation tactics are not remarkably different for other inmates, but one must be aware of their cognitive deficits. If you use language that is too sophisticated, you may elicit more frustration and anger within the inmate by making them feel stupid (and one thing I can guarantee—they have been called stupid and worse their entire lives). In addition, many such inmates are subject to 'magical thinking'(CHAPTER 1 & 27), and their beliefs about the world, and their own powers and vulnerabilities often don't conform to reality. Sometimes, correctional officers can use these beliefs to help calm this type of inmate—as you would with a child. On other occasions, one must be aware of these beliefs to keep the situation from escalating out of control.

53.1 CAUTION: Terminology

Another term, equivalent to developmental disability is 'intellectual disability.' These two terms can be considered equal. Another phrase, 'mental retardation' was the medical diagnostic term until 2014, when it was officially changed to the other two terms mentioned above. 'Mental retardation,' 'mentally retarded' and the like are now considered to be insults.

One might shake one's head how a term, previously acceptable is now, all of a sudden, the equivalent of a curse word, but so be it. If you choose to use the older terminology, and this is recorded on film or in paperwork, you actions will be questioned, however effective and ethical they may have been. I am well aware that terminology is changing so rapidly these days (as I discussed in the forward of this book) that it is hard to keep track, and it seems, at times, as if it is a 'set up' for others to feel morally superior and devalue a person's actions by any little supposed flaw in what you say.

The complaint is real and, in some cases, it is justified. However, unless there is an ethical or moral reason, worth losing one's job over, NOT to use the currently acceptable terminology, then shrug your shoulders, learn the current phrase and get on with life. The truth is, one you get used to using a certain word or phrase, it soon becomes second-nature.

If you try to control such an inmate based on their physical age and appearance, say a 250 pound, 35-year-old male, for example, things can go wrong very quickly. Most of my associates have found that once we make eye-contact, we can usually estimate the *emotional age* of the person with developmental disabilities very quickly: they are, emotionally, either a 'little kid,' or a 'pre-teen.' Speak to them at their emotional age.

However, regardless of the inmate's emotional age, you can't permit their apparent childishness to compromise your physical safety. As with children, inmates with developmental disabilities can be quite impulsive and unpredictable. Unlike a child however, they have the physical strength of an adult, and even more dangerously, may not recognize their own strength. For this reason, the tactics for evasion, self-defense, or taking the inmate into custody are unchanged.

Correctional officers can still use tactical paraphrasing (CHAPTER 46) with an enraged developmentally disabled inmate. In this case, however, don't just sum things up calmly. Use a more dramatic voice, and over-emphasize certain words. For example, "YOU are REALLLLLY upset about having to go back to court! You really don't want to go!" Your tone is a combination of drama and enthusiasm. In essence, you are trying to catch their attention with charisma, a kind of energy in which you change the dynamics of the relationship through your voice and demeanor. Your dramatic voice validates how important the situation is to the inmate. They will find themselves in an interaction where there is no 'fight' coming from you, but they perceive you as really taking them seriously.

Following the crisis, which was undoubtedly frightening and confusing to the inmate, correctional officers can certainly acknowledge and validate their feelings. For example, "Mark, that was really scary. I'm glad that's over. I want you to sit in this chair now. Yeah, know you were scared, but it's over now." [NOTE: That may be a 'restraint chair' that you are telling them to sit quietly in, until you are sure that they can maintain calm.] A detailed critique or discussion of what they did wrong or even "where things went wrong," is almost always a mistake. Because of the developmentally disabled inmate's cognitively limitations, his or her memory after an incident is usually sketchy. They are unlikely to recall or retain detailed information. Emotionally, they may react to your debriefing as a new attack. Your concern should be behavioral stability (no new attack) and reassurance because they are very likely afraid that you will punish them for their behavior.

> **53.2 Author's Experience With an Assaultive Developmentally Disabled Individual**
> A woman with fairly severe developmental disabilities once grabbed my finger, trying to break it. I neutralized her attempt by shifting the angle of my hand as she yanked, and as she was at the emotional age of about eight years old, rather than commanding her to "Let go!" I said, "I know you want to hold my hand. You don't have to twist my finger. We can hold hands as much as you like. Sure, we can hold hands." She suddenly let go and dropped to the floor, crying like a small child.

53.3 Review: De-escalation of the Developmentally Disabled Person
- Speak to them at their emotional age, not their chronological age.
- Use tactical paraphrasing, summarizing not only what they are apparently thinking, but what they are doing.
- Put some drama in your voice, so it makes what you say sound really <important!>. And this makes them feel important, so they are more likely to do what you say.

CHAPTER 54

Mob Rage: Feeding Frenzy

54.1 Rage State and Possibility of Violence

This discussion covers both the rage state and the possibility of violence. Pack behavior can easily escalate and therefore, it is impossible to separate rage from violence in this discussion. The discussion here concerns situations where you don't have sufficient forces to manage the mob.

Mob behavior amplifies hot rage exponentially, with one person's behavior and arousal amplifying that of those around them. The more people there are, the more likely that they will coalesce into an enraged mob, a beast of many heads, but one terrifying, destructive mind. Individually, members of a mob will display any or all of the types of rage that have been discussed throughout this section. An aggressive bluffer may try to entice those he/she is trying to impress into violence. Sometimes,  mob frenzy is created and stoked by one predatory inmate who uses the mob as a weapon or distraction. When faced with such a situation the best possible solution is to escape and summon help. However, if escape is impossible attempt the following to control the mob:

Overwhelming force Quite simply, the most powerful method of de-escalation is a demonstration to the mob and its members that they will be stopped. Each member of the mob suddenly feels alone: "The first to go down."

Isolating the leader as the one individual who will face the consequences—a possible, but low percentage strategy. All of your psychological energy should be focused on the leader. This is particularly effective when the leader is hiding behind the power of the mob. If you perceive that the leader is manifesting manipulative, bluff, or predatory rage, make it clear that whatever happens, they will be destroyed. The goal is definitely not to shame them, especially before the mob. Instead, presenting yourself with a quiet, grave, yet powerful calm and allowing the leader to save face are essential if you have any hopes of causing him to draw his forces back. However, in most prison mob situations, there are 'many leaders,' and the situation is chaotic to begin with. Therefore, this is rarely a viable alternative

Build up the leader's ego by clearly identifying them as one worthy of conferring with. This is for the purpose of either drawing him away from the group, or appealing to his grandiose narcissism. If his goal is to appear important in the eyes of his mob, you may have given him what he really wants, without the need for violence.

Break the pattern, as discussed in CHAPTER 45, you do something so unexpected or outlandish that none of the individuals in the mob knows how to react.

To review, the best option when facing a mob is to escape and summon assistance. If you do intervene, be aware that you may have to fight for your life. Your best hope, were this terrible situation to develop, and go 'berserk.' Fight like a wolverine in a trap with teeth, claws, and anything else you can use, tear your way free; trying to maim your attackers as savagely as you can. The goal is to become so violent yourself that each member of the group wants to get away from you. As they recoil, hopefully, an escape route opens up.

> **54.2 Author's Experience: 'Breaking the Pattern' in a Potential Mob Attack**
> About forty-five years ago, I was hitchhiking. Still a kid, I was malevolently dropped off in a very dangerous area of a city during a very volatile period of racial strife. A crowd began to coalesce around me. I grabbed a stick I found on the ground, began cackling and shrieking like I'd lost my mind, hitting myself in the head, and then began dancing and whirling down the street, attacking moving cars with my stick. Everyone pulled back, and I heard all around me, "That dude's crazy!" "Whoa, keep away from me, you crazy muthaf*ckr." I continued for about ten blocks until I reached a safer area.

CHAPTER 55:

Deceptive Rage:
Snake in the Grass

As is obvious by the subject of this book, many criminals have concurrent mental illnesses; others have spent time in a forensic unit somewhere for evaluation purposes; still others are there because they were able to fake mental illness so that they could be moved to a hospital either for a more attractive environment, or for the purposes of escape.

What do you think such individuals do, particularly the manipulative and sociopathic, while in the forensic unit?
- They victimize more vulnerable inmates, either directly, or indirectly. The opportunities to torment the genuinely mentally ill are endless.
- <u>Beyond such predation, they study</u>. Perhaps the behaviors of a truly individual suffering from mental illness may prove advantageous someday. Perhaps it will prove useful in convincing an evaluator that they are genuinely mentally ill and of diminished capacity, not responsible for the crime they committed. Furthermore, perhaps it will give such a person an opportunity to catch someone, even a correctional officer off guard.

Such an individual obscures his/her intentions behind a 'screen behavior': the imitation of genuinely individual suffering from mental illness whom they have observed. They pretend to be psychotic, in a state of terror, distressed or needing your help. All this is for the purpose of either conning you into leaving them alone, or more dangerously, drawing you close enough so they can harm you.

Imagine a snake coiled in the leaves, pattern almost indiscernible from the ground, ready to strike.

The 'de-escalation' strategy here is simple: deal with the behavior, not the cause! Imagine you have stopped a confused, psychotic appearing inmate walking down one of the hallways. What you don't realize is that a moment earlier, he was walking smoothly. Spotting you coming, he began walking in a gimping fashion, his head lolling. When he gets close, he looks frightened. You tell him to identify himself, and he replies, stumblingly, that he was just released from a crisis unit and transferred from another prison, and he's on D block, and his eyes are a little teary, and he looks so intimidated and he hunches over a little as he cries and you can't see his hands (!!!!!!!!!). What should you do? <u>Obviously, you get some distance between you, put a hand on your weapon or your weapon in your hand, depending on your best judgment and you order them to show you their hands.</u> One of two things will result:

- As predatory individual, they slowly remove their hand and exercising due caution, you pat them down and find a shank.
- They are genuinely mentally ill or developmentally disabled, and at your sharp command, they begin crying in terror. You are now in the position of helping them. Once you ascertain everything is safe, you kindly but firmly tell them that you are going to teach them the rules of how to talk with correctional officers. "I'm sorry you were frightened. But you did something that looked dangerous. I'll tell you right now how you should act so something like this won't happen again."

CHAPTER 56

The Aftermath: What Happens to the Aggressive, Inmate Suffering from Mental Illness After an Aggressive Incident?

Rage and even more so, violence, are exhausting experiences—both emotionally and physically. Many people get the 'shakes' after such an incident. So much blood has 'pooled' inside the core of their bodies to prepare for combat that they feel cold and start to tremble. Most inmates have a significantly impaired ability to remember what happened in sequence. They may have a patchy memory of a few events. Much of the rest of the incident is a blur. Although they may even be remorseful, they usually don't remember what happened, how it started, or who was responsible. Even more drastically, they can lapse into a state of defensive confusion where they no longer recall what happened at all, or they distort the incident in their memory completely, thereafter taking no responsibility whatsoever.

Others may feel profound guilt. This might be positive, were it to lead them to reflect on their own responsibility, but for most inmates, guilt is so unpleasant that they project responsibility onto the person who 'makes' them feel guilty. Thus, they soon shift to resentment and begin to blame the other person.[33]

Humiliation, the feeling of having one's faults or vulnerabilities involuntarily or forcibly exposed to others, is quite common, and here, too, many people become defensive. One humiliation is the almost inevitable loss of the fight with the correctional officers. People describe humiliation like being flayed alive. Many respond by becoming enraged all over again. Their thinking seems to be, "If I feel this bad, someone must be doing it to me." What is almost universal is a post–crisis fatigue, a combination of the depletion of energy stores in the body and the cumulative effect of all the mood and cognitive changes described above.

Managing Risks Post-Crisis

In some situations, consequences or punishment will be required. In this case, correctional officers must clearly convey the processes and procedures of detention to the inmate. Dependent on the nature of the situation, correctional officers must try and arrange for the transfer of the inmate into a treatment facility or segregation unit as appropriate.

Once the crisis has been resolved and the inmate is stable and willing to talk, clear and unambiguous limits regarding future behaviors must be imposed. Without the imposition of limits and the reiteration of consequences for violating those limits, the inmate will simply repeat their aggressive behavior. Through de-escalation and/or control, you have established control over the inmate, and you can't relinquish that control simply because the crisis has passed. Reassure the inmate that you are not out for revenge, but neither will you pretend that nothing serious happened nor are you going to reward them just because the aggression is over.

Consequence must be imposed swiftly, and can include more restrictive incarceration, or a sanctions hearing. This depends on the nature of the actual incident, and the judgment and discretion of the correctional officers.

If the inmate suffering from mental illness is really frightened or devastated by what happened, the first priority is **reassurance and orientation**. For inmates who are disorganized, psychotic, or otherwise in a fragile mental state, you may have to explain to them what has happened, what is going to happen, and why. With inmates who don't have the mental capacity to really understand the details or implications of what happened, the best approach is to be calming and reassuring, and not detail attempts at problem-solving.

If the inmate has the cognitive ability to understand, then an **educative follow-up** is necessary. Of course, this may be delayed until the inmate has been released from custody, or hospitalization for their mental illness. Still, the incident should be reviewed with the inmate in order to clarify and reiterate the consequences of similar behavior in the future. Discuss with the inmate what other tactics they might have used to get what they desired, assist them in recognizing patterns that lead to aggression and how to avoid such situations in the future, and return the inmate to a sense of dignity and integrity.

Consolidation of Gains

Another important factor is to consolidate whatever gains you made. Just because the inmate seems to be listening doesn't mean they understood or even heard what you said. There are several strategies you can use to ensure that your statements are heard and agreement established.

- Paraphrase their understanding; "So, John, we've agreed that you will… and I will …."
- Have the inmate repeat your instructions back to you.
- Have the inmate read and sign a written copy of the instructions and stipulations of their supervision plan. Although the inmate will have signed a copy of the rules and regulations at their initial interview, the recent incident may call for a modification of that plan.
- Establish a time frame for follow through with any promises you may have made, such as placement in a treatment program. Failure to uphold your end of the bargain will lead to feelings of betrayal, making future de-escalation more difficult.

CHAPTER 57

Managing Threats to Your Family

Anyone working in the field of corrections is much more disturbed by threats made toward their family than they are with threats toward themselves. By threatening your family, promising to attack when you are not there, inmates can create in you a feeling of helplessness and desperation. The threat, meant to terrify you, is usually empty, made in the heat of the moment, or as means of additional defiance. You must, however, take any such threats seriously, because it is almost impossible to know when the threat is real or not. And, truth be told, a bit of preventative planning, and educating family members as to their need to be mindful and aware is never a bad thing.

Basic safety concepts (SECTION II), are easily transferrable toward enhancing the safety of your home and family, although the author has also expanded that list with the recommended strategies listed below. Remember, as in the work environment, the development of a safety plan is not enough, and your plan should be reviewed regularly with your family.

Inform your family of any threats and of the need to take protective action. In regard to children, your responsibility is to explain everything they *need* to know, but no more. Furthermore, if you display your own fears excessively, you will only frighten your family members. To this end, I strongly recommend that you acquire two books by Gavin de Becker, listed here for your convenience: *The Gift of Fear* and *Protecting the Gift*.[34]

Inform local law enforcement. Police officers will assist you in drawing up a safety plan as well as considering what, if any, action they can take on your behalf.

Review home security. Are you a soft target or a hard target? A soft target is easily accessible, predictable, and unaware of danger. A hard target is not easily accessible, or predictable. Adequate lighting and the use of quality locks, doors, and windows will limit the ability of an intruder to enter your home. Consult with your local police department, if need be, as to how to make your home more secure. Some departments will be more willing than others to send an officer out to walk through and around your home to inform you of security gaps. There are also excellent books on home security available. Consider having a home alarm system installed.

Concerning firearms. Should you decide to purchase a firearm for home security, each member of your family must attend a firearm safety and instruction course. Firearms should be stored and cared for as delineated in the course.

Concerning dogs. In many ways dogs are a better security option than a firearm. Unlike humans, a well-trained dog, particularly certain breeds, won't hesitate to act when they perceive a threat. Dogs will also provide you with an early warning system, detecting sounds and smells that you can't. Further discussion of dog breeds and training is well beyond the scope of this book, but a good dog can be one of the most important aspects of home security.

Scan your surroundings. Your family members must learn to scan their surroundings and note anything out of the ordinary. Remind family members to report suspicious people and cars. (You can make this a game with your children so that their situational awareness is enhanced).

Inform employers and schools so they are aware of the identity of the potential assailant. Make clear to school officials exactly who is allowed to meet or pick-up your children.

Change your routine. As much as possible, travel by different routes and at different times. Be unpredictable.

Safety in numbers. Neither you nor any of your family members should be the last to leave their workplace or school. Enlist co-coworkers, coaches, teachers, etc., to be part of a team.

Notify your office and family of travel plans. Ask that they not reveal any travel plans or other schedules.

Be careful about giving out personal information. This can be difficult with children, as they happily exchange information with their friends or others. Remind them to be careful of strangers, and to report any such inquiries. <u>Don't forget about social networking sites such as Instagram, Facebook, Snapchat, even MySpace, texting, Twitter, and other dangers of the Internet.</u>

Plan an escape route. Figure out the best ways to escape from your home and rehearse this with family members. You can combine this with fire drills—something the children are already familiar with from school.

Plan how to ask for help if in public and how best to call for help if needed. If your children are alone and there are no nearby police cars, the best stranger to ask for help is a *woman*, as women are far less likely to be a threat. Of course, this is not the case if a woman is the threatening inmate, or if a male inmate has a female associate outside. Nonetheless, on a random basis, women are far safer than men.

Concerning code words. Teach your children a code word or challenge that must be answered by strange individuals. This includes neighbors, and in some cases, relatives. For example, a person approaches your child after school and says, "Tasha, your mother and father were injured in an automobile accident. The police told me to take you to the hospital! Please come with me now." Your child should have been taught to keep her distance, looking for escape routes as she asks "What's the word?" If the person does not reply immediately with the correct word, the child should run to a safe haven and describe the individual as best they can.

Post emergency numbers near each telephone in your home. Establish safe havens to escape to in times of danger. If possible, enlist your neighbors in your safety plan.

CHAPTER 58

Conclusion

The history of mental health services has intertwined with the work of law enforcement for decades. As funding for social policies have waxed and waned, populations in prisons have expanded and mental health facilities decreased. Time has shown that legislation, laws and policies have little impact on the population of the mentally ill in prisons and prisons. Sweeping changes in the past sixty years intent on moving individuals with mental illness from state hospitals to community mental health centers and primary care doctors have failed to meet the needs of the people it intended to serve. Thousands of mentally ill people come in contact daily with the prison system, sometimes after years of bouncing from the streets to jails to hospitals to probation, until they finally commit a felony and they are lost in the prison system. Our prisons have become the treatment centers of last resort.

This book and the material covered herein demonstrates the perspective that change occurs when officers recognize the need for training, recognize a problem can be addressed and encourages the search for answers. This starts at the individual level, with awareness and recognition of how an officer responds to the work, how an officer breathes, views the environment, and interacts with the inmates. Recognition is key: being aware of abnormal behavior and having the ability to label and define behaviors creates new opportunities to engage, interact, and communicate. <u>Practice, however, is vital.</u> Once you've made a commitment to change or try a new process be consistent, be persistent, and seek out additional information.

Correctional officers have a primary mission protecting society from 'bad' guys. If this book assists in moving the 'sad, but dangerous' guys to a place of greater stability, and assists officers in more effectively managing such inmates when they are incarcerated, then time reading this book is time well spent.

SAFE WITHIN THE WALLS

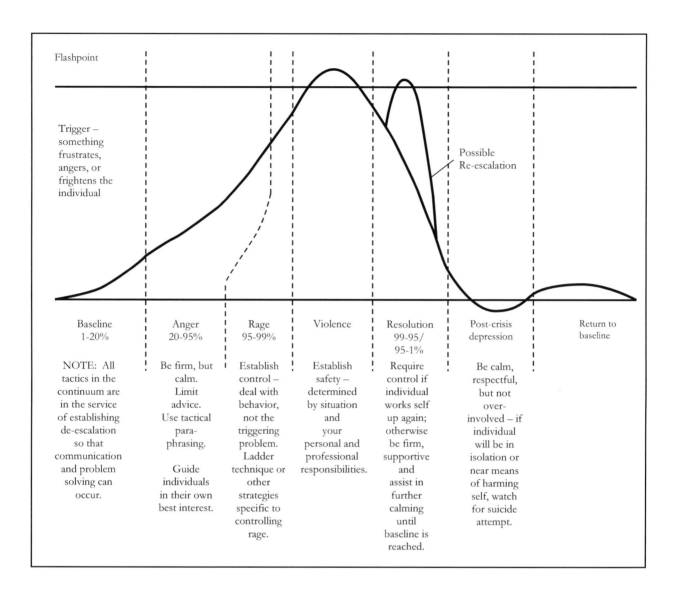

Appendices

APPENDIX A

The Question of Positional and Compression Asphyxia
by Gary M. Vilke, MD, FACEP, FAAEM

Background on Positional Asphyxia
- The concept of "Positional Asphyxia" was originally based on research that had significant methodological flaws (Reay, et al 1988)
- The premise of positional asphyxia was that if you left a patient in a hobble restraint position, he would tire, go into ventilatory failure and then asphyxiate into cardiac arrest.
- The hobble position is defined as prone with hand cuffed behind the back and ankles restrained with a device that is then pulled up and tethered to the handcuffs leaving the knees bent.
- The original research and dozens of papers since have NEVER shown hypoxia (low oxygen levels in the blood) to develop in the hobble position.
- The original research and dozens of papers since have NEVER shown hypercarbia (elevated CO_2 levels in the blood) to develop in the hobble position.
- In fact, the only paper to report that the hobble position results in positional asphyxia, actually demonstrated that oxygen saturation levels IMPROVED in all subjects who were left in a hobble position.
- Subsequent studies evaluating obese subjects also have demonstrated that when left in a hobble position, they will not asphyxiate.(Sloane, et al 2014)
- All of these studies prove that people left on their stomachs in a hobble position will not die from asphyxiation, which includes both thin and obese individuals.

Best practices
When encountered with a patient in a hobble restraint, certain assessments of a patient are critical and the documentation of the findings in the pre-hospital record is essential.

A. Assess the level of consciousness. Is the patient awake or not and is he verbal?
B. Assess perfusion. Is his skin color good and does he have a strong regular pulse?
C. Place on a monitor as soon as feasible and document first rhythm.
D. Place on pulse oximeter as soon as feasible and document O2 sat. If placing on a finger, make sure the hand is getting good perfusion through the handcuff if the O2 sat reading is low.
E. If the patient can be safely transferred to a supine position with approved 4-point restraints secured to the gurney – this is the optimal position as one has full access to the patient's airway and direct visualization of the face and access to the chest.
F. If the patient cannot be safely transferred out of the hobble position, attempt to transfer the patient in a lateral decubitus position on the gurney – preferably with the face and chest facing the EMS personnel to optimize monitoring.

G. Face down on the gurney in the hobble position is the least desirable position as the patient cannot be easily monitored or accessed if the physical status changes. If utilizing this position for transport, care must be taken to assure the airway is clear and not obstructed by sheets or the mattress.
***Despite all of the data supporting the safety of the hobble position, this is the position that will have the most scrutiny in a lawsuit if a patient deteriorates into cardiac arrest.
H. Ongoing monitoring and vigilance is important. The issue of medical concern is not the actual hobble position, as this is deemed physiologically neutral, but rather the concern is the underlying medical condition (drug induced or not) that required the patient to be hobbled in the first place.
I. These recommendations are meant to supplement, not replace, existing EMS protocols (blood glucose assessment, IV fluids, etc)

Background on Compression Asphyxia

- The concept of "Compression Asphyxia" evolved after the theory of positional asphyxia was essentially debunked. (Chan, et al. 1997, Chan et al 1998)
- The premise of compression asphyxia was that a certain amount of weight is often placed on the back of an individual to get a him into custody and handcuffed. Often this weight is multiple officers holding the person down with hands, forearms or knees. During this time period while the weight is being applied, the theory is that the subject would tire, not be able to breathe (ventilate), go into ventilatory failure and then asphyxiate into cardiac arrest.
- Research with up to 225 lbs of weight on the backs of healthy volunteers has not demonstrated physiological changes that would indicate that asphyxiation is likely with these weights. (Michalewicz, et al 2007)
- Studies with weights on the backs of normal subjects has also shown that cardiac output and blood pressure are not impacted.(Savaser, et al 2013)
- If an individual is alive, moving and breathing after the weight has been removed and then subsequently goes into cardiac arrest, the weight did not cause compressive asphyxia. ***There is not a delayed asphyxiation***, it either happens while the weight is on or it does not occur.
- Even if the weight on an individual is so great as to restrict adequate ventilation, if the subject is breathing once the weight is removed, the person will breathe out the retained CO_2 and will recover. The effects of the weight are not lasting and a breathing individual will self-correct very quickly.
- It takes a great deal of weight, consistently placed over the ventilatory muscles of the back, for a significant length of time with essentially complete impedance of ventilation without breaks to breathe in order to theoretically cause a death due to compressive asphyxia.
- If a person is vigorously and repeatedly yelling or screaming, he is moving air in and out of his lungs and thus is not meeting the "complete impedance of ventilation" criteria and thus is not in a position at that time to cause asphyxiation.
NOTE: That being said, other medical emergencies CAN present with the *sensation* that one cannot breathe, when in fact they are ventilating fine but are suffering from a myocardial infarction or ischemia, for instance. These patients should be carefully evaluated.

Best practices
When EMS encounters a patient who had weight placed on him to get him into custody, certain assessments of a patient are critical and the documentation of the findings in the pre-hospital record is essential. Basically the patient will either be spontaneously breathing with a pulse, or not. If he is spontaneously breathing with a pulse, then he did not suffer from compression asphyxia and should be assessed and documentation should follow as per the "Best practices" for positional asphyxia (above).

If the patient is not breathing or does not have a pulse, treatment is basically standard advanced cardiac life support measures. Documentation optimally should reflect the events that led up to the cardiac arrest. Often EMS is present or staged within viewing distance of the event. If so, some of the following observations can be critically useful in evaluating the case for quality review or a subsequent legal action:
- How many officers where physically involved?
- Where were they located on the subject? (i.e. holding legs, holding head, knee on back, hands on shoulder, etc)
- How long was weight on the subject?
- Was the weight moving and shifting (did the subject arch up, roll over or was he just laying flat on his stomach)?
- At what point did the subject stop yelling in relation to the cardiac arrest?
- Was the change in status sudden or gradual over time?
- Was there weight on him at the time of the cardiac arrest and if so, how much?

Pearls
Careful monitoring – you will likely be unable to prevent a patient who is suffering from Excited Delirium Syndrome from going into cardiac arrest. Additionally, rapid recognition and treatment is unlikely to change the ultimate outcome for the patient, but careful charting and documentation is extremely beneficial for subsequent legal actions that are likely to arise.

ETCO2 - If possible, document the earliest possible end tidal CO2 level. Pre-intubation with bag-valve-mask is best if feasible, as this value if low or normal, will support that the individual did not asphyxiate, as CO2 levels are high in patients who asphyxiated.

Careful accurate documentation with details as clear as possible. These cases in which there is a cardiac arrest often end up in litigation, so clear documentation of what was observed and reported with specific details is incredibly helpful in evaluating the case.

Appendix A CAUTION

Medically evaluate the subject carefully, even if the person is vigorously and repeatedly yelling or screaming. It may be obvious that he is moving air in and out of his lungs and thus is not in a position at that time to cause asphyxiation – however other medical emergencies, like myocardial infarctions or ischemia can present with the sensation of difficulty breathing and should be considered during the assessment.

References

Chan TC, Vilke GM, Neuman T, Clausen JL: Restraint position and positional asphyxia. Ann Emerg Med 1997;30(5):578-586.

Chan TC, Vilke GM, Neuman T: Reexamination of custody restraint position and positional asphyxia. Am J Forensic Med Pathol 1998;19(3):201-205.

Michalewicz BA, Chan TC, Vilke GM, Levy SS, Neuman TS, Kolkhorst FW. Ventilatory and metabolic demands during aggressive physical restraint in healthy adults. J Forensic Sci 2007;52(1):171-175.

Reay DT, Howard JD, Fligner CL, Ward RJ. Effects of positional restraint on oxygen saturation and heart rate following exercise. Am J Forensic Med Pathol. 1988 Mar;9(1):16-8.

Savaser DJ, Campbell C, Castillo EM, Vilke GM, Sloane C, Neuman T, Hansen AV, Shah S, Chan TC. The effect of the prone maximal restrained position with and without weight force on cardiac output and other hemodynamic measures. J Forens Leg Med. 2013 Nov;20(8):991-5. Epub 2013 Aug 30.

Sloane C, Chan TC, Kolkhorst F, Neuman T, Castillo EM, Vilke GM. Evaluation of the Ventilatory Effects of the Prone Maximum Restraint Position (PMR) on Obese Human Subjects. Forens Sci Int 2014;237:86-9. Epub 2014;46(6):865-72. Epub 2014 Feb 14.

APPENDIX B

Suggested Response Protocol for Correctional Facilities Concerning Suspected Excited Delirium Incidents
By Lieutenant Michael Paulus

Appendix B 1: Excited Delirium is a Chaotic Rage State

As discussed in detail in **Chapter 49**, **Excited Delirium** is a medical syndrome that is included within a general category: Chaotic Rage. It should not be incumbent upon either correctional officers to distinguish between excited delirium and other similar, equally dangerous forms of chaotic rage. The author of this book, therefore, suggests that protocols in your facility be coded for chaotic rage, with a clear understanding that this term encompasses excited delirium and other similar states, whatever the cause. **Medical staff will sort out the genuine excited delirium cases from others, and render appropriate aid in each case. The officers' protocol is the same, whenever someone presents with a chaotic rage set of behaviors.**

When considering a response to suspected Excited Delirium Syndrome incidents, it is important to understand what the correctional officer is facing. Dr. Deborah Mash of the University of Miami Brain Endowment Bank has called Excited Delirium, "a medical emergency that presents itself as a law enforcement problem."

Keeping this in mind, correctional officers are presented with a dilemma comparable to dispatching the fire department to a bank robbery. They do not have the appropriate equipment or training to handle the high-risk nature of a bank robbery. By the same token, EMS personnel are only dispatched to domestic disputes in order to tend to injuries to any of the parties—they are not expected to intervene in either legal issues or stopping the violence between the involved parties.

Similarly why would correctional officers be expected to manage to a medical emergency that requires a minimum of an advanced life support ambulance crew to address? There is nothing on the officer's duty belt or in their work area, or normally in their facility that will address hyperthermia, acidosis, cardiovascular collapse, or other life-threatening issues that are common in an Excited Delirium Syndrome (ExDS) incident.

Dr. Michael Curtis, of St. Michael's Hospital in Steven's Point, Wisconsin has said, in reference to Excited Delirium, "The legal issues can wait, the life-threatening medical emergency will not." This points out that, in a very important sense, correctional officers do not have the primary role in these incidents, but they do have a critical backup role. It just so happens that this 'back-up' comes first. Unless the individual is under complete physical control, medical assistance cannot be rendered. For this reason, correctional personnel must get the right resources to the scene as quickly as possible. In doing so, the inmate is given the best possibility of surviving.

In order to get the right resources in place, it is necessary to develop a multi-disciplinary approach to adequately respond to this multi-faceted problem. Some of the most common stakeholders in such a plan include: law enforcement, corrections, EMS personnel, fire personnel, telecommunicators, emergency room physicians/nurses, coroners, medical examiners, mental health professionals/consumers, risk managers associated with the corrections facility and the appropriate State/District attorney. Your facility may have different stakeholders, maybe more or maybe less—but the critical issue is to identify those that are, or should be, part of a best practices response to these, all too often, fatal incidents.

What is proposed here has been a successful multi-jurisdictional response since July 1, 2008 in Champaign County, Illinois. The American College of Emergency Physicians (ACEP) put out a white paper in September of 2009 that expressed the ideas that were in place in Champaign County almost a year prior. It is offered for use as a template to help gather interested parties to the table to establish a protocol that works within the confines of the resources you have available.

Correctional officers are presented with numerous situations to observe the common behaviors of ExDS. Whether it is from drug use, alcohol withdrawal, or mental illness, corrections face the same challenges when dealing with this medical emergency as do law enforcement in the field. The response to suspected ExDS incidents really does not change between the street and the correctional facility. Awareness of the behavioral cues followed by the call for additional resources to be dispatched is of primary concern.

Correctional officers must be vigilant to the signs that may indicate an inmate might be in the throes of an ExDS incident.

There are stories of prisoners being held within a facility with no known history of drug abuse, mental illness or other factors associated with ExDS. Suddenly, the inmate is in a full-blown ExDS incident requiring isolation, cell extraction, and then transport to the psychiatric ward.

Correctional staff should avoid the tendency to 'diagnose' the reasons for the inmate's behavior. Awareness of the common behavioral signs that signal a possible eminently life-threatening medical emergency must be dealt with as soon as possible regardless of the cause.

Like law enforcement, correctional staff must realize that any criminal charges or institutional violations can wait. The medical emergency cannot and will not wait but is moving forward and requires rapid and aggressive medical intervention to give the inmate the best possibility of survival.

The effectiveness of this protocol relies upon correctional officers' understanding of what they are dealing with as soon as is humanly possible, and then, immediately calling for additional backup and medical response. This protocol extends to the dispatcher/call taker as well to reasonably identify incidents that require sending additional resources to the scene as early as possible.

The correctional environment presents both opportunities as well as challenges when dealing with a potential ExDS incident. The opportunities include having inmates generally contained for the most part. This, unlike law enforcement in the field, means that unless there are exigent circumstances present, correctional personnel can develop a plan for how to get control of the inmate prior to any physical contact with the inmate. Correctional staff will usually have some knowledge about the inmate prior to contact that may give them some indication for the behavior as they plan their response.

Video surveillance also allows correctional personnel to possibly observe any sudden onset of behaviors consistent with an ExDS incident. This helps cut down on the time the inmate is experiencing the incident before medical attention is brought to the scene.

Generally, in the correctional environment, there is also enough staff present to be able to gain rapid control of the inmate prior to turning them over to medical personnel. This includes more correctional officers that might be able to go hands-on with the inmate, but also most correctional facilities have some sort of medical resource on hand. This can range from a nurse with basic medical response up to more fully equipped infirmaries. The number of personnel sent to the scene will be defendant on what resources are available, but four to six correctional officers should be dispatched to the scene, when possible, as well as a supervisor. Interagency agreements are common that allow various departments to share resources in times of emergencies such as these.

When correctional staff is dispatched, EMS should be sent as well. This will save precious time in getting the medical personnel and equipment to the scene as quickly as possible. Some communities have a combined EMS/Fire Department. Those that don't will then need to consider if sending a Fire Rescue truck is a possibility, along with EMS. Some jurisdictions have, as part of their City Ordinance that any "medical emergency" requires a Fire Rescue truck be sent. If this is the case, expect the EMS crew as well as the Fire Rescue personnel to be dispatched to the scene. The Fire Rescue's role will be discussed shortly.

Depending on the situation, it should be considered by correctional staff to create a quick action plan and wait until EMS/Fire Rescue has arrived before making physical contact with the subject. The reason to wait has to be balanced between the safety of the subject, the correctional personnel, other first responders, and other inmates. One of the toughest decisions a first responder will make could be containing the situation until the medical personnel arrive instead of physically contacting the subject. <u>We know we are repeating ourselves, but sometimes emphasis is necessary: whenever possible, correctional officers should wait until Medical has arrived before making physical contact with the subject.</u> Of course, this is contingent on how immediately dangerous the subject is to himself or herself, the correctional officers, other first responders, and bystanders. This is where the role of the correctional officer trained in verbal de-escalation and control tactics *may* help the subject and where the verbal control strategies for Chaotic Rage **(Chapter 48)** may prove helpful. There is no guarantee that the subject in the midst of an ExDS incident will be able to be talked down, but the benefit of having staff trained to recognize a person in crisis and then attempt to use the verbal de-escalation and control techniques to reach an 'island of sanity,' as the author of the text calls it, is worth the effort.

One way to help officers understand the dangers that individuals in excited delirium states present to themselves is the concept of 'capture myopathy,' a term from the veterinary sciences that deals with the issues related to capturing animals and the physical stressors that accompany their capture. Capture myopathy is a physical condition that may result in death. Relating this to the capture of the suspected ExDS subject is an easy one considering that the longer the struggle goes on with first responders the greater the risk for the subject. To repeat: if it is possible have EMS on the scene before going hands on with the subject, in order to lessen the potential for making the current condition of the subject worse.

However, correctional officers must not wait for Medical arrival when there is imminent risk of serious injury to either officers or to the subject. Officer safety is of primary importance as it is those officers who are primarily responsible for getting this situation under control. Furthermore, standing by until Medical arrives, while the subject starts to or continues to injure themselves runs counter to the goal of getting them to the hospital as safely as possible.

The EMS unit should stage closer to the subject than is usual in many other situations; however, this is not to say they should put themselves in needless jeopardy. Given that EMS personnel have the training and resources to deal with the medical emergency, it is critical that they be in a position to see the subject, do an eye-sight physical and behavioral evaluation as soon as possible. The important point to remember is that this is a potentially life-threatening medical emergency and the inmate must receive rapid and aggressive medical intervention as soon as possible.

As discussed in the multi-disciplinary approach above, if there is a field sedation protocol in place, it will be important for the EMT's/medical staff to observe the subject to estimate the amount of medication needed, or at the very least, to call in to the Emergency Room to get orders from the attending physician. It is, of course, incumbent upon the correctional officers to keep the EMS personnel safe, as they do not have the means to protect themselves from serious injury should the subject attack.

It might be a good time to briefly discuss the types of medications that your EMS Medical Director could consider using in these situations. To be clear, this is not a medical document, as it is designed for correctional staff. There are no *recommendations* on medication here; whatever medication EMS brings to the scene is *their* choice, not one guided or recommended by non-medical people. Nonetheless, it is essential that all stakeholders understand something about the medications that are used for field sedation, so that they can put in place restraint procedures best suited to facilitate their administration.

One common sedative that most ambulances currently carry is midazolam, which also goes by the trade name, Versed®. Another drug that increasing numbers of EMS Medical Directors are currently using on the ambulance rigs is Ketamine. This is a dissociative anesthetic that has been used for a long time, mainly in the Emergency Room, not in the field. This has started to change and is being considered and used in more and more areas. Whatever your EMS crews carry, it is incumbent on correctional officers to know the best way for the Paramedics to deliver the drug to the subject, correctional officers can position the subject to facilitate that delivery.

The role of the Fire Rescue personnel is to support the EMS personnel with the treatment of the inmate. This can be through driving the ambulance from the scene to the hospital, or by helping with the treatment of the subject in the back of the ambulance. If EMS and Fire are separate, it is important to note that the rescue truck does not have to have a code response. It is also important to make sure they don't park too close, which might make it hard for other emergency vehicles to enter or exit the scene.

As the first responding correctional officers arrive on the scene, it is important to assess what is actually happening. This will minimize the potential for missing important information, such as dangerous environmental conditions or other people with injuries that are not recognized because your attention is too focused on the inmate.

As soon as reasonably possible, correctional officers along with EMS/Fire personnel should develop a plan to address the incident. This will mean officers will need to know if the EMS paramedic will sedate the inmate. This decision is the sole discretion of the Medical staff and not correctional personnel. Correctional supervisor or someone designated should be in charge of the incident, a quarterback, if you will, to assign personnel and keep track of what is going on. This does not have to be the highest-ranking person at the scene, just someone who is running the operation.

The quarterback will assign what limb each officer will be responsible for as well as the less lethal weapon officer, if one is available. Advising the capture officers of the EMS decision on whether or not there will be a sedative given, will let the officers know what steps will be taken once control is gained over the inmate.

Once there is a plan for capturing the subject that includes EMS, it is important to consider which less lethal weapon options are available to the officers.
- OC spray may temporarily blind the subject, but it cannot be counted on to incapacitate a subject in this extremely agitated state.
- Electronic Control Devices (ECDs) (i.e. Tasers®) provide a means to knock the subject down from a distance as opposed to tackling the inmate. It must be understood that voluntary compliance is unlikely when a person is in this state, so the number of deployments should focus only on getting the person to the ground, and allowing the officers to get into a position to control the limbs. If an agency equips their officers with ECDs, the subject can best be put under control and restraint through 'cuffing under power.' This tactic has been taught as a part of the ECD

usage and works well when dealing with resistive arrest subjects and may prove effective with the Excited Delirium subject as well. A clear distinction must be made between this procedure and any attempt to use an ECD device to *elicit* compliance.
- Some agencies have less lethal impact rounds known as bean bag rounds, as well as plastic impact rounds. These could also be used as knock down options, provided they are available at the scene, or close by. However, unless the inmate is incapacitated, they will, almost surely, just get up again.
- The last option would be for a physical takedown of the inmate. There are studies that have shown that going 'hands on', physically grabbing, wrestling, or fighting an inmate, has the greatest potential for injury to both the inmate as well as the officers involved. We must get physical control of the subject, and that requires hands on control, but the takedown should be viewed as a last resort in lieu of other less lethal means.

After capturing the subject, they are placed face down with arms out to their sides and feet spread apart. This position makes it the hardest for the inmate to resist or attack the officers. This position is also consistent with the arrest and control tactics used most often by correctional officers. This means that learning a completely new control tactic for an incident that may happen infrequently is not necessary.

The physical control tactic described below is adapted from a method of control originally developed by Chris Lawrence, of the Ontario Police College in Ontario, Canada. I refer to it as **Multiple Officer Control Tactic (MOCT** – see step-by-step illustrations at the end of this section). The tactic isolates the shoulders of the subject by placing the armpits of the officer on the back of the subject's shoulders, raising the subject's wrists, turning their palms to the sky, placing the officers legs in a position so it is the legs (through leverage and positioning) that are keeping the subject's arms raised, and finally moving the arms above the shoulder-line to completely isolate the shoulders. This makes the shoulder a weak joint, and does not allow the subject to bring their arms under their body, which would otherwise enable them to continue the struggle.

The legs are controlled by separating them and having the officers put their chests on top of the subject's legs, just above the ankle. Whether the officers are back to back, or in between the subject's legs, the subject will not be able to keep moving forward, something that could enable them to continue the struggle. If there is a fifth officer available, this person should be up at the subject's head, pushing down on the shoulder blades. This would be the best position for the quarterback, because this person has the best view of the entire control process.

One of the advantages of this MOCT is that there is no one lying on the inmate's back or lower abdomen. Concerns about restricting the inmate's breathing from too much weight on their back are alleviated because it is based on the mechanical control of each limb in such a way that prevents the subject from moving, not weight on the subject's back. Another benefit of the MOCT is that it is gross motor skills based. Because individuals in this condition are often sweating profusely, possibly covered in blood, the fine motor arrest tactics often taught in some academies, are not very effective. The gross motor tactics of the MOCT allow officers to control the arms and legs of these subjects effectively in the sometimes cramped conditions that they face.

This MOCT position can be accomplished with four officers, and as few as three officers. Fewer than that, and there is no reasonable way to prevent the subject from continuing to struggle. The MOCT can be performed by EMS and Fire personnel in coordination with law enforcement. As long as personnel understand the mechanics of how to isolate the different limbs, the inmate can be controlled. In communities where there are only one or two correctional officers available, having two EMS personnel and/or Fire personnel could give you enough people to capture and control the inmate.

Once the inmate's limbs are controlled by the personnel on the scene, this is the point that the sedation can occur, if EMS has a sedation protocol in place. The type of sedative used will dictate the best position of the inmate to administer the sedative. If there is to be an injection of the sedative, the buttocks and the thigh are positioned as to make this possible. If the EMS company uses a nasal-atomized sedative as part of their protocol, it is better for the subject to be mechanically restrained prior to placing the inmate on their back in order to deliver the sedative. As stated previously, the decision to sedate or not sedate is solely the paramedics, not the correctional officer.

There are going to be incidents where either there are not enough officers present or EMS has advised that sedation is not going to take place which will mean the process may have to be adapted to the situation at hand. **It is important to understand that whatever means correctional officers and EMS personnel use to capture the ExDS inmate, there must be frequent training that involves ALL of the participants. This develops the common understanding of what each of the responders will do or can do to assist in getting the subject controlled.**

There have been several recognized emergency medical experts, along with mental health professionals, that suggest that the person in such a state is in need of rapid sedation. The sedation allows the EMS personnel to begin to treat the inmate's underlying life-threatening medical issues as quickly as possible. It has been documented in numerous incidents that the inmate in this state will continue to struggle with the very people that are capable of helping him or her. It is important to understand that the field sedation does not directly address the multitude of medical issues the EMS personnel are facing. It just allows them access to the inmate so they can begin to treat the acidosis, the hyperthermia, etc.

Once the sedation has been given, or if there is no sedation protocol in place, or the paramedic does not choose to sedate the person, the inmate will need to be restrained in such a way as to allow the EMS personnel to treat the subject safely and then transport them. This is accomplished by using multiple sets of handcuffs so as to allow the subject to be placed on their back with their arms down by their sides. This gives the EMS personnel access to the subject's veins in the arms to get IVs started. Remember, that the hands must be cuffed with chain link handcuffs, not hinged handcuffs, as hinged cuffs will torque the wrists when the subject is lying on their back. Once the arms are secured with enough handcuffs, a minimum of three in a daisy chain configuration, then the legs are restrained with a hobble restraint.

There are various types of hobble restraints, but a simple nylon web restraint with a couple of cam buckles allows the legs to be secured quickly together and then tied to the backboard. This will prevent the subject from kicking the EMS personnel in the ambulance, as well as the ER staff at the hospital. It is also easily removed at the hospital by either correctional or nursing staff.

After the arms and legs are secured, the subject should be placed in the "recovery position," on their left side, pending placement of the inmate on a backboard. This position is recognized by EMS personnel as beneficial for the inmate's heart, as well as preventing the inmate from aspirating their own vomit. If the EMS crew is already on hand, the subject will be placed directly on a backboard, and loaded into the ambulance.

The subject should be secured onto the backboard, in the supine (face up) position, with whatever standard restraints are used by local EMS crews. Some will use larger nylon straps with buckles, or they may use "spider straps" to keep the subject secure on the backboard. Once they are secured on the backboard, they are loaded onto the gurney and then placed in the ambulance, where at least one correctional officer will ride with the ambulance crew. The quarterback will need to make this assignment to ensure someone rides with the inmate. The correctional officer's role is to advise the EMS personnel of what occurred with the inmate before the ambulance arrived. The officer is also on hand to be able to release the inmate from the handcuffs should this be needed by the EMS personnel. The officer should take notes on the actions of the EMS personnel with the inmate, while en route to the hospital for future documentation.

Upon arrival at the hospital, the officer should advise the ER staff of the inmate's actions before they arrived on the scene as well as actions taken with the inmate after their arrival. This will give the ER staff a better idea on what has happened to the inmate since correctional staff and EMS arrived to treat the inmate. **The request for a core body temperature should be made as soon as possible.** Subjects with very high body temperatures are consistent with people in this state. Unfortunately, if the core body temperature is not taken, a valuable piece of evidence is missing, which could help to explain the dire state the subject was in, at the time of correctional officer involvement.

There are several other tests, in addition to the core body temperature, that the ER physician can order that will help them identify the medical state the subject is in and what direction the treatment will take. This can be a "work up" of several tests that include:
- Initial vital signs
- Arterial Blood Gas
- Serum Lactate (acid level)
- CBC (red and white blood cells) and Complete Metabolic Panel
- Total CK and CKMB, Troponin (for heart attack)

- ETOH (alcohol)
- TSH (thyroid)
- Ten drug urine (drugs of abuse), urine HCG (females only)
- EKG, CXR
- Head CT without contrast

This is not a complete list, but one that will help the ER physician get an idea on the current status of the inmate. These tests are for the physician to help treat the inmate, but if the inmate dies, they then become critical evidence of the profoundly dangerous medical condition the inmate was in when correctional staff made contact.

One reason that these tests are so important is if the inmate does not die, the opportunity is usually missed for further investigation. The incident may be memorialized in the station house story of the "naked guy who was brought in last winter, who bashed his head against the wall during booking"—this is legend, not data. Neglecting to administer proper medical testing loses a valuable opportunity to document what Dr. Mash has called "flicker events" in which a person gets into this excited state and then works their way out of it. These flicker events could be predictors of future incidents that portend a dire ending.[52]

If the inmate dies, there will most certainly be a thorough investigation. One consideration, made in conjunction with your coroner and your medical examiner, should be to harvest the brain sections from the inmate who has just expired. This must be done, generally, within twelve hours and the samples sent to Dr. Deborah Mash from the University of Miami's Brain Endowment Center for analysis. Dr. Mash is able to test for heat shock proteins and cocaine levels in the brain of the inmate that can help investigators, coroners, and medical examiners in identifying the incident as an ExDS incident. Specimen kits are available from Dr. Mash and should be kept available in the event that a sudden in-custody death has occurred and it has the signs and behaviors that are consistent with a suspected Excited Delirium case. In the case of death, someone should request a copy of the EKG strip, if such an exam was carried out. This will be of value to detectives, medical staff, and Medical Examiner and can be made part of the permanent record as well.

Appendix B 2: Deal with the Behavior, Not the Cause

To underscore one more time, your protocols must not be predicated on the inmate actually being in a medically "certifiable" Excited Delirium Syndrome condition. Just as the Correctional Officer is not required to know if an inmate's gasping for air is due to an asthma attack, aspirated vomit, or a half-swallowed object—the facilities protocol is behaviorally coded for Chaotic Rage. If it turns out to be ExDS and the protocols are properly initiated, very likely the inmate's life will be saved. If it turns out to be some other, similar appearing condition that is caused by other factors, nonetheless, the initiation of this protocol will also very likely save the inmate's life.

All too often the focus of the investigation is on the use of force needed to get control of the inmate, instead of the numerous behavioral cues of a possible ExDS incident. The focus of this investigation should be on recreating at least the last twenty-four hours before the incident, but preferably longer. This will create a complete picture of the various factors that led to the involvement of correctional staff and EMS. The force used to gain control of the subject will be reviewed for reasonableness, but the investigation should not remain at that level.

There are numerous incidents where the subject was demonstrating superhuman strength, seemingly unlimited endurance, and incredible pain tolerance. These behaviors are what have led correctional officers to use force that is needed to get the subject under control and to the hospital. If the inmate dies, then the investigation tends to focus just on the force and not what might have caused the behavior in the first place.

Investigators should attempt to collect as much medical information as possible about the subject. This may indicate the serious medical condition the inmate was in at the time that corrections and EMS were contacted. If the medical tests were done, as previously stated, for medical purposes, then the results will be available for investigative purposes as well. The goal is to completely explain what happened, and what actions were taken in order to give the subject the best *possibility* of survival. This is often referred to as a "Psychological Autopsy," and it should include detailed personal and criminal history, as well as any information that might suggest a pre-disposition for Excited Delirium: this can include a history of chronic drug use, or episodic use of such substances as "bath salts," PCP or so-called "Sherm," which can precipitate such an episode without years of chronic drug abuse, as is more typical with such substances as cocaine or methamphetamine. In addition, investigators are often able to get information about so-called "flicker events," where the individual ramped up, momentarily or episodically, into what appeared to onlookers to be a delirium state, but one that was resolved without injury.

Investigators should attempt to collect information from the subject's criminal, medical, psychiatric, social worker, hospitalization, and jail/prison histories. This could give the investigator clues to other underlying causes for the subject's behavior. Evidence regarding the subject's prescribed medications as well as if the subject was compliant or non-compliant with those prescriptions should be located.

Witnesses and responders should be interviewed as soon as possible for their observations of the subject and the timeline of those observations. This will help the investigator understand the progress of the subject's behavior leading to their involvement with law enforcement personnel. The longer witnesses go without being interviewed, the greater the potential for failed or distorted recollections.

Since the officer was only concerned with the recognition that the subject needed to receive medical attention, and not with what caused the subject's behavior, it is now the investigator's task to seek to identify the cause of the incident. Primary emphasis should be on stimulant drug abuse and then possible psychiatric causes. The investigator will face a difficult task if the medical testing mentioned previously was not done.

The investigator and administrator should understand that it is usually *after* the subject has already reached an out-of-control state that the call goes out for assistance. This puts correctional staff behind the curve on the inmate's condition. If you liken this ExDS process to a "metabolic freight train to death," then if the correctional staff arrives as the inmate is already "pulling into the station," it may be possible that the correctional officers were dispatched to just observe the inmate's demise. The officers are then left in a state of confusion, wondering what could have been done differently.

If the investigation focuses on just what the officers did and not the condition of the subject, the potential for inaccurate conclusions is possible. This will not help the family of the subject, the officers involved, the agency, or the community to understand the incident.

SUMMARY

To summarize, dispatch personnel should gain as much information from the caller, on the condition of the subject, as possible. It is important to understand this could be a *medical emergency* that requires the appropriate number of correctional personnel, EMS, and Advanced Life Support (ALS) to be dispatched to the scene.

If the correctional officers observe the inmate acting in an agitated, chaotic manner *before* the call comes in or goes out from dispatch, they should assume that this is likely a *medical emergency*, and call for additional backup and EMS as soon as possible. The officer should assess the situation and determine the need to make contact with the inmate, dependent upon the circumstances. It is preferable to wait to make contact until EMS is on scene, unless the previously described exceptions are present.

A plan, in conjunction with EMS, should be made as quickly as possible in order to capture the subject. Once the subject is face down on the ground, consider using the MOCT (Multiple Officer Control Tactic) to quickly overcome the subject's resistance. If sedation has been decided upon by EMS personnel, it is necessary to control the inmate until that is accomplished. Restraining the subject with enough handcuffs to keep the subject's hands down by their sides as well as restraining their feet, to keep them from kicking first responders needs to be done in an organized manner. Remember the use of chain link handcuffs on the subject's wrists instead of hinged handcuffs to prevent possible injury to the subject's nerves.

The subject should then be secured to a backboard, face up, and loaded onto a gurney. Correctional staff should assist EMS in loading the subject into the ambulance. At least one officer should accompany EMS personnel to the hospital. It is necessary for the officer to articulate the subject's actions prior to the arrival of EMS, and any and all actions taken by law enforcement and EMS on the scene prior to arriving at the hospital.

Careful documentation of each incident, especially those that survive, can paint a clear picture of the tense, uncertain, and rapidly evolving situation faced by the first responders.

This guide may be used as a template to develop your own multi-disciplinary response to this multi-faceted problem based on the resources available in your facility.

If you have questions about this protocol, please contact Michael Paulus at michael@michaelpaulustraining.com

Multiple Officer Control Tactic (MOCT) – An Illustrated Guide

Figure#1- (Pin#1) Patient's arms are above the shoulder line with the officer's armpit on top of the shoulder. Patient's arms are controlled by officers by use of "figure four" along with a chain-link handcuff. Patient's arms are raised by using the officer's outside leg. Weight is kept off the patient's back to isolate the patient's shoulder.

Figure#2- (Pin#2) Patient's legs are moved out from the centerline of the body to limit their power. Officers wrap the patient's leg with their arms and tuck the heel under the armpit on the outside of their body. Weight is kept low towards the patient's ankles.

Figure#3- (Pin#3) Skeletal isolation is maintained by having two officers on the arms, two officers on the legs and then one officer at the patient's head. The officer at the patient's head is pushing down on the patient's trapezius muscles and monitoring the patient's status. This can be achieved by as few as three officers.

Figure#4- (Sedation#1) - EMS IM injection is achieved after the "quarterback" has confirmed that the arms and legs are controlled enough to allow EMS to approach the patient. EMS will move in from the sides which allow better access to buttocks or upper thigh of the patient.

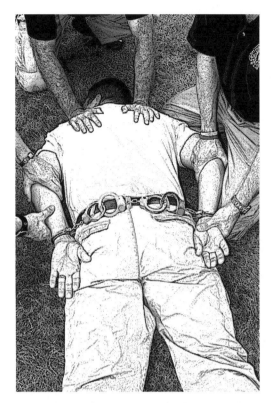

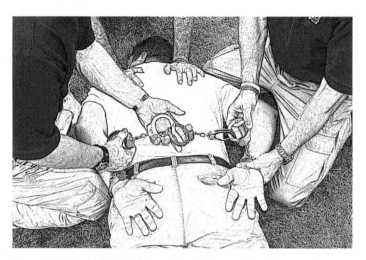

Figure#6- (Cuffing#2) - If the subject is larger, then four or more sets of handcuffs should be applied so that the patient can be placed in the supine position.

Figure#5- (Cuffing#1) - Once sedation has been given, officers will bring one arm behind the back at a time and apply at least three sets of handcuffs in a daisy chain configuration to allow the patient to be turned to a supine position. This will allow EMS to access the arm to establish an IV if warranted.

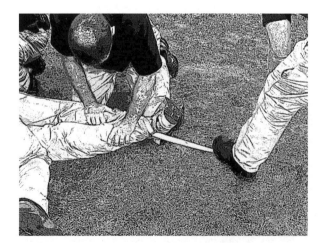

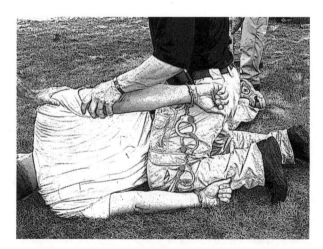

Figure#7- (Cuffing#3) - The patient's legs are brought together, ankles crossed if possible, then the nylon hobble is applied and pulled away from the patient. The other officer holds the patient's legs to keep them secured.

Figure#8- (Recovery#1) - If EMS is not on scene when the patient is captured, the officers are advised to place the patient in the left recovery position until EMS arrives on scene. Sedation can still be administered in this position.

SUGGESTED RESPONSE PROTOCOL FOR CORRECTIONAL FACILITIES

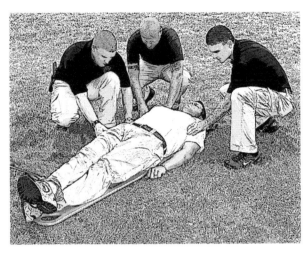

Figure#9- (Backboard#1) - The patient is placed on top of the backboard with the series of handcuffs under their back. This starts to limit the patient's ability to resist.

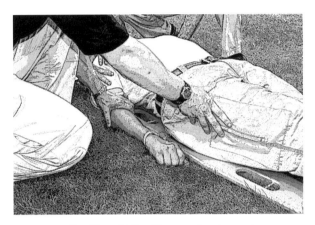

Figure#10- (Backboard#2) - Close-up showing patient on top of handcuffs while on top of the backboard.

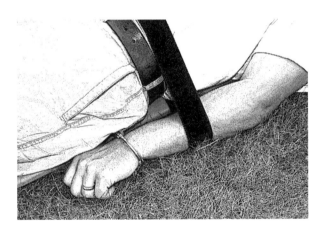

Figure#11- (Backboard#3) - Close-up of patient's arms while handcuffs are under the body and spider straps are applied. Notice that an IV could be started while in this position.

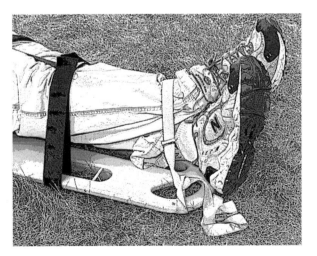

Figure#12- (Backboard#4) - Close-up of patient's legs secured to the backboard using the spider straps and the nylon hobble tied to the end of the backboard.

295

Endnotes

1. The rest of this chapter relies on the work of Sgt. Michael Blake, who first presented it in our companion work, SAFE BEHIND BARS: Communication, Control, and De-escalation of Mentally Ill and Aggressive Inmates *A Comprehensive Guidebook for Correctional Officers in Jail Settings* Ellis Amdur, Michael Blake & Chris De Villeneuve

2. Goldman, Marc, ""When People with Complex Disabilities Break the Law: Forensic Issues and Solutions," NADD Bulletin, V II, #2, Article 1, February, 2019

3. Petersilia J. (1997). Doing justice? Criminal offenders with developmental disabilities. California Policy Research Center.

4. See Rhodes, Richard. (1999). *Why they kill: The discoveries of a maverick criminologist.* New York: Vintage, on the work of sociologist Lonnie Atkins, who coined the phrase "violentization," to describe the process in which a victim of violence becomes a perpetrator. Atkins focused on the family, but violentization can also occur later in life. On the other hand, prior incarceration can also work to the institution's benefit. Some inmates are so familiar with the system that they fall into its natural rhythm. They will even ask the intake officer to tell the officer that runs inmate programs that they are back in prison. In an example of the 'abnormal becoming normal,' some officers are happy to see the 'good laundry worker' or 'floor guy' back in custody.

5. Ibid.

6. This author observed an informal study by a neurologist at a youth detention facility. He noted signs of closed head injury (through neuro-psych evaluation) in approximately fifty percent of the male inmates.

7. The Religious Land Use In Prison Act (RLUIPA) requires prison administration to develop policy and subsequent training for staff in order to ensure compliance with its tenets.

8. Issues of religion are almost always brought in the medical interview as many religions have dietary restrictions.

9. Example: cheeking - http://www.youtube.com/watch?v=DzLFquT2jTQ

10. This author first heard this method presented by author David Grossman. Also see his book: Grossman, D. (1996). *On killing: The psychological cost of learning to kill in war and society.* Santa Ana, CA: Back Bay Books.

11. Personal communication

12. You will sometimes see the same thing with people for whom English is not a first language.

13. An extremely valuable book regarding OCD is: Schwartz, Jeffrey (with Beverly Beyette). (1996). *Brain lock: Free yourself from obsessive-compulsive behavior.* New York: Regan Books.

14. This behavior certainly is seen severely developmentally disabled individuals, as well as profoundly disabled elderly people either at home or in long-term care.

15. https://en.wikipedia.org/wiki/Dirty_protest

16. https://www.miamiherald.com/latest-news/article1938250.html

17. One of the best books on manipulation, well-known to older correctional officers is the famous 'yellow book,' is: Allen, B., & Bosta, D. (1981-2002). *Games criminals play: How you can profit by knowing them.* Berkeley, CA: Rae John.

18. Hare, Robert. (1999). *Without conscience: The disturbing world of the psychopaths among us.* New York: Guilford.

19. In Greek mythology Sisyphus was a king who, as a punishment from the gods, was made to roll a huge rock up a steep hill, but before he could reach the top of the hill, the rock would always roll back down, forcing him to begin again, dooming Sisyphus to an eternity of frustrations. Today, pointless and frustrating activities are often described as Sisyphean.

20. Arieti, Silvano. (1994). Interpretation of Schizophrenia (2nd ed.). Jason Aronson.

21. Amdur, Ellis, (2016) BODY AND SOUL: Toward a Radical Intersubjectivity in Psychotherapy, Edgework Books,

22. Other major categories of stalkers are:

    Relational stalkers. Often an extension of a controlling or violent relationship, this stalker is either keeping tabs on his/her partner, or pursuing them once they have left.

Obsessive stalkers. The classic stalker—a hyper-focus on the victim as prey, not necessarily to kill or even harm, but always to control. Like ordinary obsessive-compulsive disorder, this stalker can be well-aware that the victim does not desire contact, and may be afraid of or hate him/her. But just as the germ-obsessed obsessive MUST wash his hands 50 times despite *knowing* that they are clean, the obsessive stalker has to have the attention of his/her victim.

Terroristic stalker. Such an individual may certainly have been in a relationship with or be obsessed with his/her victim. In addition, there is considerable 'ego' involved—this stalker's psychological energy focuses on self rather than the victim. A true predator, he/she is doing something they enjoys—simply because they can (for amusement), or because the victim, in some way, offended them (for revenge). At least in the professional context, correctional officers are most at risk from obsessive stalkers, who get fixated on them, or terroristic stalkers, who decide to target one officer for revenge, hatred or amusement.

23 Our thanks to Aaron Fields of the Seattle Fire Department for another version of this intervention.

24 An actual incident. The engineer was killed trying to jump clear when the person in the manic state wrecked the train.

25 Researchers note that a mixture of alcohol and cocaine is particularly dangerous, as the body synthesizes them together into a new substance, coca ethylene. Retrieved from http://jpet.aspetjournals.org/ content/274/1/215.abstract

26 U.S. Dept. of Justice 2010 Key Indicators Strategic Support System Demographics.

27 These same questions can and should be used if the suspected suicidal person is a fellow officer and you, as a friend, are trying to convince them to seek services.

28 This chapter is a brief discussion of a much more complicated issue. It is beyond the scope of this text to go into such planning in detail as this involves a lot of players beyond correctional officers, and gets into a lot of 'political' issues on how one responds to the distress of mentally ill or emotionally disturbed people.

29 A remarkable example of "the relationship" saving a correctional officer's life can be seen on this YouTube video: http://www.youtube.com /watch?v=s1FR6YjHbYE As described in an article in "Mail Online," dated November 6, 2009: "Previtera, the commander of Hillsborough County's Department of Detention Services, said the inmates had 'saved the deputy's life'. 'The response of the inmates in this case, I think, speaks volumes as to the fact that we treat these men and women . . . in our facilities with a lot of respect,' he added. Letters of thanks were sent to the attorneys of the four inmates who came to Deputy Moon's rescue, to be delivered to a judge on their behalf. Deputy Moon himself was admitted to the hospital for his injuries but quickly released. When asked why they had bothered to help him, the inmates' answer was simple: He was a good guy and they liked him."

30 The author owes the image of the hands as a fence to Geoff Thompson, who has authored a number of books on his career as a doorman in violent British pubs, as well as exemplary books on self-defense.

31 The author owes a debt for some of the basic information in this section to a form of training called Professional Assault Response Training (PART), thanks to a workshop I attended approximately thirty years ago. I have made major changes in their basic four-part schema, as well as adding a significant amount of new data. Therefore, my approach is, in many aspects, quite different, and it should not be confused with PART's procedures.

32 See: Salter, A. (2004). Predators: pedophiles, rapists and other sex inmates: Who they are, how they operate, and how we protect ourselves and our children. New York: Basic Books. My gratitude for the formulation of the overwhelming force/professionalism concept that she presented in a great story during a seminar. Dr. Salter uses the term 'respect' rather than professionalism. The latter is better because one has to maintain professionalism even we people we can never respect.

33 This projection of guilt is one of the reasons that lifestyle criminals have a difficult time rehabilitating. Guilt is the opportunity to take moral inventory. By projecting guilt and blame on the other, they avoid the moral confrontation that is the beginning of true rehabilitation.

34 See: de Becker, G. (1997). The Gift of Fear: Survival signals that protect us from violence. U.S. and Canada: Little Brown; and (1999). Protecting the gift: Keeping children and teenagers safe (and parents sane) New York: Random House, New York.

ABOUT THE AUTHOR

Ellis Amdur

Edgework founder Ellis Amdur received his B.A. in psychology from Yale University in 1974 and his M.A. in psychology from Seattle University in 1990. He is both a National Certified Counselor and a State Certified Child Mental Health Specialist. He has written a number of books concerning communication with mentally ill and emotionally disturbed individuals and the de-escalation of aggression.

Since the late 1960s, Amdur has trained in various martial arts systems, spending thirteen of these years studying in Japan. He is a recognized expert in classical and modern Japanese martial traditions and has authored three iconoclastic books and one instructional DVD on martial arts subjects.

Since his return to America in 1988, Ellis Amdur has worked in the field of crisis intervention. He has developed a range of training and consultation services, as well as a unique style of assessment and psychotherapy. He has also written seventeen books in the area of tactical de-escalation, crisis negotiation and effectively managing aggressive and out-of-control behavior. All of his work is based on a combination of phenomenological psychology and the underlying philosophical premises of classical Japanese martial traditions. Amdur's professional philosophy can best be summed up in this idea: "The development of an individual's integrity and dignity is the paramount virtue. This can only occur when people live courageously, regardless of their circumstances, and take responsibility for their roles in making the changes they desire."

Ellis Amdur is a dynamic public speaker and trainer who presents his work throughout the U.S. and internationally. He is noted for his sometimes outrageous humor as well as his profound breadth of knowledge. His vivid descriptions of aggressive and mentally ill people and his true-to-life role-playing of the behaviors in question give participants an almost first-hand experience of facing the real individuals in question.

For more information on books and training by Ellis Amdur, please refer to his websites at www.edgeworkbooks.com and www.gullaamdur.com

Made in the USA
San Bernardino, CA
05 January 2020